Echoes of the Call

Echoes of the Call

*Identity and Ideology Among
American Missionaries
in Ecuador*

JEFFREY SWANSON

New York   Oxford
OXFORD UNIVERSITY PRESS
1995

Oxford University Press

Oxford   New York
Athens   Auckland   Bangkok   Bombay
Calcutta   Cape Town   Dar es Salaam   Delhi
Florence   Hong Kong   Istanbul   Karachi
Kuala Lumpur   Madras   Madrid   Melbourne
Mexico City   Nairobi   Paris   Singapore
Taipei   Tokyo   Toronto

and associated companies in
Berlin   Ibadan

Library of Congress Cataloging-in-Publication Data
Swanson, Jeffrey.
Echoes of the call : identity and ideology among
American missionaries in Ecuador / Jeffrey Swanson.
p. cm.   Includes bibliographical references and index.
ISBN 0-19-506823-8
1. Missions, American—Ecuador.
2. Protestant churches—Missions—Ecuador.
3. Evangelistic work—Ecuador.
4. Ecuador—Church history.   I. Title.
BV2853.E293   1995   266'.023730866—dc20
94-9012

Page v constitutes an extension of the copyright page.

1 3 5 7 9 8 6 4 2
Printed in the United States of America
on acid-free paper

Preface

This book grew out of a study made possible by the wholehearted cooperation of the missionary community of HCJB-World Radio in Ecuador. To all those Mission members who kindly shared with me the stories of their lives, who generously filled out cumbersome questionnaires, who befriended and inspired and encouraged me during the year of my sojourn in their midst, I offer deepest thanks.

Support for my fieldwork in 1982 and 1983 came in the form of a doctoral research fellowship at Yale University, funded in part by the National Institute of Mental Health. During the intervening years, my efforts in writing this book were supported (or at least tolerated) by several institutions at which I was supposed to be doing mainly something else. These included the Department of Psychiatry and Behavioral Sciences at the University of Texas Medical Branch at Galveston; the Institute for the Medical Humanities (also at Galveston); the Cecil G. Sheps Center for Health Services Research at the University of North Carolina at Chapel Hill; and the Division of Social and Community Psychiatry at Duke University Medical Center.

I am grateful to my mentors and colleagues in several disciplines who took an interest in this project at one point or another, offering invaluable insights, practical advice, and friendly criticism. At Yale, it was Jerome Myers who first encouraged me to undertake a dissertation study in Ecuador and who guided me over various practical hurdles in getting there. Nancy Ammerman, then a fellow graduate student in sociology, shared my concerns in balancing personal with scholarly interests in studying evangelicals and fundamentalist Christians. Later, as I began to convert my dissertation into a book, she provided an extremely useful review of the manuscript from the viewpoint of someone who had "been there" in more ways than one. Charles Forman of the Yale Divinity School also gave a careful reading to early drafts of each chapter, offering a trenchant critique from one who is both a distinguished historian of missions and a former missionary. Kai Erikson went beyond the call of duty as my dissertation director; he was at key moments an inspirational mentor, incisive editor, wise counselor, and trusted friend.

Since leaving Yale for Texas and then North Carolina, a number of fellow academic travelers have walked along with me on the road to completing this book—especially Paul Adams, Tom Cole, and my brother Tod Swanson. Each of them contributed in significant ways to my thinking and writing about American evangelical missionaries, though the book would have been better if I had been able to apply more of the lessons they tried to teach.

My parents, Charlotte and Wallace Swanson, inspired my interest in missions and missionaries from the beginning. They have always had something meaningful to say and have said it well, not only with words but with their whole lives.

Pamela Mydske Swanson deserves a great deal of credit for this book, more than she would care to admit. Her critical and personal insight into the missionary experience improved and corrected my work in a number of ways. But beyond this, truly it must be said of Pam: "Love bears all things, believes all things, hopes all things, endures all things"—even life with someone writing a book.

Finally, whereas authors customarily thank their children, too, for suffering absences and distraction during the writing of a book, my own three offspring deserve no such commendation. Happily and without regret, I have Angela and Alex and Matthew to thank for making me take eight years to finish a thing that might have been done in one or two—but would have been a lot less fun.

Durham, N.C.   J. S.
April 1994

Contents

Echoes of the Call

1

Beginnings

Wallace Swanson was born in 1927 in a modest two-story frame house in Minneapolis, the fifth of Clara and Arvid Swanson's eight children. A decade earlier Arvid had set sail for France to fight in the Great War, leaving his immigrant parents and older brother tending the family farm up north. Then he had returned—doughboy helmet intact and some change in his pocket—to marry Clara Mattson from neighboring Isanti and to seek his fortune with her in the city. Eventually, Arvid had found steady work as a deliveryman at the Franklin Creamery. At age twenty-four, he had paid five thousand dollars for a three-bedroom house at 817 East 22nd Street, in which he and Clara would spend the next sixty years of married life.

The Swansons made a kind of second home at First Covenant Church a few blocks away on Chicago Avenue. Founded by a group of Bible-reading, mission-minded Swedish pietists who had renounced the "unconverted" religiosity of the Old Country's state Lutheran church and likewise the "dead formalism" of the Augustana Synod in America, First Covenant was bursting with congregants in those days. Minneapolis Swedes packed in by the hundreds on Sunday mornings and evenings to hear the fiery, spirit-filled preaching of Gustaf Johnson and the carefully crafted Bible exposition of his successor Doctor Paul Rees (a man Wally Swanson often referred to in later life as "a real prince of the pulpit").

Wally remembers Arvid as a principled patriarch who kept his children in line with a strong hand. Never one to accept lame excuses for infractions such as late arrival at dinner, he would dispatch the hapless straggler summarily to the basement to await a dose of razor-strap discipline. A taciturn Scandinavian given at times to melancholy, Arvid—with a family of ten in the 1930s—was a man with a great deal to worry about. Still, his children remember knowing that he loved them dearly and that he prayed for them every day of his life. Clara was a painfully frugal but nurturing mother, and a devout soul who sang hymns and read to Wally and his sisters and brothers nightly from the biographies of great missionaries.

Most of what Wally would be inclined to recall from his store of childhood memories is ordinary stuff about a boy growing up in the Midwest during the Great Depression. He remembers sandlot baseball games and visits to his grandparents' farm near Harris and the magic of the midway at the State Fair in August. He speaks of endless summer days spent swimming at Lake Calhoun, and of cold winter nights when he sketched scenes of cowboys and Indians, built balsa models of fighter planes and battleships, marshalled his lead soldiers, and imagined grand adventures beyond the borders of Minnesota.

But there was something unusual about Wally Swanson—a spiritual sensibility that tended to set him apart, even at a very young age. His siblings describe him as a pious child, always the one to accompany his mother on snowy winter's walks to prayer meeting

Wednesday nights, the one who sang gospel songs as he played with his toys and who seemed to relish going to missionary conferences at First Covenant more than most children would. Despite his toy-soldier fantasies, Wally's real heroes were the soldiers in God's army—the missionaries who arose in his imagination like giants from the pages of the stories Clara read: William Carey, Hudson Taylor, Adoniram Judson, and David Livingstone. Sometimes he could almost hear their voices join his own as he stood in the pew at First Covenant and sang, "We've a story to tell to the nations" and "So send I you."

Of slight build and small stature, Wally was by nature a rather timid child who was little noticed, but sometimes attracted the attention of neighborhood bullies. (Once he bought a bicycle with money that he had earned peddling newspapers. Another boy promptly stole it, disassembled it and sold the parts.) Still, Wally felt compelled to witness to his "unsaved" schoolmates, sometimes carrying his Bible to public junior high school. For a boy with his natural modesty and shyness this was not an easy thing to do, but he remembers feeling genuinely concerned for the eternal souls of the children around him.

By the time he finished high school at the Covenant's Minnehaha Academy, Wally had articulated his life's highest goal. He wanted to be a missionary doctor, perhaps in China, Africa, South America, or "wherever the Lord would lead." In human terms it seemed like a "pipe dream"—at least the doctor part—because a medical education would cost ten thousand dollars, an enormous sum in 1945 for the son of Arvid and Clara Swanson. Still, he had a growing sense that this is what God was calling him to do. Somehow he could not put the thought of it out of his mind—the image of himself, Wally, traveling down a jungle river in a dugout canoe, on a mission to heal the bodies and souls of people who had never heard the gospel of Christ.

In 1946 Wally enlisted in the U.S. Navy and sailed for China. He worked as a carpenter, repairing other vessels in the Pacific fleet. But his real mission was of a different sort; he organized regular prayer and Bible study with a half dozen shipmates, and attempted vigorously to evangelize the other men. On a ship with over nine hundred American sailors, Wally was convinced he and his five brethren were the only Christians. On shore leave in Tsingtao, eighteen-year-old Wally soberly watched his fellow sailors staggering drunk back to the dock, and felt a pain in his heart matched only by his anguish at the sight of homeless Chinese children scavenging food from the ship's garbage.

After two years at sea and abroad, Wally returned home eager to begin preparation for the missionary work to which he was now convinced God had called him. Paul Rees directed him to Asbury College, a Methodist-Holiness school in Kentucky where he immersed himself in premedical and Biblical studies, his tuition financed by the G.I. bill. What he felt he lacked in natural academic quickness, Wally more than made up in determination and sleepless nights. By the time he graduated, he had an offer of admission to the Bowman Gray School of Medicine in Winston-Salem, North Carolina. Meanwhile, he had met Charlotte Dillon, a Methodist minister's daughter from Nebraska, whose intense motivation to become a foreign missionary rivaled Wally's own and was rooted as deeply in her childhood experience. The two were married after college graduation in June, 1952, and moved to Winston-Salem, where Charlotte taught school and Wally plodded through medical school.

A doctor at last, Wally began inquiring about medical missions around the world. He had thought that God might call him back to China, but that country was now closed to missionaries. He learned about many other places where doctors were needed, and he began to wonder how he would find the place he had always dreamed of—the place of service for which he felt God had so long prepared him. And then one night as he was praying, Wally heard an extraordinary but somehow familiar voice that he recognized as God calling him to Ecuador. For the rest of his life, he would insist that his call was unmistakably of divine origin.

Five years later Wally found himself in a dugout canoe, headed down the Pastaza river into the Atshuara tribal territory of Ecuador's Amazonia. He would later recall the scene many times, a moment of serene fulfillment in which his sense of calling and his life story finally converged: He glances down at the black satchel filled with medical examining tools and pharmacopoeia. He gazes over at the trees soaring up from the riverbank against the tropical blue sky, and at the clouds suspended above the steamy forest canopy. He thinks of Charlotte and his young children, days behind him through the jungle. He remembers his parents and friends back in Minneapolis and imagines they can see him now, as they place their missionary offering in the collection plate on Sunday morning at First Covenant. Finally, his eyes fall on the dark young men poling the canoe in front and in back of him, chattering in a tribal tongue he doesn't understand. And then, in his soft, sweet tenor, Wally Swanson begins to sing the song that his sons and daughters one day would be unable to forget. "There is a balm in Gilead, to make the wounded whole. There is a balm in Gilead, to heal the sin-sick soul."

This book is a sociologist's account of a special world and of a special sort of life story, that of evangelical Christian missionaries abroad. It is also an attempt by a son of missionaries to come to terms with his parents' vocation and what their views of life might mean to him. In 1982 I set off from New Haven, bound for Ecuador on a mission of my own, quite different from my father's mission a generation earlier. I was a twenty-five-year-old Yale graduate student, burdened (I thought) by little more than a dissertation prospectus, a tape recorder, and a suitcase full of blank cassettes. But I was also a missionaries' child coming home—literally moving back in under my parents' roof in Quito. I had arranged to spend a year observing life and work among members of the World Radio Missionary Fellowship,[1] the mission my parents had belonged to for two decades. I was going to interview their friends and colleagues, the people I had once called aunt and uncle.

As a sociologist, I was developing some academic ideas about the significance of the missionary vocation, about moral careers, and about the role of the stranger. I had (somewhat loosely) proposed an investigation of how these ideas might play out in the social construction of divine-calling experiences among missionaries. Having heard missionary stories all my life, I now wondered how these narratives came to be, what purposes they served for the individuals who told them and listened to them, and how they worked for a whole community of people who cared deeply about such testimonies. Hearkening back to my parents' accounts of being "set apart" and "called" by God to the mission field, I wondered now whether such notions as set-apartness and calling might emerge as a rhetorical key to missionaries' identities, giving a sort of thematic coherence to the fragments of their life stories and defining the boundaries of their group as cultural strangers abroad.

As I had begun to examine the American missionary worldview from an academic perspective, I had been struck to realize that, in one sense, this was a vocation bound up in a cultural-historical matrix whose time had long since passed. It seemed as if the Protestant missions movement had been pretty well summed up in 1899:

Commerce and civilization follow as inevitably as education in the wake of Christian missions. Gradually idolatry is undermined; pagan temples fall to ruins;

profligate priests lose their hold upon their peoples; the Christian home puts to shame the harem and the female slave-herd; reeking cannibals and murderous chieftains become gentle and kindly; and not infrequently whole peoples are transformed, passing from barbarism to civilization, from cruelty to mercy, from vileness to purity, from lust to love, from darkness to light, and from Satan to God (Lhamon, 1899:19).

The missionary calling appeared to derive its meaning from a commitment to ancient articles of faith refracted largely through the cultural imagery of the nineteenth-century Anglo-American world. I discovered that most of the scholarly attention that had been focused on missionaries was the work of historians, often stopping short of 1920, and this was understandable. Any serious student of Western civilization's expansion between the French Revolution and the first World War would squarely encounter the Protestant missionary movement as a significant force. Likewise, the question of how Christianity got to be a global religion could hardly be answered without coming to terms with the era of American "manifest destiny" and British colonialism (see Latourette, 1949; Neill, 1964; Hutchison, 1987; Stanley, 1990).

I began to see why popular culture tends to portray the Protestant missionary as a creature left over from the nineteenth century. The images and ideas ordinarily associated with the missionary impulse—religious colonialism, adventure on the frontier, cultural redemption, moral crusade, urgent millennialism, divine calling, individual piety, disinterested benevolence, romantic sacrificial heroism, and even Victorian prudishness—all of these were, in a sense, important themes in the Anglo-American culture of the period that Yale historian Kenneth Scott Latourette had aptly called "Christianity's Great Century."[2] Missionaries of the time embodied the ideals of a nation that saw itself as morally set apart from the world. They were pioneers and Biblical primitivists, born in a country that very much defined itself in pioneering and Biblical terms. They lived in a world full of virgin frontiers to be spiritually claimed for American Christendom (see Phillips, 1969).

But what about American missionaries today? What were they doing in the latter part of the twentieth century, after the colonial proconsuls were gone, and the Puritan boundaries of their own country had all but vanished in what scholars were interpreting as a multicultural, post-Christian (even postmodern) world?[3] Why did they still feel compelled to "go into all the world and make disciples of all nations"? Historian James Reed (1983) has observed that "the Protestant missionary movement began to wane in the 1920s and, despite periodic atavism and latter-day nostalgia, the decline continues to this day." But William Hutchison (1987) terms this "a bit of conventional wisdom that was both accurate and wildly incorrect." On the one hand, if defined as a significant movement of the Protestant establishment within the mainstream of American culture, Hutchinson points out that foreign missions had indeed diminished almost to extinction by the mid-twentieth century. But on the other hand, marginalized fundamentalists and independent evangelical "faith missions" had picked up (and even expanded) the foreign missions enterprise where the liberalized mainline denominations had left off.

By 1990, the legions of U.S.-based Protestant missionaries working in foreign countries reached unprecedented numbers—about 71,000, representing 692 different agencies, and taking in a combined $1.7 billion a year. They were growing at an annual rate of 2.4 percent, up from 1.9 percent in 1985. But except for the Southern Baptists, the traditional mainline denominations accounted for only a small fraction of these missionaries. The Protestant mission powerhouses of the 1980s were conservative groups such as the Assemblies of God, Wycliffe Bible Translators, New Tribes Mission, the Christian and Missionary Alliance, the Evangelical Alliance Mission, and the Seventh Day Adventists. In Ecuador alone, for example, there were 752 missionaries from U.S.-based agencies working in 1989. However, all together the mainline denominations such as the Methodists, Episcopalians, Presbyterians, Lutherans, United Church of Christ, and General (not Southern) Baptists accounted for only 5 percent of the total number of American missionaries in that country. The formerly active Church World Services of the National Council of Churches–USA had no missionaries at all in Ecuador in 1989.[4]

The missionaries I had known in Ecuador were people who believed fervently in the literal, historical truth of the Bible and were convinced that born-again faith in Jesus Christ was the only way to escape a certain fate of eternal hellfire in the hereafter. They were the cultural heirs not only of the Puritans, spiritual colonialists, revivalists, and moral crusaders of earlier centuries, but of the 1920s fundamentalists who had come into their own in the wake of something James Hunter (1982) has termed "the disestablishment of Protestantism"—a thorough reshaping of American religious sensibilities that affected Bible believers with a profound and lasting sense of strangerhood.

It occurred to me then that American evangelical missionaries were strangers in several ways that might be symbolically interrelated. First, they viewed themselves as spiritually set apart from the secular world around them. Then they had been separated physically from their own culture and country of origin. And they were temporal strangers, too, insofar as their basic motivations seemed to be out of sync with larger humanistic-cultural developments that defined the historical moment in which they lived. Finally (I suspected, based on the stories of missionaries I knew), they were individuals who had experienced various kinds of separation and psychological estrangement in their early developmental experience.

I began to formulate some basic questions: How do missionaries in the present day construct and maintain their identities and their commitment to a vocation founded upon premodern (or early-modern) views of the world? How do missionaries understand themselves and the development of their calling? How are they able to integrate the various layers of marginality and strangerhood in their life stories, and to what end? I was not certain these were all the right questions. But I knew enough to be sure there was a sociological richness hidden in the missionary's moral career, in the missionary's experience as a figure on the boundaries of familiar and strange social life. I was eager to return to Ecuador to talk and listen to these people I had always known, but who were becoming more interesting to me the more I thought about them.

I now see that it was an uncommon privilege for me to conduct such a study under the rubric of a dissertation in sociology. The idea begged a number of questions that might have given my academic mentors serious pause. First, there was the matter of my personal and value-laden connection to the subject matter. Was I really a missionary myself, disguised as a sociologist? Did I have an axe to grind one way or the other? A perceptive teacher could have seen that the "layers of strangerhood" and the "tensions" I wished to uncover in the missionary vocation had as much to do with my own psychological ambivalence and search for identity as they did about the life stories of the people I intended to study. How would such a personal agenda affect my focusing of the sociological lens? I could see my professors arguing that, indeed, going back to Ecuador and talking to missionaries might be helpful in my efforts to construct an adult identity for myself, but didn't promise a significant contribution to social science.

Then there were the inevitable questions some sociologists would have raised about my proposed method (or the lack of it)—recording individual life stories and trying to understand what they meant on their own terms. Unfortunately, the natural affinity most people possess for telling and hearing stories tends to come under assault in the professional training of a sociologist, or is often pushed aside to accommodate the cant of reductionistic theories, quantitative research methods, and data analysis. Becoming a sociologist supposedly means deciding that generalities about group phenomena are academically more interesting than individual persons and personal development. Too often, graduate school is overly effective, and the newly minted sociologist emerges with little residue of interest in individual utterance for its own sake—whether of dancers, doctors, or death row inmates—but only in what the talk represents about larger social categories and variables related to each other in quantifiable ways hypothesized by social theory. That is not primarily what I was interested in doing.[5]

Fortunately, about midway through my graduate training I got to know Kai Erikson, who agreed to direct my dissertation.[6] In topical terms, it seemed an unlikely match of professor with student. I was seeking guidance for a study in social-psychological matters involving religion and mental health, which I hoped would take me back to Ecuador. Erikson was identified at the time as an American Studies scholar with an historical interest in the social functions of deviance, and in the nature of community and community loss.[7]

While Kai Erikson's first academic position had been in a department of psychiatry, he had made his sociological reputation as a proponent of the labeling theory of deviance that was widely applied in critiques of psychiatry in the 1960s. When I met him, he made it appear almost as if he had lost interest in the sort of developmental, interpretive approaches to mental illness (or religion, for that matter) that I might have found seductive. He was fond of saying that sociologists didn't have a methodological place to stand in trying to understand such phenomena in terms of individualized experiences—that the "ways of God and the furnishings of the human mind are equally inscrutable, at least to a sociologist."

Nevertheless (almost paradoxically), Erikson was a champion of using narrative data to tell a sociological story, exactly the kind of data that some sociologists find tedious and untidy and "nongeneralizable." Furthermore, he recognized that many times the sociologist herself or himself is an important part of that story. He insisted that academics must attend to the ways in which their own biographical events and guiding personal myths were bound up with their interests as scholars and researchers. And of course, being, among other things, editor of the *Yale Review*, Kai Erikson cared about the esthetics of language and authorial voice.

In Erikson's opinion then, sociology remained intellectually impoverished to the extent that it concerned itself only with abstractions cleansed of the lived experience of real people in real historical moments—including (sometimes especially) the experience of sociological authors. He didn't see why a thing had to be specified ahead of time as a "sample" or a "specimen" of some larger, more important category in order to qualify for sociological attention. He thought that a perfectly good warrant for studying a special setting or group might be provided not by the subject itself, but the investigator's unique relation to it.

Taking this wisdom to heart came to mean doing social observation a bit backwards from the way it is sometimes taught as "normal science." Instead of starting with questions posed by past theory and moving forward to hypotheses and then to observation, Erikson's method was to start with the present moment—what we see as relevant here and now, and how we talk and feel about it—and then to move back through the selective filters (including theoretical ideas) by which we have come to view the past in light of what has happened to us, and finally to ask the right questions. The questions we formulate in this manner should be the ones that future generations would most like to know the answers to, when they come to wonder who we were and to ponder the important things that occurred in our lifetimes (see Erikson, 1984). In the end, we might retell our story as a seamless, coherent chronology from beginning to end—people tend do that naturally—but we would understand our own role in crafting a kind of interpretive reality that is only one of many possible realities, though nonetheless "true."

Finally, Erikson helped me to see that I really could go back to Ecuador and study missionaries' lives with a bit more confidence than I felt at the time. He suggested that my personal background—in conversation with sociological ideas—could transform what some would call "subjective bias" into a fund of sociological sensitivity and imagination. And it was he who asserted, long before the thought ever occurred to me, that all of this would be a book one day. He said he knew "a few people" who would be interested in reading it. As it happened, his friend and former Yale colleague, novelist John Hersey, was at that time writing his career-crowning work about a missionary in China—a character who turned out to resemble no one so much as Hersey's own father. If Erikson knew about this, he never mentioned it. But when I finished my dissertation, he presented me with a copy of *The Call* personally inscribed by Hersey, along with the author's address in Key West and a suggestion that I write to him. I wish I had done so. Hersey died in 1993.

I was not quite five years old when my family moved to a small settlement at the edge of the jungle in the Ecuadorian Oriente, province of Pastaza. The surrounding region was inhabited by a dwindling population of Quichua and Shuar Indians interspersed with a few scattered settlements of white and mixed-race *colonos*. We lived in a large tropical-style house on stilts, with unpainted lumber siding, screened windows, and a covered veranda graced by a flowering bougainvillea that wound up a trellis to touch the sloping tin roof overhead. It was a very large house that came with two boarders inhabiting the guest rooms when we arrived. It was situated in a mission compound on the outskirts of a village called Shell, named for the Dutch petroleum company that had set up a base camp in the 1940s to look for oil. By the time we arrived in 1961, the company had long since abandoned its quest, and the Ecuadorian military had established an outpost there to take advantage of the airstrip. The former Shell camp was occupied by missionaries from the Gospel Missionary Union who had established a small Bible Institute there. Almost adjacent to the Institute, on the opposite side of a single-lane gravel road that ran through town, was our compound—bordered by jungle on three sides, and encompassing a couple of houses, an outpatient clinic building, and a twenty-bed hospital. Beyond the trees in the foreground, the far horizon beckoned with the gray-blue outlines of the Andean highlands, and—on a clear morning—the snow-covered peaks of the volcanoes, Sangay and El Altar.

My father was one of two doctors who staffed the hospital that served a huge area of Ecuador's eastern jungle. Patients would be flown in on a single-engine missionary airplane, or would arrive by bus from towns further up the road, or would even straggle in on foot after several days of walking through the forest. Those who made it to the hospital were often gravely ill or injured, had pregnancy complications, or had some equally serious problem. In my mind, my father was a hero who saved people's lives, sometimes in the dead of the night. Since we lived right next to the hospital, I could see the patients arrive and I could see him attend to them. On many occasions Mother would send me over to the clinic to tell Dad it was time for dinner, and then I would return and we would eat without him. Sometimes he would go on trips down the river and be gone several days, bringing back an Indian blowgun, a feathered headdress, a monkey, or a boa constrictor that he'd traded for penicillin. Once he brought home a gift from a Quichua elder who suffered from tuberculosis—a parrot that turned out to have a chronic cough.

My mother was perhaps a more influential presence in my early life than was my father (despite his looming stature as a heroic figure in my imagination). Mother had been a teacher and had pursued graduate studies in Latin American history prior to entering the missionary vocation. Rather than sending us children away to a boarding academy in Quito, Mother created her own version of a Nebraska country schoolhouse in our home, and soon found herself teaching not only us, but a half dozen children of other missionaries stationed in Shell. The public school in town was an option my parents never considered, since it would not have qualified us for subsequent study at the U.S.-accredited Alliance Academy in Quito, and beyond that, for college back in the States.

My older brother Tod and I spent endless hours exploring the jungle around our house, building lean-to forts with palm branches, and trying to catch fish in the streams nearby. Aside from Sunday School, we had almost no contact with Ecuadorian children from town. We learned Spanish from lessons in school, from the maids in our home, and from employees around the hospital. When Tod was about seven or eight, one of the hospital maintenance workers—a Quichua man named Agustin Tapui—took him under his wing. I was too small to be included, but Tod was allowed to tag along with Agustin as he fished and set traps and hunted for monkeys, ocelots, and birds in the jungle. Before he was ten, Tod had become fairly adept at knocking small game out of trees with Dad's twenty-gauge shotgun. I, meanwhile, developed an elaborate fantasy featuring myself as an international airline pilot. My parents commissioned a local tailor to sew a blue pilot's uniform with gold braid on the sleeves and shoulders, which I wore with a certain august bearing to Sunday School every week. Before long, the Shell townspeople had taken to calling me *Capitán,* and the name stuck.

When we returned to Minnesota for a furlough after five years, I was enrolled in third grade at a suburban public elementary school. I was something of a curiosity. Boys I admired brought G.I. Joes to school for show-and-tell. I, instead, brought a snake skin from Ecuador—twenty-two feet long. Then I produced a blowgun and a hunting spear made of chonta palm wood, and a long feathered headdress from the Atshuaras. I let it slip that I could speak Spanish. The teacher informed the principal, and he was so impressed he invited my parents to address the whole school at a special session. The Richfield newspaper ran an article: "Local Doctor Returns from Ecuador Jungle Mission." But after a while, my celebrity status grew thin and tiresome, and I just wanted to fit in. I wanted to have friends and, to my parents' chagrin, I began to covet a G.I. Joe. I begged and pleaded, and eventually they relented and bought me one. ("After all, Charlotte, I had toy soldiers when I was little. I don't suppose this is much different.") I carried my new status symbol to school the next morning in a paper bag. Mrs. Olson eagerly introduced me at show-and-tell time, and my classmates peered at me in wide-eyed anticipation, trying to imagine the exotic treasure I had concealed in the bag. I pulled out the G.I. Joe. They stared in silent disappointment. Then came a good deal of nervous laughter. Mrs. Olson finally asked, "Is there anything special about that G.I. Joe? Did you buy it with your own money or something?" I said "No, my parents just bought it for me." After an awkward silence I returned to my seat trying to understand what had gone wrong.

At First Covenant Church, my parents were treated like the returned heroes that they were, and some of the aura rubbed off on us kids. In my third grade Sunday School class, the teacher asked me to lead in prayer and insisted I tell the class what it was like to be a missionary boy in the jungles of South America. Later that fall when it came time for the "Swansons' report from the Ecuador field," the church was packed to the rafters. We children dressed up in Amazon Indian costumes and paraded on stage to sing gospel choruses in Spanish. Dad showed slides from his river trips, and Mother regaled the folk with spellbinding tales of what God was doing in Ecuador.

All of us longed to be back in Shell. But when our furlough year ended, Dad was reassigned to the Mission's city hospital in Quito, a bitter disappointment to my brothers and sisters and me. In the city we moved into a two-storied green stucco house with a tile roof, surrounded by a high chain-link fence, Mount Pichincha looming behind it. The house was situated among a cluster of other missionary residences and institutional buildings on the north side of Quito—a concentrated foreign presence that included the HCJB-World Radio compound, Hospital Vozandes, the Alliance Academy and adjoining student dormitories, and English Fellowship Church. We were enrolled in the Alliance Academy, a school for missionaries' children run by the Christian and Missionary Alliance and accredited in the States. Many of my fourth-grade friends lived in adjacent dormitories and had parents working in remote parts of Ecuador or other South American countries. Life for us revolved around the school, which was almost hermetically sealed off from the surrounding community.

Inside the high walls of the school compound, we often passed our days without seeing a single Ecuadorian person except for a few janitors, gardeners, and Spanish teachers. Apart from one required class in Spanish, all of our academic instruction was in English—including chapel services and daily Bible lessons. We used Spanish mainly to interact with snack vendors around the school and the maids who worked in our homes. We celebrated American holidays like Thanksgiving and dressed up for Halloween. We played American football and baseball among ourselves, and basketball and soccer against Ecuadorian schools—almost always on our home turf. We wore "Stateside" clothes and shoes that our parents had brought down in barrels. On Sundays, we attended English Fellowship Church and Sunday School.

In 1969 Dad received an urgent call from the Wycliffe Bible Translators who sponsored a mission among the Waoranis (then known as Aucas), the famous tribe that had speared to death five American missionaries in 1956. One group of Aucas had converted to Christianity and settled around the missionary airstrip and compound on the Tiwaeno river. But for many years, the rest of the Aucas had remained in their jungle habitat completely out of touch with white civilization. In our student prayer sessions at the Alliance Academy, we were frequently encouraged to "pray for the downriver Aucas, that they might be reached with the Gospel." Finally, a group of them had been enticed out of the forest to rejoin their kinspeople in the Tiwaeno settlement. Having no immunity to outside diseases, many of the new arrivals were promptly stricken with a febrile illness causing muscle paralysis and respiratory difficulty. Almost none of the Christian Aucas were affected. It soon occurred to the missionary woman on site that the downriver Aucas might suspect that they had been bushwhacked with powerful unseen weapons. Tensions mounted and two retaliatory spearings took place, despite the efforts of the Christian Aucas to reassure the new group, and to care for their ill members. Undeterred by the warning of the missionary in Tiwaeno about the risk that the situation posed for a male outsider, Dad was flown in to try to diagnose the illness and treat the sick. Mother said goodbye wondering, she later told us, if she would ever see Dad alive again. But the massacre never occurred. The disease was polio, and it left strong warriors unable to walk. Dad did everything he could do under the circumstances. Before the epidemic had passed, sixteen Indians had died.

A year later our family went back to Minnesota for another furlough. Many rolls of 35mm slides had been taken of the Aucas during the polio epidemic, and Dad appeared in a number of dramatic photographs. He developed an audiovisual production telling the story and presented it in churches throughout the Twin Cities. We kids usually went along, so I got to see it many times and still remember the opening line of Dad's narration: "Polio! The forgotten plague of our present generation still strikes along the headwaters of the Amazon." I attended Richfield East Junior High School. A social studies teacher there took me under his wing and suggested that I enter the Optimists' Oratorical Contest with a speech about my life in a foreign country. I prepared a speech giving tribute to my father and the missionaries in Ecuador, extolling the sacrifices they had made and the wonderful things they were doing for less fortunate souls abroad. I entitled my remarks rather grandly "The American Image Overseas" (being oblivious to the Vietnam War protests raging at the time.) I won a large silver trophy and displayed it proudly for many years.

Back in Ecuador, Dad was reassigned to the Shell hospital but I stayed in Quito—a day's drive away—to attend school at the Academy. I lived with the family of a teacher whose son was in my class. My brother and sister each lived with a different family. I saw my mother and dad and two younger siblings during school vacations, and a few other occasions when they visited. My parents assured me that if I ever needed them, they would be there for me.

By the time I was a senior in high school, the cool thing to do was to act like a touring hippie from California. My friends and I wore Otavalan Indian ponchos over our Levis in a bemused act of parody. We played guitars and carried cameras around and took pictures of the mystifying people and sights we had seen all our lives. We spoke Spanish with exaggerated gringo accents. We listened to ball games on American Armed Forces Radio, and we bided our time, longing to get back to the States. Then suddenly it was over, and we stepped on a plane and headed north for good.

In the fall of 1975 I entered Westmont College, a small Christian liberal arts school in California. The campus was an American evangelical paradise—a former private estate in the hills overlooking Santa Barbara and the Pacific Ocean, inhabited by several hundred Christian young people and their able, dedicated professors. Westmont students were beautiful, bright, athletic, clean-cut kids who did well and had a lot of fun at it. It was an expensive school; I had gotten a scholarship to go there and had announced my intention to study premedical science and eventually become a doctor. My parents were thrilled. It should have been a wonderful place to spend four years—and in some ways it was. And yet, the expected feeling of "coming home to America"—a feeling of belonging to a place that I had yearned for as a missionaries' kid—completely eluded me. I made few friends and I felt alone much of the time. I endured a kind of melancholy that I couldn't understand and didn't disclose. Instead, I poured myself into my studies.

On Sundays I frequently went down into Santa Barbara to attend a Spanish-speaking Mexican church. It was a struggling little congregation of mostly older people who—for various interesting reasons—were not Catholic. They viewed my presence among them with a kind of perplexed indifference and insisted on responding to me in English when I addressed them in Spanish. The sermon was often delivered by a silver-tongued Westmont professor of Cuban extraction. My mind tended to wander as he spoke, the rising and falling of his Latin cadences washing into the recesses of my memory like waves on the Pacific shore. Before long I would find myself back in Shell, a towheaded six-year-old in a blue dress-up uniform, surrounded by dark faces listening earnestly to the *evangelio* while dogs straggled in from the rain that beat down on the tin roof above.

In the summer after my first year at Westmont, I secured a minimum-wage job in a window factory and warehouse in San Leandro. Almost all of my fellow workers, including my foreman, were Mexicans. They didn't know quite what to make of me. I affected the persona of an expatriate Ecuadorian (originally from Minnesota by accident of birth.) I spoke Spanish with all the *modismos* I could muster. I even sent my parents a cassette tape describing my life as a factory worker—all in Spanish as if, in my transformation, I had somehow forgotten my mother tongue and expected them not to notice.

I returned to Westmont, and by the middle of my sophomore year abandoned plans to be a medical doctor (which I had constructed as a kind of father-son crisis that it never was), and declared a major in sociology. I began to realize that I could employ my unusual background to write successful term papers in various timely courses. One of my first was a descriptive analysis of my recent experience in the window factory, applying the ideas of Erving Goffman and Theodore Caplow. I took a course in social deviance and wrote about foreigners as deviants who form a "subculture of the uprooted." I took a course in the sociology of religion and wrote about culture and Christianity in Hispanic America—a paper about the "meaning and belonging functions of religion" illustrated with personal reminiscences ranging from my childhood fear and loathing of the Catholic church in Ecuador to my alienating reverie among the Mexican Baptists in Santa Barbara. As I went along, the sociology of this-and-that became a new vehicle for self-discovery. My encounters with philosophy, religious studies, history, and literature also served this function, though perhaps less successfully. (For a creative writing seminar, I crafted a now-laughable short story that I imagined to be a sort of Steinbeck-meets-Hemingway, Cain-and-Abel tale of two rum-besotted American brothers searching for sunken treasure off the coast of Ecuador, ending implausibly with an underwater fratricide.)

Then about midway through college I went back to Ecuador to visit my folks, and to spend the summer volunteering with a mission project that involved training Indian health workers in the Oriente. Tod was going to be there too. Dad had started training indigenous "health promoters" about ten years earlier, and the endeavor was now incorporated rather grandly and bureaucratically as part of the Community Development Department of HCJB's Health Care Division. The Mission had gotten some consultation and technical assistance from an Illinois-based outfit called Medical Assistance Programs, which in turn had helped them secure a demonstration grant from the Agency for International Development (USAID). As part of the grant, a program evaluation was supposed to be conducted that included a baseline health survey in selected communities of the Shuar and Atshuara tribes in the province of Morona Santiago. Tod and I were the household survey interviewers, working in Spanish through Shuar interpreters.

Near the end of the summer, Dad decided to accompany his two sons on our last survey trip to the jungle—out to a remote region of the Atshuara territory that he had not visited since his early days in Shell. When he had last gone there many years before, the only means of access was by canoe. Now there was a tiny airstrip carved out of the jungle on a bluff overlooking the river. The three of us were flown in on a single-engine missionary plane and dropped off for an eight-day sojourn. We had no means of contacting the outside world in the meantime; just before leaving Shell, we had discovered that the portable, battery-powered radio usually taken on such trips was not working. We would be about three days' walk from the nearest place that had two-way radio communication.

A couple of days into the week, I became extremely ill with a pounding headache and a stiff neck, which Dad diagnosed as cerebro-spinal meningitis but didn't say so out loud. The only remedy he had brought along was a container of one hundred capsules of an antibiotic. Dad let me know he had enough medicine for me to take five capsules every four hours until the plane was scheduled to come in at the end of the week. (What he didn't mention was that this amounted to less than half the recommended dosage to treat such a serious and life-threatening infection, and that the medication really ought to have been administered intravenously.)

I took the pills, and I asked Dad if I was going to be all right. He said that I was in the hollow of God's hand. I lay on a bamboo mat, staring up at the palm thatch overhead, while the Atshuaras hovered about drinking chicha and commenting inscrutably in hushed tones, and the thought came to me: I really could die out here, and Dad might not be able to do anything about it. If I lived, it was going to make a terrific missionary story but that was not exactly a foregone conclusion. (If I died it might make an even better story, but I wouldn't be around to care.) As the evening wore on, and after our hosts had gone to bed, Dad sat up beside me. He said he was going to pray. He put his hand on my forehead and he asked the Lord to touch my body as the Great Physician, and to make me well if it should be His will. As I drifted off to sleep, Dad was softly humming a tune I knew well. There is a balm in Gilead.

The Moral Career, the Stranger, and the Call

> *I am a stranger here,*
> *within a foreign land;*
> *My home is far away,*
> *upon a golden strand;*
> *Ambassador to be*
> *of realms beyond the sea—*
> *I'm here on business for my king*
>
> E. T. CASSEL[8]

Whose story is this? And who is the stranger? Perhaps there are several kinds of "stranger stories" to be told here, each providing a different filter for interpreting the fragments of missionary talk that will appear throughout the book. First, there is my own tale of growing up in Ecuador as a missionaries' son, coming of age and going away, and returning to interrogate my parents' world with the secular device of a dissertation. According to that story, the things that missionaries say—and especially the ways in which I choose to quote them—express indirectly my own ambivalent struggle to integrate past and present chapters of my life.[9]

At further remove, there is the chronicle of the social movements in which the missionaries that I interviewed continue to play a part—American evangelicalism, fundamentalism, and the modern foreign missions movement in particular. Here the words of my research subjects serve to situate their lives within a larger saga of a collective set-apartness, and to illuminate a significant social history and reveal the changing cultural conditions that have shaped the missionary vocation.[10]

Then there is the alternative story (many stories, really) belonging to the people whose conversion to Christianity has been the earnest goal of evangelical missions for at least three centuries. Missionaries offer only glimpses of their hosts' lives when they speak of "Ecuadorians," "Indians," and "nationals"—as if they were the strangers. Still, it will be important to interpret the ways in which these others have been (and continue to be) objectified in missionary rhetoric, as such images reveal the religious nuances of a Euro-American domination which has altered irrevocably—for good or ill—the cultural history and experience of indigenous people throughout the world, and which is bound up with their possible futures as well.[11]

I have had to overcome the conceit that I should (or could) somehow weave these alternative "stranger stories" together and do them justice. Each of them would require its own telling for a distinctive purpose; each calls for a different sort of voice and language (not my own, often enough). In consequence, I have given none of these stories much direct attention, though I view them as important subplots that will approach the surface of the text at various points throughout the book.

The story that I intend to feature, rather, is a sociological account of *strangerhood* as a *moral career*—as a complex narrative theme in the self-understanding of a group of individuals who have embraced a missionary *calling*. In this rendering, I will try to show how these particular American evangelical Christians in a foreign setting employ the ideological abstraction of *life-as-testimony* to organize diverse existential and cultural conditions of estrangement in their lives. I will try to show how these missionaries' moral careers emerge and develop as such people reflect on their condition of set-apartness in the light of culturally stylized ideas about conversion and divine calling; and how, in the end, they manage to domesticate their foreignness and transcend disenchantment through a reformulation—and reappropriation—of the imagery of *mission-as-sacrificial-hero-quest*.

The exegesis of strangerhood in missionary testimonies perhaps offers some insight into the larger cultural context that encloses American evangelicals, i.e., as social actors whose presence and posture in a postmodern world would seem to call for explanation. Clearly, however, my work does not provide a comprehensive or systematic interpretation of the intellectual-historical and cultural matrices of the Protestant-missionary lifeworld. That task has been (and continues to be) performed admirably by others—social historians and missiologists (e.g., Hutchison, 1987; Carpenter and Shenk, 1990; Bosch, 1991; Taber, 1991; Neill, 1986; Hesselgrave, 1988; Van Engen, Gilliland, and Pierson, 1993) as well as sociologists who have examined the significance of mission ideas that have emerged and influenced evangelicals and fundamentalists in their own natural habitat (e.g., Ammerman, 1987; Warner, 1988; Hunter, 1982, 1987).

Alternatively, a *moral career* approach places on center stage the formation of a missionary *self*, and inquires after cultural patterns, movements, and historical events only insofar as necessary to identify certain significant "texts" that these individuals employ in their repertoire of social performances—specifically those performances that serve to consolidate a distinctive missionary identity. The question becomes what must we learn, especially from the missionaries' own points of view, about the cultural worlds to which they are (often tenuously) connected, in order to understand their accounts of missionary identity *as strangerhood*? An answer will emerge gradually, as we see how different individuals shape their missionary careers and their identities from the elements of various cultural situations, which they confront with an ambivalence arising from experiences of withdrawal and engagement, conflict and embrace, and dependence and personal empowerment.

The key terms used throughout this study were thus chosen to frame an understanding of the sorts of testimonies that evangelical missionaries relate; to show how missionaries use certain symbolic images and narrative forms to invest their lives with meaning and interpret that meaning for various audiences (including themselves); and to illustrate how, in so doing, they develop thematic accounts of becoming the people they now see themselves as being. The expressions I employ to convey such an understanding—*the moral career, the stranger, and the call*—have an ordinary-language ring to them, but contain broader connotations that may illuminate hidden facets and functions of missionaries' testimonies. These deeper symbolic meanings bear sociological scrutiny.

Moral is a complex term in social theory, defined more often in terms of how it works than what it is. In the tradition of Durkheim, the *moral order* is conceived as a sort of collective conscience, transcending individual interests and making society's equilibrium possible by providing a consensual basis for the rules that govern and sanction the conduct of social relations. But *moral* can also refer to the inner life of a person in confrontation with those social rules and sanctions, encompassing a person's internalized responses to the ways others seem to view him or her. And a *career* can refer to a "trajectory through life . . . in the service of both the physical being and the symbolic self" (Goldschmidt, 1990). A *moral career*, then, is the connected line of any person's experiences with others in society from which there emerge his or her most profound and lasting judgments of self.[12] Different patterns of social experience tend to produce different judgments of self over time—which is to say, different kinds of moral careers.

The pathbreaking study that made the term famous in sociology was Erving Goffman's (1961) essay on "the moral career of the mental patient." Goffman described the process by which persons may gradually *become* mental patients in response to the dehumanizing judgments of others with more power, who treat them as if they had no self apart from the deviant role of mental patient. Goffman called this process "mortification," evoking the death and transformation of the mental patient's other potential self or selves. Eventually, said Goffman, such persons may reconstruct their entire biography as an explanation of how they became a mental patient, and come to view their future in terms of that "institutional self" or "master status" as well.

In this light, we can see *moral experience* as that which accrues from the life changes affecting people's most basic, lasting views of how they are connected to (or disconnected from) the social world around them, and of their own sense of significance, destiny, or fate within that world. Likewise, *moral ideas* emerge from the stories people tell that give some account of the origin, character, consequence, and trajectory of their lives. And importantly, one's moral career is connected to one's own telling of the story for an audience that includes both the self and others; it is a constructed, narrated, *socially mediated* as well as *self-mediated* account of personal identity.

The lives of missionaries provide an unusually rich study of moral careers, though differing in obvious ways from those Goffman examined. Building on Goffman's insights, we shall see that becoming a missionary also tends to involve a distinctive kind of socially induced "mortification" of the self, and that missionaries, too, tend to reconstruct their biographies as an explanation of how they became what they are. In more positive terms, though, they tend to view their unfolding life stories as emerging testimonies to the Christian message of salvation for the world around them. As such, a mission becomes more than something they do; it is something they embody, as it encompasses not only their work but their basic sense of identity.

We shall see that the role of the *stranger*—and the symbolic imagery of *strangerhood*—are featured significantly, if not always explicitly, in missionaries' moral-career narratives. Why is the stranger important to missionaries, and thus for the task of understanding their lives? One reason is that the arrival of a stranger makes a good story, provoking interest and creating dramatic intrigue; and missionaries are in the business of telling good stories with a purpose. Another reason is that the *unknown one* brings to the social world that he or she approaches an experience that is exogenous to everyday life in that world, and thus offers the possibility of *otherness*—of transformation to a new and extraordinary way of being. Moreover, the stranger's unique perceptual frame becomes a reflective device through which those around him or her can view themselves and their local world as if they were standing in a distant *elsewhere*. Thus, the figure of the stranger tends to draw out self-illuminating reactions from other characters and potentially brings about some sort of transformation in their lives. That is what missionaries—in many different ways—say has happened to them, and it is what they desire to accomplish in other lives.

The figure of the stranger is also important in a broader sociological sense, because it provides a symbolic idiom for understanding the commonalities among different ways of being set apart,[13] i.e., across diverse forms of *estrangement* captured in the social-psychological experiences of being excluded, rejected, abandoned, or left behind; but also in the features of such culturally typified characters as the voyager, the newcomer, the pilgrim, the prodigal, the pariah, the other-worldly seer, the prophet, the ambassador, the scapegoat, the sinner, and the saint.

For evangelical missionaries, the primary archetype of strangerhood has been the figure of Christ, as refracted through hagiographies of earlier missionaries. According to this view, missionaries—like Christ—come into a world that is not their own, suffer rejection by those who fail to understand where they have come from and what they are about, give themselves sacrificially for the lives of others, and finally complete their earthly sojourn by "going home" to be with God. Moreover, since the earliest American missionaries appropriated the Christ story as a paradigm for their own sacrifice and other-worldly strangerhood, future generations of evangelicals have tended to legitimate the mission calling not only through the direct use of Christological imagery, but by echoing the powerful use of such images by their heroic predecessors at the dawn of the missions movement. Consider, for example, the rhetorical and thematic parallels in the following composite passages from the journals of two young missionaries, separated in time by more than two centuries:

> Such fatigues and hardships as these serve to wean me more from the earth, and, I trust, will make heaven the sweeter. . . . For a very considerable time past, my soul has rejoiced to think of death in its nearest approaches, even when I have been very weak. . . . I am willing to tarry awhile in a world of sorrow; I am willing to be from home as long as God sees fit it should be so . . . but oh, when will the day appear, that I shall be perfect in holiness, and in the enjoyment of God!

> Oh Lord, deliver me from the spirit of this faithless generation. . . . God, I pray Thee, light these idle sticks of my life and may I burn for Thee. Consume my life, my God, for it is Thine. . . . Father, take my life, yea, my blood if Thou wilt, and consume it with Thine enveloping fire. I would not save it, for it is not mine to save. Have it, Lord, have it all. Pour out my life as an oblation for the world. Blood is only of value as it flows before Thine altar.

The words in the first quotation were written by the Puritan missionary David Brainerd, not long before he died at the edge of the forests of New England in 1747.[14] The words in the second quotation were written by an Illinois college student named Jim Elliot, a few years before he was speared to death by the Auca Indians in the jungle of Ecuador in 1956.[15]

Clearly, there are other sorts of moral careers besides missionaries' that may revolve around a sense of heroic strangerhood passed from one generation to another. Among academics, anthropologists in particular have often embraced the role of the stranger, i.e., the stranger and heroic cartographer of exotic *ethoi*. Along these lines, Clifford Geertz (1988) renders Levi-Strauss's *Tristes Tropiques* as the enacting of the myth of the stranger's quest:

> The departure from familiar, boring, [but] oddly threatening shores; the journey, with adventures, into another, darker world, full of various phantasms and odd revelations; the culminating mystery, the absolute other, sequestered and opaque, confronted deep down in the sertao; the return home to tell tales, a bit wistfully, a bit wearily (Geertz, 1988:45).

As have others, I view the stranger as an apt image (though a complex one) to use in portraying the missionary's moral career.[16] The missionary's most formative and defining experiences are received on the outskirts of social life, in a liminal zone where ordinary expectations are suspended or challenged—which is perhaps where moral understanding and "identity work"[17] is most called for. Georg Simmel (1904) might have been describing missionaries' ambiguous relation to various social worlds when he wrote that the stranger is one who is "inorganically appended" to a group—who does not belong to it, yet confronts it. Simmel showed how strangers embody a paradox. They are near to the group, yet remain far from it. They have freedom to wander, yet are limited by a kind of remoteness. Elaborating on Simmel's stranger, Alfred Schutz (1944) described the subjective conditions entailed in the stranger's relation to groups. He described these conditions as showing several layers of separation; first, and most generally, from the social world of one's origin; second, from interpretive devices—the "recipes"—for meaningful action and for attaching meaning to everyday experience; and third, from the self which is created reflectively and sustained through social interaction.

The exemplar for Simmel's and Schutz's notions of strangerhood was the immigrant. One who is uprooted from a homeland and confronts a foreign country must initially endure, to some degree, a loss of social being. The missionary's experience resembles the immigrant's in some ways, but key differences arise from their distinctive underlying motives and expectations. Immigrants typically manifest an economic motivation to get involved in their surrounding community and to become as much a part of it as they can. Immigrants to America in particular have traditionally seen themselves as successful in their host country insofar as the structure of their economic, social, cultural, and emotional exchange with the host community approaches a kind of symmetry. To that extent, being a stranger is a temporary condition that may be overcome as the immigrant gradually becomes bonded to the new country and eventually gives children over to its ways, planting new roots for the family line.

According to Schutz (himself an immigrant to America), this process involves reconstructing one's personal identity with respect to a new cultural pattern.[18] Clearly, an immigrant's recasting of identity becomes more complicated in contemporary host communities whose members may represent many cultures, each somehow resisting assimilation into a dominant (or polyglot) culture. But the point is that immigrants succeed in a new life by initiating and sustaining interaction with the community (or communities) around them; by giving and receiving, in more or less equal measure, and thus capitalizing on their strengths to make up for their weaknesses. By the same token, though, immigrants can remain marginal, dependent, and relatively powerless if they possess few resources needed or desired by members of the host community, yet manifest great needs that only the host community can fulfill.

Missionaries, in contrast, tend to remain marginal not because of some unbalanced dependency upon the host community, but because of their autonomy from it and their distinctive motivation for approaching it. Their economic and social needs are supplied largely by unknown sources outside the community, while they control and offer unilaterally certain resources needed (they think) by those living around them. Missionaries conceive of their foreign sojourn as a spiritual act that involves going out, conducting a mission, and eventually returning home. They tend to view themselves as religious ambassadors sent out to represent an other-worldly kingdom, and it is this self-perception that sets the tone of missionaries' confrontations with their host country. It provides them with a rationalization for the persistent lack of balance in their exchange with members of their target community.

Success in their mission ultimately removes missionaries' basic reason for staying in a particular place—but if they are rejected, their sense of strangerhood only grows stronger while they remain. Thus, in a sense, missionary strangerhood is inherent; their giving and receiving, knowing and being known in a host community can never be quite commensurate, due to their outside means of support and locus of accountability, their temporary and tentative status in the host community, and their ulterior motives for entering that community in the first place. Such asymmetry is not primarily a social fact arising from unequal distribution of resources—though this sharpens it—but rather, a normative principle at the core of evangelical missionary ideology.

As this study will show, missionaries' experiences of set-apartness in a foreign country are linked to preceding stages of their moral careers. In one way or another, strangerhood emerges as a theme running through missionaries' entire lives, connecting and organizing both positive and negative events and conditions that affect them. Opposite or very different sorts of early-life experiences may be imbued with similar significance from the later vantage point of the missionary vocation. Among the missionaries whose testimonies I recorded, one person had a physical handicap; another was an excellent athlete. One was a failing student; another was a valedictorian. One was an only child; another was the youngest of many children. One had a preacher father; another had an alcoholic father. Some felt smothered by their parents; others lost their parents at an early age. Some grew up poor in America; a few grew up comfortably in a foreign country. The point is that all of my subjects tended to redefine their prior experiences as material that God used to bring them to a point of spiritual commitment culminating in a missionary vocation. As a result, being *set apart* became *set apart for God*, and the whole complex of missionary strangerhood could be embraced as a way of living out an underlying sense of other-worldly identity.

The missionary's moral career dramatizes an important distinction (and linkage) between the objectified categories of social membership over against which the stranger exists (or is produced), and the subjective experience of strangerhood that may be connected to prior developmental events and religious other-worldly sensibilities. In this light, the locus of strangerhood may be internal and permanent, carried along as a part of the self and manifested in different formations and transformations; and it may also be an external attribute, given by an individual's position in (or distance from) a relevant social space at a particular moment.

Missionaries' life stories demonstrate that the fact of being set apart tends to suspend the taken-for-granted quality of their everyday lives, and seems to demand that a greater portion of their total experience be interpreted *morally*—i.e., by highlighting and interrogating the relationship between the self and the moral order upon which the stability of particular forms of social life depends. One important sociological question, then, that may be addressed by an inquiry into missionaries' complex strangerhood, is this: What can people on the margins tell us about conditions at the so-called center of social life from which they are set apart? Upon reflection, though, this question gives way to a second, more penetrating query: How do people such as these come to experience life on the margin as *morally central*?

A part of the answer, as we shall see, is that the people to be heard from in this book tend to organize their life stories around a liminal religious experience that comes to define their social and personal identities—the moment of a missionary *call*, or a pervasive and persistent sense of divine *calling*. Evangelicals employ the rhetoric of calling in at least two significant ways, corresponding to social and individualized forms of set-apartness. On the one hand, they speak in Biblical terms about the people of God—or the church as a whole—being called out of the world, and called to the task of evangelizing the world in their own generation. On the other hand, they construct the missionary calling as a personalized experience at the portal of a religious career, which prompts the individual to embrace a spiritual life work for which he or she is supposedly singled out by God. Missionaries' moral-career narratives often weave both of these senses of calling and set-apartness into a single underlying theme at the core of their identity. However, the second kind of call is perhaps most significant, because it becomes the watershed of the missionary's life story: Events leading up to the call are configured to foreshadow it, and developments thereafter are seen as elaborations that fulfill the call, work it out, or renegotiate its terms in one way or another.

As we shall see, some missionaries say they received the call in the moment of a dramatic personal epiphany, often at a point of crisis in late adolescence or in conjunction with religious conversion. Others construct a call as something gradually realized, a spiritual thread weaving together a whole series of circumstances whose interconnections were not discerned until much later. But in any case, the significance of the call for the moral careers to be examined here can hardly be overestimated. A missionary call sets a person apart from a local religious community as well as from the larger social world of his or her origin. It imbues past experience with transcendent meaning that previously was opaque or unnoticed, and highlights any sense in which a person has been set apart throughout his or her prior life. Finally, the call brings into focus a personal destiny of Christ-like strangerhood, which motivates action and "identity work" towards an ideal and frames the interpretation of subsequent life events.

Roots of Set-Apartness and Mission in American Evangelical History

As will become clear in subsequent chapters of this book, the embracing of strangerhood by missionaries can be understood on several levels: (1) as an elaboration of the process of "mortification" and conversion of a prior self, often rooted in early developmental experiences of estrangement or loss of significant others; (2) as a self-conscious symbolic imitation of Christ; (3) as an expression of the spiritual set-apartness that evangelicals construct as a requisite of Christian identity; (4) as an expression of the national set-apartness that has defined America's historical sense of itself as a redeemer nation destined to occupy a favored place and to exert special religious and cultural influence throughout the world.

These interwoven threads of meaning pose a sociological puzzle for interpreting individualized missionary callings. On the one hand, the broader evangelical notion of spiritual set-apartness is grounded in the ideal of a pure church, which is embodied in the cultural mythology of a Christian nation founded in the bedrock of Puritan theocracy. On the other hand, spiritual set-apartness is here played out in the experience of *individuals*—for whom the supreme manifestation of that larger social identity comes to mean leaving the community behind and embarking on a lone hero quest. For people with a particular developmental background, who are psychologically inclined towards a Christocentric identity, the missionary calling turns the American religious ideal of social set-apartness inside out: the calling to *come out* of the world into the church becomes the calling to *go out* from the church (or the Christian nation) into the world.

Where does this ambiguous notion of set-apartness come from? And how does the concept lend itself to missionaries? As with any moral idea, evangelicals believe that the "principle of separation" originates with God and is spelled out in the Bible. As evangelical scholars have put it:

> The principle of separation itself is as old as belief in the God of creation. God separated the offering of Abel from that of Cain. When God entered into covenant with Abraham, he set apart one man and his descendants as the means by which all mankind would be blessed. In Christ's teaching there was no mistaking virgins with lamps ready and those unprepared, the house built on the rock from the one built on sand. The Lord himself likened the members of his kingdom to wheat and fruitful vines, those standing outside to weeds and barren branches. Later in the New Testament Paul urged Christians not to be "conformed to this world, but to be transformed by the renewal of your mind" (Rom. 12:2 RSV). And James contended that one of the marks of true religion was remaining "unspotted from the world" (James 1:27 RSV).
>
> In light of this biblical evidence, Christians have always seen a clear difference between the children of God and the children of the world (Woodbridge, Noll, and Hatch, 1979:183–184).

Evangelicals' rhetorical use of Biblical events, characters, and themes to interpret their own contemporary experience sometimes tends to obscure their sense of being shaped by a more recent cultural past. Their overarching view of the sweep of human history—incorporating their own time—thus extends from Genesis to the Apocalypse of John. Embedded in this perspective is the idea that, since the Bible defines and transcends history, Biblical principles must be treated as timeless absolutes, which are not bound or modifiable by human culture across generations. The problem for evangelicals, however, is to fix the rules by which the Bible can be applied as an ethical guide to action in the surrounding culture, but without admitting that such rules of engagement are given by their own culture and thus a part of it. Evangelicals must somehow acquire a culture-specific theology, addressing the particular dilemmas of the moment, but then act as if they could have received it by no other means than reading the Bible in the company of the Holy Spirit.

It is sometimes difficult to uncover the trail along which key ideas, events, and social developments have followed each other beneath layers of ideological reformulation of the record. Nevertheless, American evangelicals have a story to tell, one that tends to locate the idea of set-apartness in the matrix of a larger culture in conversation with the Bible. As George Marsden (1980:224) writes:

> In America, for the first two centuries the Bible had played a role in shaping the culture for which there was no European parallel. Lacking a strong institutional church and denying the relevance of much of Christian tradition, American Protestants were united behind the principle of *Scriptura sola*. . . . This Biblicism, strong among the Puritans, gained new significance in the early nineteenth century. In the wake of the Revolution, Americans saw themselves as inaugurators of a new order for the ages. The new order was conceived as a return to a pristine human condition. For Protestants this ideal was readily translated into Biblical primitivism. The true church should set aside all intervening tradition, and return to the purity of New Testament practice.

From Jonathan Edwards to Dwight Moody, to Billy Graham and Pat Robertson, voices of revivalist pietism have resonated with a robust element of Reformational-orthodox Christian belief that has pulsated through American life (though its influence has waxed and waned, its facets have been diverse, and its relation to various institutional forms and structures in American society has undergone profound changes, especially since World War II). Expressions of Biblical faith have hardly been limited to Protestant churches on Sundays; rather, they have seeped through American culture. Social historians of religion trace an almost continuous thread of evangelical experience in America: from Puritan beginnings, to the First and Second Great Awakenings in eighteenth-century New England, to the widespread pietistic revivals and moral reform movements of the nineteenth century, to the ascendance of a denominational society dominated by Protestant institutions, to the "modernist" controversies and beleaguered fundamentalism of the 1920s, to the post-war reestablishment and restructuring of evangelicalism in the middle class, to the social and political resurgence of a polarized conservative Christianity on the margins of a secularized culture in the late 1970s and 1980s (Ahlstrom, 1972; Marsden, 1980; Marty, 1984; Wuthnow, 1988b).

Along the way, each generation of Biblical primitivists has interpreted the ideals of set-apartness and mission in the light of their own cultural experience. But the seventeenth-century Puritans of New England provided the archetype—the model of spiritual and cultural set-apartness, infused with a sense of mission—that took on special significance for their evangelical successors, and remains in many ways apropos to the contemporary mission community that I went to study in Ecuador.

Like the present-day missionaries who hearken back to them, the Puritans had been set apart from their own time and culture in the Old World. As Kai Erikson writes:

> [The Puritans were] remote from the political drifts of their own age, living in a kind of cultural suspension. . . . They had been drawn away from many of the cultural landmarks which give each people a sense of their place in human history and human society—the folklore and traditions, the art and literature, the monuments and memories which become a part of their national identity (Erikson, 1966:48).

For them, "the world" (from which they were to be set apart) corresponded primarily to the edifice of medieval and Anglican religious tradition—the cathedrals, the vestments, the liturgical rituals, the clerical hierarchy—all of which they saw as so much "foliage obstructing [their] view of God" (Erikson, 1966:48).

When the Puritans arrived in the forests of New England, however, their new experience—seen in the light of Biblical ideals of moral set-apartness—transformed their prior estrangement. Now they were not merely set apart, but rather, divinely commissioned as a social "model of Christian charity" in the wilderness. This was to be their mission in the world, as John Winthrop so memorably exhorted his fellow sojourners aboard the Arabella on the eve of their 1630 landing at Massachusetts Bay. They were a New Israel, a City on a Hill, and the visible body of Christ in the world. They were a people set apart by God to show his grace on earth. The settlers' ideals for a new social order and a pure church were practically indistinguishable. Both were supposed to consist exclusively of regenerated Christian believers. Public testimonies of conversion were necessary, but insufficient for social membership. Truer signs of divine election were needed: submission to authority and law, acts of charity, and labor in the common good.

A key facet of the Puritan archetype for the worldview of evangelicals in future generations was their transhistorical perspective on the Bible, and their belief not only in its literal truth but its literal significance for the minutiae of their daily lives. Again, Kai Erikson makes a trenchant observation:

> The Bible was not just an announcement of God's purpose. . . . It was a catalog of all possible forms of human experience, a digest of history both past and yet to come. Events which occur in the lives of men and give them an illusion that time is passing in some orderly fashion are no more than echoes of thoughts in the mind of God, registered permanently in the Scriptures. And so the Puritan world took its form by analogy rather than by sequence of time. Everything that happens in the present world is only a flickering reproduction of something that has happened before, a repetition of some divine truth, and the Puritans assumed that they could discover the archetypes from which their own experience was derived by careful study of the world around them. In a very real sense, they knew that there is nothing new under the sun (Erikson, 1966:51).

The Puritans embraced the Bible's missionary mandate primarily as a corporate task to be accomplished by setting a social example to the nations, as a City on a Hill. Nevertheless, a number of Puritan individuals did feel called to take the gospel directly to the prior inhabitants of the New World. As Sydney Ahlstrom noted, "[The] Puritan attitude to the Indians (despite a propensity to liken their total experience to that of the Children of Israel) is by no means summed up in the parallels they on occasion drew between American savages and the Canaanites" (Ahlstrom, 1961:169–177). In fact, the Massachusetts charter itself stated the hope that the colonists might "win and invite natives of that country to the knowledge and obedience of the only true God and Savior of mankind and the Christian faith" (Latourette, 1949). John Eliot, who arrived in the Bay Colony in 1631, is perhaps best known among early missionaries to the Indians, primarily because he translated the New Testament into the Algonquin language. But he was not the first in the colonies and did not labor alone. In 1649 the Society for the Propagation of the Gospel in New England was chartered by Parliament, in order to support missionary work among the Indians as well as spiritually needy colonists.[19]

Clearly then, the Biblical ideals of set-apartness and mission did have individual as well as corporate meanings among the Puritans, though the corporate meanings were primary. With time, however, the connotations of these ideas began to shift to accommodate new experience. The first generation of Puritans had attempted to produce a social world consisting only of a purified church of "converted" believers who had renounced the corruption of the Old World. At first, everyone belonged and everyone professed conversion. But inevitably, a definition of purity based on being set apart from religious apostasy across the ocean lost its immediacy and sharpness. A crisis arose when second and third generations (though progeny of the elect) did not necessarily experience conversion. Should they be excluded outright from church (and thus, community) membership?

The early congregationalists' "half-way covenant," adopted in 1662, provided only a temporary solution. Eventually, the primary locus of purity was shifted from the church as a community to the heart of each individual standing alone before God. This was, in fact, to become the dominant emphasis during many subsequent seasons of revival, and it persists among evangelicals today. Beginning with the Great Awakenings in New England, the primary appeal of evangelical revivalism has not been for purified churches, but for individuals to get their souls right with God (Ahlstrom, 1972).

Daniel Bell has written that the "thought of Puritan theocracy is the great influential fact in the history of the American mind" (Bell, 1980:256). And yet certain contradictions emerged within the Puritan ethos, beginning with the Enlightenment in the eighteenth century, that eventually threatened to dissolve the other-worldly ideals of set-apartness and mission into the secularization and disenchantment of modern life. Echoing Max Weber, Bell writes:

> [T]he very conditions of American life, the need for self-reliance and the evidence that one could change the world by one's own efforts, gradually eroded the other-worldly foundations of Puritan New England, and stressed the need to find one's self, one's achievements, one's salvation in the here and now (Bell, 1976:56).

Thus, when conservative evangelicals in the present day hearken back to America's founding fathers as their spiritual forebears, critics like to point out that Protestant-religious influence had declined a great deal by the time of the Revolution. The Republic was chartered by enlightened, this-worldly political visionaries who assigned God a remote role in human affairs and, in any case, were more concerned with keeping religion out of the affairs of state than with founding a government on the precepts of the Lord.

In that light, one is at first hard pressed to reconcile a seemingly paradoxical fact: that evangelical Protestantism resurged with a vengeance in antebellum America and built up a head of steam that fueled a global missionary movement lasting over a hundred years. Looking deeper, it becomes apparent that while the Enlightenment put religion on the defensive, it defined an ethos of innovation and renewal that found an affinity with revivalism; and, of course, it provided the secularized stage against which revivalism could thrive. Moreover, as Wilbert Shenk (1991) has noted, the Enlightenment set in place a worldview that made global missions possible through a tacit alliance with the cultural and technological forces that propelled the expanding hegemony of the West.

> Where people managed to hold in tension inward piety and outward concern for the world, renewal movements became engines of wide-ranging innovation, the modern mission movement being one of the most evident fruits (Shenk, 1991:x).

The nineteenth century was ushered in by widespread spiritual awakenings on both sides of the Atlantic and culminated with a modern missions movement that would inspire a historian's designation of the era as "The Great Century" for the expansion of Christianity throughout the world (Latourette, 1938–1946). In American culture, it was a time shaped by "the dynamics of unopposed revivalism," (Marsden, 1980:224) as Biblical notions of set-apartness and mission were woven into the fabric of a cultural consciousness that combined individual Christian piety with expansive nationalism (Hutchison, 1987).

To be sure, evangelical understandings were molded by economic relations and regional sensibilities as well as national historical events. At midcentury, for example, outspoken Protestant churchmen were to be counted among southern slave owners as well as northern abolitionists. Both appealed to the Bible to make their respective cases, and both were convinced of God's favor. When the Civil War finally erupted, there were Americans on each side who understood the conflict in the apocalyptic terms of the Bible. Nevertheless, throughout most of the century America as a whole was thought of by its citizens as a "Christian nation." Many of its most significant institutions—in education, politics, business, the professions—were dominated by evangelicals (Thomas, 1986). Woodrow Wilson, born in 1856, spoke for a cultural era and an intellectual establishment when he said that "America was born a Christian nation for the purpose of exemplifying to the nations of the world the principles of righteousness found in the Word of God" (Woodbridge, Noll, and Hatch, 1979).

It is in this light that one understands the actions of men and women who turned the New Testament's "Great Commission" into a worldwide, mass movement that still reverberates throughout the developing world today. Although neither the Reformers nor their Protestant successors in the intervening centuries were indifferent to missions (Gensichen, 1960), it was not until 1792 that the modern, global movement of Protestant missions was launched. This is the date when an English cobbler named William Carey, deeply affected by the Wesleyan "awakening," published an enormously influential 87-page tract entitled, "An Enquiry into the Obligations of Christians to Use Means for the Conversion of the Heathens." Carey argued persuasively that the New Testament's commission to "preach the gospel to all nations" was as literally binding for Christians of his day as for the first apostles (Carey, 1979 [1792]). He also became the first Baptist missionary to India, where he worked continuously for forty years.[20]

Mission histories often mention Carey's knowledge of John Eliot's and David Brainerd's missionary work among the Indians in New England, and of his reading of Brainerd's journals. But his global missionary vision—his sense of the world as a finite universe of perishing heathens in need of the gospel—was sparked rather by his reading of *The Last Voyage of Captain Cook*. This, of course, hints at larger connections between the missionary movement and the urge of colonial powers to discover, conquer, and civilize a newly emerging world. Some historians have charged that the modern mission movement was merely a religious gloss on the wider quest of Euro-American societies to establish economic and cultural dominance throughout the world. As Shenk (1991) observes, missions were thus "stained by their association with Western imperialism":

> [T]he missionary drama was played out on the same stage as the powerful political and economic developments of the period. . . . By virtue of its global reach the movement became a primary carrier of modernity, and the artifacts and institutions associated with modernity early became hallmarks of missions. But there is more to be said. Missions released influences that contributed to the subversion and eventual overthrow of colonialism in its many forms (Shenk, 1991:xii).

Beyond these sociopolitical matters, when we consider the individual lives of people who initiated and carried the missions movement along, we cannot understand them except by admitting that they had a remarkable experience—at the personal level—of being "set apart by God" and "sent into the world." American foreign missions are customarily said to have begun in 1806, when a handful of earnest young men were somehow touched by the spirit in their now-famous "haystack prayer meeting" at Williams College. It is noteworthy that evangelical lore cites the date of a spiritual experience, and not of some human charter or declaration, as the beginning of the foreign missions movement.

These young New Englanders (lead by Samuel Mills, who had personally felt the call several years earlier while plowing his field in eastern Connecticut) set the steps in motion for the founding, in 1810, of the American Board of Commissioners for Foreign Missions. Two years later, five of these brethren were officially set apart and commissioned to take the gospel to Asia. Their leader was the Brown College valedictorian, Adoniram Judson, who had joined the others at Andover Seminary. In an excellent history of the first fifty years of the American Board, Clifton Phillips evokes the mood of that sending:

> On a midwinter Thursday in February, 1812, while much of the nation talked of war, an event which looked toward greater conquests than Canada took place quietly in the little seaport town of Salem, Massachusetts. On that day five young men of "highly respectable talents and attainments" were ordained as "Missionaries to the heathen in Asia." Common curiosity and a concern for the extraordinary purpose of the occasion attracted an unusually large assembly to the otherwise familiar Congregational service in Tabernacle Church. "A season of more impressive solemnity," ran the official report, "has scarcely been witnessed in our country" (Phillips, 1969:1).

Other missions were soon founded to spread the gospel both at home and abroad. In addition to the organizational efforts of the Protestant denominations (Presbyterians, Baptists, Methodists) to reach the "heathen" overseas, many societies were founded about the same time for home evangelization and Christian education. As Martin Marty (1984) notes, "[a] catalog of the societies for mission and reform at that time suggests the moral oxygen and energy that filled the air." He cites the American Bible Society, the American Home Mission Society, the American Sunday-School Union, and the American Tract Society, all started within a few years in the early part of the century.

Understandably, foreign missions efforts abated somewhat throughout the Civil War, but afterward missionary activity resurged and reached unprecedented levels during the 1880s and 1890s. During these years, in conjunction with D. L. Moody's widespread revivals, students at Princeton, Yale, Harvard, Dartmouth, and Cornell (as well as Edinburgh, Oxford, and Cambridge) felt called by the thousands to complete the task of "the evangelization of the world in this generation." As a result of an 1886 student revival at Moody's conference grounds at Mt. Hermon, Massachusetts, the enormously influential Student Volunteer Movement for Foreign Missions was founded. In the succeeding years, tens of thousands of students attended the SVM's conventions, receiving the call and signing what was known as the Princeton Pledge: "I purpose, God willing, to become a foreign missionary" (Ahlstrom, 1972:343–345).

During this period, in some evangelical circles, the sense of being set apart by a missionary call became so generalized that one almost had to have a sort reverse call or defect to justify staying home. It was assumed, if one was able, that one would consider going abroad as a foreign missionary. Robert Speer, one of the most influential leaders of the SVM, expressed this idea in an essay on the subject, in which he quoted a famed missionary to Arabia named Keith-Falconer:

> Whilst vast continents are shrouded in almost utter darkness, and hundreds of millions suffer the horrors of heathenism, or of Islam, the burden of proof lies upon you to show that the circumstances in which God has placed you were meant by Him to keep you out of the foreign mission field (Speer, 1901a:3–6).

Sympathetic histories of Protestant missions often highlight the fact that many early missionaries from America were remarkably talented, highly educated (often Ivy League graduates), and that they went abroad not only as emissaries of the Christian gospel, but as representatives of the best that their nation had to offer to "less fortunate people." Rather than being set apart *from* American culture, such missionaries were seen as *embodying* the culture abroad. In return, the strong ties they maintained with sending churches provided what Sydney Ahlstrom termed "the great American window on the non-Western world" (Ahlstrom, 1972:345). One could hardly overstate the effect such missionaries had on their home churches:

> India, Africa, China, and Japan came to be regarded as spiritual provinces of the American churches from the Nebraska plains to New York's Fifth Avenue. . . . Statesmen could not treat these vast "mission fields" as diplomatic pawns (Ahlstrom, 1972:345).

Nevertheless, many of the early missionaries were set apart from the larger currents of culture emanating from the more heterogeneous urban centers of America—human conglomerations that would eventually make "diversity" the American religion. Phillips suggests that missionaries for the most part came from a different "center," which was the "heart of evangelical America" in the hinterlands:

> Not many from the cities or coastal towns felt impelled to plant the standard of the cross abroad. Rather it was the farm boy and villager who dreamed in their homes in the Berkshires or the Mohawk Valley of the evangelical conquest of distant shores. The case of Samuel Mills of rural Litchfield County, Connecticut, provides a characteristic image. "While toiling at the plow," his pious biographer wrote, "was his heart touched with compassion for the heathen world, and he bid adieu to his farm, to obtain an education on purpose to carry the Gospel to millions who perish for lack of knowledge" (Phillips, 1969:30).

Of course, nineteenth-century America faced a massive moral frontier closer to home, in the westward expansion of its population on the continent (Ahlstrom, 1961). It would seem that if American evangelicals needed a missionary challenge, it could be found not only in the Puritan archetype of building a Christian society in the wilderness as an example to the nations, but, as Phillips points out, in the task of converting "uncounted hordes of pagan aborigines" on the edges of their own civilization (Phillips, 1969:30). Why should talented young Americans leave this work behind in favor of a mission abroad?

Part of the answer lies in the symbolic power of the imagery of foreign missions, which held out the possibility for ordinary folk to achieve the Christian ideal through romantic exile and spiritual heroism—an imagery that was made even more compelling by the fact that many missionaries died abroad and thus became martyrs. From the call, to the commissioning ritual, to the lengthy period of passage[21] between America and the "heathen" world, to the dangers encountered there, to the precarious return home as a transformed super-mortal, the saga of the missionary in many ways resembled the classic hero myth (Campbell, 1949). A characteristic book written at the end of this period was entitled "The Romance of Missionary Heroism: True Stories of Intrepid Bravery and Stirring Adventures with Uncivilized Man, Wild Beasts, and the Forces of Nature in All Parts of the World" (Lambert, 1907).

The nineteenth century may have been America's great Christian age. But even as the Protestant missionary movement in its most American expression was reaching a climax, the seeds of an extraordinary cultural transformation were being sown. George Marsden (1980) argues that, in consequence, a significant subgroup of American evangelicals (who later became known as fundamentalists) underwent something quite like an immigrant experience during the first several decades of this century. In Marsden's view, they were literally alienated by the massive changes that swept America into the twentieth century: large-scale urbanization, the swarming of Catholic and Jewish immigrants from Europe, huge and far-reaching advances in technology, and a shifting worldview among the religious elite that seemed to replace prophetic Biblical images of history (and America's place in it) with secular notions of scientific progress.

In many ways, the cognitive and cultural landscape so dramatically changed around the fundamentalists that they became like foreigners in their own land. As did many of the recent immigrants in America's cities, Bible believers found themselves confronting a strange new establishment that spoke with an unfamiliar voice, drowning out their cries of protest. As Marsden (1980:204) observes: "Faced by a culture with a myriad of competing ideals, and having little power to influence that culture, [the fundamentalists] reacted by creating their own equivalent of an urban ghetto."

As they split off from mainline denominations that were taken up in the modernist spirit of progressive social and theological liberalism, the fundamentalists formed their own network of independent congregations, Bible schools, institutes, camps, conferences, and faith missions. Their leaders fiercely championed a "dispensational" theology of history and literalist interpretation of Scripture as God-inspired and factually inerrant in its every word. Outwardly, the fundamentalists seemed to signal their rejection of secular culture and its sensate pleasures through modest dress and a dour countenance that turned away from all "worldly" practices such as drinking, smoking, swearing, dancing, card-playing, gambling, theater attendance, and popular music.

In effect, what had once been the Protestant establishment gradually disintegrated, leaving a remnant of evangelical belief that had shifted toward the periphery of American cultural consciousness, downward in social class, and away from the large urban and intellectual centers. But like their Puritan forbears, American fundamentalists and evangelicals throughout the twentieth century have continued to embrace cultural strangerhood as a spiritual calling:

> God calls out his people to be strangers and pilgrims, as many of America's early settlers knew so well. He calls them to repent of their sins and to avoid conformity with the world . . . our renderings to Caesar, while they must be taken seriously, are to follow the values of that kingdom that stands above all earthly authority. These priorities, rather than those of our culture and nation, demand our unfettered loyalty (Woodbridge, Noll, and Hatch, 1979:222).

The World Radio Missionary Fellowship in Ecuador

Go into all the world and preach the gospel to the whole creation (Mark 16:15).

In the late 1920s, two passionate young men envisioned a way to fulfill the "Great Commission of Christ" in their own time, using a remarkable new invention called radio. One of them was Clarence Jones, the son of a Sergeant Major in the Salvation Army, an accomplished trombone player, and an associate of the Chicago-based radio evangelist Paul Rader. The other was Reuben Larson, a trailblazing jungle missionary in Ecuador. In due course, these two visionaries founded a tiny "faith mission" with a very large name and an even larger goal: The World Radio Missionary Fellowship, Inc., would employ a miracle of modern technology to virtually blanket the earth with the message of salvation by faith in Christ.[22]

The urgency of this word for Bible believers in 1920s America hardly needs emphasis.[23] The heathen were dying unsaved, thousands each day passing into a Godforsaken eternity. The stage was set on earth for the drama of the End Times, the second coming of the Lord. Every ear needed to hear the message; there was little time to waste on traditional missionary journeys. Larson, already something of a legend in the Ecuadorian jungle, used his political connections in that country to secure permission to begin broadcasting from Quito. Situated on the equator at nearly 10,000 feet in the Andes, the capital city seemed to provide a fitting venue for this twentieth-century *axis mundi* of Christian redemption. And on Christmas Day, 1931, the first program of the pioneer missionary radio station was broadcast from a converted sheep shed on the outskirts of Quito. Using a 250-watt transmitter, Jones played his trombone, and a handful of associates bravely intoned the hymn "Great Is Thy Faithfulness" for anyone who might be listening on the six receivers then existing in the country.

Sixty years later, the Great Commission continues to inspire and compel the inheritors of Jones and Larson's World Radio Mission—now numbering nearly three hundred members in Ecuador. Their 250 watts of radio transmitter power have increased to over one million and their annual income to nearly ten million dollars (Roberts and Siewart, 1989), as the Mission now broadcasts in more than a dozen languages and literally covers most of the globe with its short-wave signal and network of local stations linked by satellite. Listeners from as far away as Russia, Japan, and Australia send over 75,000 letters a year, while the Mission presses earnestly toward its stated goal of *The World by 2000*—that by the end of the millennium every member of the human race will have access to the Christian gospel message by radio or television, in a language that he or she understands.

The Mission has diversified its media and now focuses a great deal of attention on local ministries in Ecuador. Yet its message and commitment remains the same: "In view of Christ's last command and recognizing the lost condition of all those who fail to accept the gospel message, we believe in the urgency of every Christian's responding to the great commission of Christ. . . . [We are] committed to communicate the gospel of Jesus Christ to all nations, via international shortwave radio (HCJB), local AM/FM radio, television, health care services, the printed page, schools, churches, evangelism, correspondence courses, and training."[24]

HCJB-World Radio has firm roots in American fundamentalism and the faith missions movement of the early twentieth century,[25] as is evident in one of the Mission's self-descriptions in a 1983 brochure: "No religious group sponsors HCJB. . . . We are *fundamental* or *evangelical* and each missionary has come to know the Lord Jesus Christ as his or her Savior. . . . [We are] a faith mission, dependent upon God as He moves the hearts of interested individuals [and] local churches . . . to meet financial needs." Being a member of the Mission requires signing the group's "statement of faith" each year to ensure continued assent to orthodoxy, including the defining canon of Biblical inerrancy: "We believe that the Bible is the Word of God, verbally inspired and without error as originally written, and that it is the only infallible rule of faith and practice." And in their lifestyle, World Radio members continue to avoid those personal and social practices traditionally viewed as "worldly" by American fundamentalists.

And yet, certain themes in the Mission's historical sense of itself resonate with earlier, traditional views of the American character—echoes of pioneering on the frontier, of Yankee ingenuity, and the subduing of nature (see Pike, 1992). Some of these themes are especially apparent in various renditions of what might be called the Mission's founding myth. For example, in Lois Neely's chronicle of the beginnings of HCJB, *Come Up to This Mountain* (1980), Reuben Larson is depicted (favorably and without a modern apology) as the quintessential civilizing missionary in league with the colonial masters. But he also appears as a sort of of Daniel Boone with a radio:

> At the junction of two swift rivers, the Tena and the Missauwaali, headwaters of the mighty Amazon, Grace and Reuben had put up a little shelter, hardly more than a grass shack, and tried to make contact with the Indians. As possible trading material, Reuben had brought with him cloth, beads, knives, machetes—all the trappings of a jungle trading post. . . .
>
> The very next morning, Reuben looked up to see two Indian dugout canoes pulling in to shore. "We have come to be your Indians," they said. . . . "We want to help you clear the jungle and build a better house." They called Reuben "patron," a Spanish term that wraps into one word the roles of father, banker, judge, arbiter, and overseer. Now these Indians slashed away with their machetes, cutting and splitting the bamboo for a proper house, enlarging the clearing, and planting pineapple and coffee trees. . . . Machete in hand, [Larson] joined with the Indians as they hacked their way through the jungle, clearing a muddy trail wide enough for a horse to negotiate. . . .
>
> Remembering the Indians' initial reluctance to come out of the forest, Larson began to visualize a "singing radio" hanging from the branches of a bamboo tree. Would this be the way to get the gospel out to the Indians of the jungle? . . . Could they use this new tool, radio, to "reach even further into the darkness?" (Neely, 1980:57–59).

In Neely's telling, Larson's remarkable success as a missionary pioneer and civilizing presence among the jungle Indians earned him such favor with Ecuadorian officials that they permitted HCJB to start a Protestant radio station in that (very Catholic) country—notwithstanding that the first contract referred to these fledgling broadcasters as "foreigners and heretics." When the permit was granted, Larson is said to have remarked, "The hearts of kings are in God's hands."

The Larsons' unusual and increasing rapport with the Indians, a previously unruly people, did not go unnoticed. One day a government representative stopped by the Dos Rios hacienda. "Would you be superintendent of schools in the Oriente?" . . . "Would you supervise road building?" . . . "Will you handle the salt sales?" . . . "And the gold the Indians are collecting, would you see that it gets to the Banco Central?" . . . Soon this jovial, efficient, politically astute American Swede had earned the nickname, "King of the Oriente." Larson's consistent success in everything he tackled won him great acceptance with government officials, and they sought ways to show their appreciation, summoning him to the Presidential Palace for a hearty commendation.

Regarding Clarence Jones, Neely (1980) contrasts his divinely inspired innovation with the more conservative impulses of fundamentalism. "In those pioneer days of Christian radio," she writes, "there were the conservatives who could not see 'using the devil's tool' for mass evangelism, so some were preaching against radio even while God was blessing the [programs Jones produced]" (Neely, 1980:34).

Thus, the cutting edge of civilization—and of technology in particular—served as a metaphor for the missionary task of claiming a moral frontier for God. Signaling God's preeminence over nature (and thus over human technology that seeks to harness nature), the lore around the Mission's beginnings includes the story of how Clarence Jones, with divine assistance, outsmarted the best technical advice of the 1920s on the subject of where to put a radio station:

> According to the experts of that day, they said [sic] it would never work to broadcast from so close to the equator and in the mountains. Today we know this has been an ideal location and the Creator knows best (WRMF brochure, 1983).

Inspired by Jones over the ensuing decades, World Radio engineers designed and built much of their own system of transmitters, steerable antennas, computer networks for automated program control, and two hydroelectric power plants in the rugged Andes. In 1954 the Mission built a hospital in Quito that was for many years unrivaled as the most advanced health care facility in the Ecuadorian capital. A second hospital was built in the jungle town of Shell four years later, and then replaced by a larger, more modern facility in the mid-1980s. Currently, HCJB is completing a major renovation and expansion of its Quito hospital—at a time when many missions around the world have backed away from hospital-based health ministries.

The "ideal location" for radio and the other ministries of HCJB also turned out to be a fine place for a large congregation of foreigners to form their own model of an organic Christian community—a social body set apart for a purpose—with each member's inner-worldly labor joined by a common spiritual vocation and goal. A page from one of the Mission's promotional brochures evokes this goal with a map of the world, Quito at the center, above the caption, "We have come from all the world, to the center of the world, to reach the world for Jesus." The following text amplifies the theme:

> God has called a remarkable team of His servants to do His work. . . . We are communicators, engineers, doctors, nurses, audio specialists, musicians, television and radio producers, accountants, photographers, printers, administrators, secretaries, ed-

ucators, evangelists, mechanics, graphic artists, writers—and people skilled in many other areas of expertise—all with a deep desire to serve God and be used of Him (WRMF brochure, 1983).

Like their predecessors in the "Great Century" for Christian missions, World Radio members literally imagine the whole world as their field of evangelization. The tribes and "people groups" around the globe—crystal isolates of unredeemed humanity—await dissolution in the universal medium of the gospel. Significantly, this conception of the missionary vocation recaptures an ideological vision long since lost by the mainline Protestant denominations.

Late nineteenth-century evangelicals saw the missionary as a special envoy from an enlightened Christendom to a dark pagan world. The character and the boundaries of each of these worlds were objectified and clearly delineated, and the membership of each was seen as homogeneous. Moreover, the distance between these communities was great and took a long time to traverse. The lone missionary arrived (and infrequently returned) at the end of a lengthy and perilous passage. But in the transitional world of the twentieth century, the cultural landscape around the communities that sent missionaries abroad changed dramatically with the conditions of modernity—"Christendom" finally broke down (Shenk, 1993)—while the slow pace of change in many of the receiving communities kept them more or less as they had been for hundreds of years. Then, and until recent decades, becoming a foreign missionary could mean withdrawing from the battle with modern secularism, relativism, and pluralism, in favor of doing battle with less subtle, less rational, and more enchanted enemies. Taking the gospel to a preliterate tribe in Amazonia meant transporting the crusade to a foreign continent—but perhaps more importantly, to what seemed like a simpler time. The missionary there could present the gospel as an appeal from one ancient story to another, from one small-scale community to another. The physical conditions of engagement with a primitive culture were difficult, but at least the missionary's task and role seemed unambiguously interpretable.

In the postmodern situation, the social and temporal distance between the sending and receiving communities has been narrowed by advances in transportation, communications, and development in general. Traditional boundaries have broken down. Missionaries encounter a new kind of conflict in many of the self-conscious young nations they now wish to evangelize—if they are given entry at all. On the one hand, they may become enmired in conditions of massive social upheaval and political turmoil in the world's developing countries (Ostling, 1982). On the other hand, missionaries often find themselves confronting the same kind of urban modernity, disenchantment, and pluralism they left at home. Moreover, in the religious sphere, they often face a nationalism—as well as a general shift in missionary thinking—that makes them no longer masters, nor even respected advisers, but at best servants of the local church. Given these conditions, many missionaries around the world have stopped calling themselves missionaries at all, in favor of emphasizing that "every Christian is a missionary" to whatever people he or she encounters.

The contemporary global environment thus poses a dilemma for people who experience a traditional sort of missionary calling, as will be discussed in later chapters. It is a problem, in particular, for people whose life stories become organized around experiences of estrangement—with consequent affinities for the nineteenth-century ideals of being "set apart and sent into the world"—and whose financial supporters back home wish to be involved vicariously in living out a missionary mythology.

World Radio provides a unique set of options for such people. What the Mission has done, in a sense, is to recreate the nineteenth-century missionary distance by means of shortwave radio. Broadcasting from Quito to far-away lost souls in Russia and Japan takes the place of a traditional missionary journey. At such remove, the boundaries around the foreign target audiences can once again be drawn clearly, and listeners can be perceived stereotypically as if they were homogeneous and pagan. Moreover, these missionaries remain socially set apart, free to withdraw into their own enclave and to create their own exemplary community—as the Body of Christ and the Voice of the Andes—with a sense of their own significance almost resembling that of the seventeenth-century Puritans of New England.

Like their Calvinist forbears, these missionaries carry out an earthly vocation in response to a concern with spiritual election. They were born into a society that has secularized the Protestant ethic such that the words "vocation" and "profession" and "career" have ordinarily nothing to do with moral progress in a way of life, but only with engagement in some respectable way of earning a living. Moreover, most of their day-to-day work in the Mission corporation is highly rationalized, modern work. Yet somehow the meaning of their work has come to resemble that of their forbears' creative labor in the commonwealth, interspersed with efforts to evangelize the "native barbarians" who inhabited the New World around them. The peculiar tension arising between the modern missionary's "job" and "ministry" thus bears no accidental (or simple) relation to that between the Puritans' inner-worldly vocation and other-worldly election. Like the Puritans, missionaries perceive and interpret events in their lives at two levels of relevance—the level of practical, ordinary experience, and the level of spiritual imagery carried along in a transcendent Biblical story. Such a tension is one key to the moral careers about which this book is written.

Plan of the Book

The substance of this book is divided into three parts (Chapters 2, 3, and 4) which, in my view, derive their form and sequence from the ideal-typical narrative structure of missionaries' personal testimonies. The moral careers portrayed throughout all three sorts of moments in these testimonies develop around experiences of set-apartness—from parental abandonment and death, to religious ecstasy, to a kind of heroic cultural otherness.

Chapter 2 deals with themes in the recollected early lives of missionaries. These early-life narratives reveal the species' predicaments: They are bound up in the mysteries of suffering and loss, in ambivalent yearnings for both intimacy and freedom, in the experience of guilt, and in the fear of death. In these portrayed lives, core emotional and social tensions are not resolved *per se*, but are morally translated in conversion stories leading into a spiritual vocation. By listening to various narrators, it will become clear that these missionaries view themselves as having been set apart early in life, in such a way as to prefigure or to foreshadow a divine calling.

Chapter 3—the centerpiece, really, of the book—is focused on the call and the calling, as a moral idea and experience given historically in evangelical culture and personally stylized by contemporary missionaries. The call is viewed by them as a divine incursion into the life of an individual, showing a personal destiny to make Christ-like sacrifice for the benefit of others. The data illustrate how the missionary call experience and the social forms surrounding it are mutually conditioned. That is to say, the call provides career motivation for persons who already felt set apart spiritually, psychologically, and socially; it also gives some assurance of membership and status in the missionary group.

Chapter 4 places the missionary in the alien setting of Ecuador, where the calling must be reinterpreted to account for unexpected and often profoundly disillusioning experiences. But as the calling is lived out there, the missionary's cultural status as a stranger and self-image as a moral hero eventually become integrated in a unique expression of the other-worldliness that is essential to the evangelical ethos. Certain tensions in the missionary's relation to experienced social worlds—home society, host society, foreign enclave—are transformed, and given coherence by the moral construction of set-apartness.

2

Themes in the Early Lives
of Missionaries

This study draws upon two sources of primary data: self-administered questionnaires completed by 129 Mission members and open-ended interviews conducted with 107 Mission members.[1] These offer complementary ways of looking at the origins of evangelical missionaries. The questionnaire survey, on the one hand, provides uniform background information including sociodemographic characteristics, the occurrence of "separating" events in childhood (such as migration, going away to boarding school, parental death), and religious milestone experiences (such as conversion and calling). Responses were given by 75 women and 54 men between the ages of 24 and 64 who began working as HCJB missionaries in Ecuador between the years 1941 and 1983. When summarized statistically, they yield one sort of answer to the question of where the people that I studied "came from."

The interview transcripts, on the other hand, allow us to address a different question: How do people who become missionaries recall and talk about their early life experience? During extended conversations, I asked my subjects to recount the stories of their lives leading up to the time when they entered the missionary vocation. As I listened to their responses and probed with further queries, I tried to direct their attention to experiences they now considered to have been most formative of their character, to events they now believe were the most influential in pointing out the life pathways they were to take. Each of these interviews thus yielded a narrative record of a person's unique past—including whatever settings, characters, defining moments, and interpretations he or she deemed significant. Taken together, they form a group of life stories told from the perspective of a common destiny, the missionary vocation.

In my own interpretations, I approached the interview data with two different sorts of queries. First, I attended to the content of the missionaries' responses and wondered, simply, what these people were talking about. What sorts of characters, places, events, and experiences seemed to emerge as common elements and themes in their stories, and what overt significance did they attach to these? Second, I tried to look at the style and structure of the missionaries' narratives, and to ask something else: What sort of talk was this? Who were the audiences for it? What implicit rules might govern the way in which the missionaries discussed their formative experiences? How might the images common to the early sequence of their moral careers be configured symbolically?[2]

A Background Sketch

About ninety percent of the missionaries in my study were of Anglo-American origin, native speakers of English, and racially white. Three-quarters of them were from the United States and another sixteen percent came from Canada, the British Isles, New Zealand, or Australia. Within the subgroup from the United States, the majority—57 percent—were born in the heartland region of the Midwest, including the states of Illinois, Indiana, Iowa, Kansas, Michigan, Minnesota, Nebraska, North Dakota, Ohio, South Dakota, and Wisconsin. An additional 13 percent were from the Southeast or Mid-Atlantic states. The remaining minority were born in the West, Southwest, or New England.

Nearly half of the missionaries spent their childhood in a place they would describe as a "rural area" or "small town." Only one-third came from a city they would call a "large metropolis," or the "suburb of a large metropolis." The most common occupation of missionaries' fathers was the clergy or mission work (23 percent), followed by farming (19 percent), skilled work or trades (16 percent), and unskilled labor (12 percent). The remaining minority had fathers in business or professions, or did not know their father's occupation. About 60 percent of the Mission members' fathers were not educated beyond high school.

Over 90 percent of the missionaries came from church-going Protestant families and attended Sunday School regularly as children (i.e., during the period when they were twelve years old or younger). About 70 percent said they had been brought up in a home environment they would describe as "evangelical Christian." More than half had at least one parent who was active in church work. Yet only a minority of the missionaries' families had been members of mainline Protestant denominational churches. Fifteen percent had been Baptists, of which almost all described their church's theological orientation as "conservative evangelical" or "fundamental." Besides Baptists, however, only about one quarter of the entire group had a church background in any of the mainline denominations including Methodist, Presbyterian, Congregationalist, Episcopalian, Anglican, or Lutheran. The remaining majority of the Mission members had grown up in families whose churches they described as "independent Bible churches," or one of an array of conservative evangelical or fundamentalist groups including the Mennonites, Brethren, Mission Covenant, Evangelical Free Church, Missionary Church, the Christian and Missionary Alliance, Apostolic Christians, Church of God, and Pentecostals.

A sketch of the HCJB missionaries' social origins in many ways resembles James Hunter's 1982 portrayal of American evangelicals in general, based on his analysis of data gathered by the Gallup organization for *Christianity Today* magazine (Hunter, 1982). According to Hunter's profile, adult evangelical Christians in America are predominantly white and more often female than male. They tend to come from families located in the lower-middle and working classes and live in smaller towns or rural areas of the Midwest, Southeast, and Mid-Atlantic regions of the country. The group of missionaries I studied was more or less cut from this same cloth.

Hunter argues that evangelicals and fundamentalists, throughout most of the twentieth century, were markedly "removed from the institutional structures and processes of modernity," and remained "protected within the private sphere from the constraining forces of the highly rational public sphere" (Hunter, 1982). Increasingly since the 1960s, however, evangelicals have had to confront the secularizing forces and pluralism of modern society in ways they had not done previously. Hunter outlines three strategies of response—resistance, withdrawal, and accommodation (of style on the whole, rather than substance)—and argues that young evangelicals generally have opted for the latter (see also Hunter, 1987). As we shall see, HCJB missionaries provide an illuminating study of ideological strategies employed by evangelicals in the modern world, as their meaningful actions and reflective interpretations of those actions stand out in bold relief against a foreign background; and yet, the missionary career provides the possibility of distinctive responses to the social and psychological challenges of modernity—combining in unique ways the various elements of resistance, withdrawal, and accommodation.

The Shape of Things Set Apart: Child Missionaries

Sarah:[3]

My parents had eight children, and I am the second. My father was a factory worker. We were poor, compared to other people, but we lived in an old farmhouse out in the country where we could grow our own vegetables. My mother was a good Christian. She took us to Sunday School so that we could learn about the Bible, and about Jesus. And then when I was six, I heard about the five missionary men who were killed by the Auca Indians in Ecuador—that they were just trying to tell the Indians about God's love and they were speared to death. So I realized even then that there were things very wrong in the world, that there was hate and death.

Then my father—I remember him telling me, one day, that the rainbow didn't really come from Noah's ark, but it was just sunlight passing through little droplets of rain, dividing into colors. I realized my father was a pagan. We grew up with a man who had a very mean temper, with a lot of broken dishes and radios thrown across the room, and a lot of screaming and black-and-blue marks. He had quite a violent temper, really, and he would mistreat my mother and my brother especially.

I was a goodie-goodie. I memorized Bible verses, and filled in my Sunday School lesson every week. There aren't many kids who actually fill in their lesson every week, but I did. I was so righteous. I actually prayed the Pharisee's prayer, "I thank you, God, that I am not bad like my father."

But then my father became a believer in Jesus, when he was thirty-five years old. A new, young preacher had come to our church—just a kid out of Bible school—and he went on about how "all our righteousness is filthy rags." Well, my father got saved. And my first reaction was, "Who does he think he is? I'm the good person in this family!" But then I realized that there was a God who could change my father, and I suddenly realized my own sinfulness and my own need for a savior. I tried to run away from it, but I couldn't. I was a sinner, and I needed to ask God to forgive my sins. I became a true Christian at that moment.

Well, not even a year after that, my father found out that he had lung cancer, and then he died. I couldn't understand how that could be part of God's will for my father. After all, he had accepted the Lord and had become a good Christian man. He wanted to save all the men at the factory where he worked. How could he suffer and be in such pain, and then die and leave my mother with eight children? Why now? I couldn't make any sense of it.

Not only the suffering, but the worries of the future. We were already poor. What were we going to do now? And then there were the people who believed in faith healing, that if we just had enough faith, he would be healed. But he died. There's guilt with that. Then there was just the "Why?" I was not at a point where I could sit down and have a Bible study on human suffering. But I did know Proverbs 3:5 and 6, "Lean not unto your own understanding; trust in the Lord with all your heart." I struggled with that, and then I had a very, very spiritual experience—I really felt the touch of God. You can even say I felt a physical touch. That had been my favorite verse before, but I was never taken to task on what it meant, until that time. But then God just said to me, "Okay, trust in me, and I will direct your paths. Don't lean on your own understanding."

I really did not know what I was going to do with my life, but I did know that I did not want to be an old maid missionary. That was the one thing I did not want to do. But the day I got my college scholarship, I remember as a day of promise, even though it was a day of pain. It helped me to see that God had a plan for my life, and that my life was going to go on, even though my father was not. And I remember that I got down on my knees and said, "Okay, Lord. If you want me to be an old maid missionary, I'll do it." It was not until afterward, in studying the Bible, that I came across another verse in Corinthians that says to preach the gospel to the regions beyond you. I took that, and knew it was a calling to the mission field—not to stay where I was, but to go beyond me.

It wasn't easy to get here from that point. It took a long time. I fell in love with an unsaved man, and I went through about two years of intense turmoil, of conflict between the mission field and him. At one point I almost gave it up and said I would not go, that I would stay home and marry him. And at another point he said that he would go with me, that I could be a missionary and we would be together. But he finally got fed up, and one day he just said "I'm leaving," and he got on his motorcycle and went off across the country. I never saw him again. It was soon after that that I applied to come here.

Karen:

I am a preacher's kid, and I have grown up with my whole life involved in caring about other people, in trying to see other people as Jesus sees them. Let me start with when I accepted Jesus as my Savior. I was five years old, and the Holy Spirit convicted me of sin. I knew, even as a five-year-old, that I did things that were wrong. I can remember the actual feeling that I had, that Sunday morning in church, that I did things that were wrong and that I needed a savior. I needed Jesus to take away my sin. My feeling of sin was mainly from fighting with my brother, who was one year younger. I also knew, because I'd had training in my home, that Jesus had come to take away my feeling of guilt. So that day I just asked him to forgive my sins. That was the point when I became a Christian.

Then as a seven-year-old, I heard an evangelist preach on hell, and I got worried. I knew that I still did things that were wrong. And so, after the service that night, I called my dad into my room and I told him that I was concerned. I knew Jesus had forgiven me of my sins, but I still did things that were wrong. I felt like I needed him to pray for me. And so he did. I remember it real well. It was another one of those feelings. I remember that he prayed for me, that the feeling of guilt would just be lifted from me. And I remember actually feeling that sin was lifted from me.

My parents were very strict, and they had very high standards. All through grade school, one of the things was that I didn't dance. When everyone else had dancing, I stayed in the classroom. I was the only one. I had a special note from my parents. A couple of teachers even went to my parents and tried to talk them into allowing me to dance, but they would not.

We didn't go to movies. All the "no" things that Christians aren't supposed to do, we didn't do. We didn't smoke, we didn't drink, we didn't swear. We didn't even go mixed swimming, men with women. My dad, about the swimming, his thing was that it was important for a woman to be modest and careful about the way she dressed. You didn't want to put men in the position where they were always having to fight temptation. That wasn't something that brought glory to God.

I was set apart in that sense. Everybody knew that I was different. But it never did bother me. The reason was, I understood why we did what we did. My parents were consistent and loving, and they helped us develop in all kinds of ways. We never had a vacuum in our lives. We had lots and lots of things to do. I was always a top student. I was always good in music. And my friends looked up to me because of that. They respected me. They knew where I stood.

I knew my family was different. My family was so different, but such a better situation than any of my friends had. My friends were from crummy home situations. Their parents had been married two or three times. They didn't have the love, they didn't have the understanding, they didn't have the affirmation, they didn't have parents who sat and talked with them and listened to them, and let them express themselves. My home was so superior. I would take my friends home, just so they would know what it was like—just so that they would have a happy situation, and a nice atmosphere. But it was definitely set apart. I felt that God had set me apart for himself, and that I was going to serve him. I just felt that whatever I did, it would be secondary to the goal of serving God, and becoming what he wanted me to be.

Keith:

I grew up with a real hostility, anger, and hatred of people. I was very shy. I had a bad speech impediment. People laughed at me, so I just withdrew. My high school years were miserable. It's funny, you know, I was as big as I am now, in ninth grade. But because I couldn't talk right, I wouldn't be selected for football teams, or baseball teams, or basketball teams—even though I could play very well.

We had a lot of laws in our home—a lot of legalism. We went to a Baptist church. And it wasn't a question of whether I wanted to go—I *had* to go. But that just built more resistance in me, because I was mad at God. I figured he was the reason for most of my problems—particularly my speech impediment.

I did so poorly in high school. I graduated, but I think they just "socially graduated" me. I couldn't get into any colleges. I was turned down by even the local junior college. They wouldn't take me, and I thought they always had to take *anybody*. But my folks knew of a little dinky Christian college, and they knew the guy that was president. They wrote and told him the whole thing. They said, "We feel like our son's at a crossroads, and if he doesn't go to school, he'll just lose it. But nobody will let him in." And the guy said, "We'll let him in. He'll be on probation, but we'll help him." Well, I didn't want to go to this Bible school. In fact, I was so embarrassed of it, I used to say I was going to "barber school" instead of "Bible school." I would rather have been a barber than Christian.

I went there anyway, even though I hated the idea. I was the only non-Christian in the school, and everybody started praying for me. It all came to a head when we had a week of special evangelistic meetings in chapel. At the end of the week I was still resisting God. But the head of the school somehow sensed that God still had work to do in the life of at least one person, and so the preacher was asked to stay on a second week. That person was me. I finally accepted Christ. And it just—I mean, it just turned my life around. You know II Corinthians 5:17. "Old things have passed away, all things have become new." I know it's true. Everything changed.

I accepted Christ on a Monday, and I preached my first sermon the following Saturday—with no speech impediment! It was just an incredible experience. I was sitting there in chapel and the guy who was supposed to preach lost his voice. He came back and told me I had to speak. And I said, "No way." Because I knew what would happen. I would just go into this incredible stutter. But he said, "You've got to. These people are out here, and you've got to give them the Word. Just give them your testimony." He was whispering to me. He had completely lost his voice. I don't know how, but it was of God. Somehow I got up behind that pulpit and gave my testimony.

That's where it all started. The Lord gave me a burden to help others who were just like I had been. And that's the reason why that first part of my life is so important. I really can understand the lonely person, the hurt person, the hateful person, the resentful person—because I used to be like that. They don't want to be the way they are, but it's like being sucked down into a raging river. There's no way to get out, but if they could just find one thing to get a hold of, they might be able to get out. My one thing, of course, was Christ.

Maxine:

I come from a rather different family. My parents were separated when I was three, and I haven't seen my father since that time. My mother kind of gave up when Dad left—decided she wasn't going to take care of us kids. You know, the world was against her. We were going to go into an orphanage. But an aunt decided she would take care of us. She took over, and brought us up.

Mom was living in the house, but she wasn't doing anything. She was in bed, just completely out of it. She stayed in bed and did nothing except complain and fight. My grandma and grandpa were also living in the house. But when I was eight, my grandpa died. And when I was ten my grandma died. So that left my aunt and us three kids and my mom in the house. Mom was emotionally and mentally unstable. She just felt so sorry for herself. But I think she rejected me particularly because I'm the one in the family like my father. I have my father's ears, my father's personality. I bugged her all the time, because everything I did reminded her of him. She would say terrible things, but I would never fight back, because I just don't fight back, I just keep quiet.

Then one day, I was coming home from school, and they were giving out some pamphlets about daily vacation Bible school at the local church. And so I went to the Bible class. They told me that God loved me, that he had a special plan for my life, and they invited me to accept him. I couldn't believe the people in this church—they were so warm and friendly and happy. I had never come across people like that before. It was a Baptist church. They were genuinely loving. And to be able to say, "God is my father," that was really something for me, since I didn't have a father.

When I became a Christian, my mom told me to get out of the house, that she didn't want to see my face ever again. She ranted and raved—yelling and screaming and throwing things at me. Needless to say, I felt pretty insecure about the whole situation, but happy, too—that I had become a Christian. I was happy that I could have peace with the Lord.

Marie:

I come from a Christian family. My father has always been a visionary, but he has found it very difficult to hold a job because of wanting to do things for the Lord. He's done some quite amazing and strange things in his life, and this has really affected me as a person. For instance, right now he's trying to get into China. He has no money, but he has a couple of boats that he built himself. He has gone all around the South Pacific with Bibles. But he's found it difficult to work with others. He's never been happy in any church or denomination or group. So therefore, he has found his Christian desires and his Christian work to be an incredible frustration. He is a bitter man, which has affected our family very much. I think we've been affected in some positive ways, though we've all suffered. I still suffer about it.

Don:

I was born into a family of very humble people, but people who were concerned about following the Lord Jesus Christ in all that they did and said. We lived in a small town in Ohio. My father, for as long as I can remember, was an elder in the church. He was a layman—a coal miner, and later a construction worker.

We went to a church known as the Bible Church. It was a very fundamental church. But even there, my family tended to be the set-apart ones. You know, there were those leaders who were set apart, and kept the faith, and then there was that general church group who maybe started to drift off, doing some other things, and dabbling in things here and there.

I was dedicated to the Lord, probably at about two or three weeks of age, and my parents took that commitment very, very seriously. In those early years we didn't have a car or anything like that, but they saw to it that I was in church every time there was a service.

My parents say I made a decision for the Lord when I was four years old. I don't really remember that. What I do remember is about the age of twelve or thirteen, there was a tent campaign in a little town nearby and I went to it. I remember feeling very concerned. I wanted to be sure I was saved, and sure I was on the right road. So I went forward, and my dad counseled with me at that point. I went away knowing that I had been obedient, and that things were right.

I was the kind of kid that was supposedly "too religious" for most of the kids in public school. They made fun of me. I felt I was different in that sense. I was in a minority, trying to be very out-in-the-open with my Christian testimony. In high school it was the same. Even among the kids in my own church young people's group, I was the one who was kind of off to one side, because my life tended to be much more directed toward spiritual practice than a lot of the kids—even in the church.

Ralph:

From my youngest days, I felt a very heavy sense of responsibility for being a witness. Some of my earliest spiritual battles had to do with finding courage to carry on a witness among my own classmates and friends in the neighborhood. Maybe seven, eight years old—even at that stage I was feeling the necessity of trying to share my faith with people. By the time I was in junior high school, it was a big concern of mine—a daily concern. It wasn't pleasant. It was hard for me. It was embarrassing for me. But I had a strong sense of spiritual obligation—that that's what a Christian needed to do. My classmates were lost. So I would try to witness to them, and I would invite them to the evangelistic meetings at my church. As I got older, I became increasingly involved in witnessing, and increasingly bold about it. At my job, at school, it became a primary activity—organizing gospel teams in our young people's group to go down to the rescue missions, and so on.

Walter:

I was raised by Christian parents, in a Baptist church. I feel my dad was always a missionary in his own way. He was a mechanic, a gas station man, and brought up us kids in the gas station. We learned how to clean tools, how to clean the service station, and the restrooms—that was one of my first jobs. But we were always helping people. Dad would give a break to people. I remember one Christmas day, my dad and my brother and myself, we went out and we tuned up a car completely for free—plugs, points, condenser, carburetor, the whole thing. The people had just moved to the area. They needed help, so my dad helped them. And he taught us to help.

I was baptized at the age of eight, which indicated a decision in my life to follow Jesus. Our pastor came around to our third-grade Sunday School class, and said, "Well boys, it's about time to decide whether you want to be baptized." You'd probably guess this was a Baptist church. He didn't force us, but he knew us. He knew our family. He was a regular customer at our service station. He knew I was ready, and that some others in the class were ready. He baptized us, and it was a very real experience. I felt that I needed to share my faith with others, and baptism was the best way to initiate that.

When I got older I visited the Hopi and the Navaho Indian reservations with a man from our church. We took candy and clothes and the gospel, in the form of tracts and Bibles. I got an eyeful of Indians, living right in the United States, who were very poor. They needed help. And I guess I've always felt that the Lord wanted me doing something for people less fortunate than myself. Not only helping them in a physical way, but sharing my life and what the Lord has done in my life. That's always been my direction. Through my parents, there's been a divine guidance. I don't know why, because I don't think I'm anybody special, but I think the Lord has directed. He's had his hand on my life. I just think the Lord honored an eight-year-old boy's request.

Jean:

My father was a Methodist minister in a little Nebraska town surrounded by farms, which is the setting for my earliest memories. I remember the house, and the parsonage, and the church. My father had an important place in that town. And then when I was four years old, he became very ill, and he died. My mother was widowed at age thirty-four, with six children, whose ages were twelve, eleven, nine, seven—I was four—and my brother was nineteen months. This is the all-consuming event of my childhood, and it very definitely affected the rest of my life.

It was 1933. My father died in March, and the church voted to give us his salary until September. But then we would be moved out of the parsonage, and my mother had to make a decision about where to go. People came to my mother, and they told her she should not try to keep us all together. Her husband was gone, she was out of work, and they said the best thing for her to do would be to let other families raise different ones of us children. Someone offered to keep my younger brother, who was the smallest. Someone else offered Mother a job teaching in an orphanage. They said we could be part of the orphanage and she would have a job. She could see to supporting us that way, and we would have food and clothing. Another option she had was to go back to live with her own family. But they all lived on farms, and they were suffering poverty and drought. She felt she should not go back there.

But the thing about Mother is that the Lord told her just to live one day at a time. That she should just take all these ideas to him—kind of like Samuel who went through all the sons of Jesse to see who the Lord wanted to be king—and the Lord would sort of give her the nod for what she should do. She was not supposed to follow anyone's advice except the Lord's.

So she launched out in faith. It turned out that Father had insurance for two thousand dollars, and because prices were so low, Mother found a little house that she could buy for exactly that. So she bought this house with all of her money, and then she had nothing.

Every three months she got a pension from my father's church, about thirty dollars—ten dollars a month. And that was all she had.

I can remember, though, that she took us on the hill and showed us the house she had bought. She told us we would be homeowners. And from that time on, I grew up feeling kind of rich, that God was supplying our needs. We were sort of different from everybody else. I grew up feeling that other kids' daddies made money, but our money came directly from God. I always felt kind of proud and special—like God had called my father to heaven on a special assignment. It was like a child would say that his daddy had gone to Washington, D.C., on a special summons from the president. You know how that would make you feel, in a small town. Well, I just felt that we were special like that, that God had chosen this for us.

Testimonies of Conversion

What are these stories about? What do they have in common? Each is distinctive, yet a central idea seems to carry them along: that God predestines individuals for the missionary calling; that the process of divine selection often seems obscure during the painful and solitary moments of early life, but all the while God is carving out the spiritual identity of a missionary—severing layers of psychological and social tissues that bind the soul. Thus their towns are set apart from the cities, their churches from the towns, their families from the churches, their women from men, fathers and mothers from their children, a family from its home, a child from his chums—and finally the spirit from the flesh. The poor and humble are appointed keepers of the faith. A little girl sits alone in a classroom while her friends are dancing. A little boy endures his schoolmates' ridicule with Jesus in his heart.

Sarah's story in particular is a parable of estrangement. She begins by sketching a backdrop for the events of her early life, a picture of a family set apart and torn asunder. She draws the line of moral separation between her two parents. Her mother is the good parent who sends her to Sunday school where she learns about Jesus. Her father is the bad parent, the violent unbeliever. Recasting the moral boundary within herself, Sarah thinks at first that she is on her mother's side—aligned with the sacred against the profane. But then, a startling event occurs. Her father is converted, and she finds the guilt and the sinfulness that he embodied is within her as well. Somehow she is as bad as he is, needs salvation just as much, and so she accepts Jesus into her heart.

The next narrative moment, however, presents a new paradox to be resolved. Her father is now a good Christian man, ready to win the souls of his fellow workers at the factory. But he dies. Sarah faces the great problem of theodicy, timeless moral questions about the origins of good and evil and the purpose of human existence— the same questions raised in the Old Testament story of Job. Sarah's resolution is quite similar to Job's. She doesn't get any answers, but in the end simply trusts in God, in a higher understanding and a higher order of things. God appears to replace her father in a symbolic sense, resulting in a feeling of intimacy with God that is virtually physical. Sarah's story culminates in the essential portrayal of herself as a person set apart for God, destined for the mission field. Normal adolescent interests become trivial. She leaves behind her family and a potential husband to follow the

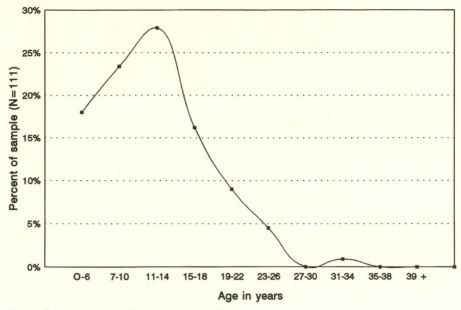

Figure 2.1. Age at time of conversion experience.

Lord, becoming the one thing that she was sure she never wanted to be—an old maid missionary.

But what are such stories for? Why and how are they told, and to whom? In my view, these vignettes are best understood as narrative fragments in the genre of the *Christian testimony*.[4] For evangelicals, a testimony is the evidence of a personal saving faith, stated in two ways. First, a testimony signals a life of moral rectitude by the avoidance of worldliness and sin. Second, a testimony is rendered as the verbal record of God's grace in a person's life, authenticating his or her membership among the faithful and confronting those outside the fold with the gospel's claim on their own lives.

Many of the testimonies that I recorded centered around the idea or the personal experience of conversion and employed a special rhetoric and imagery for separating a former *life in the flesh* from a new *life in the spirit*. Specifically, 90 percent of the Mission members I studied indicated that they had experienced a "definite conversion" and remembered their specific age at the time they "accepted the Lord as personal Savior." As Figure 2.1 suggests, conversion tends to be a normative experience for these people, occurring most typically in late childhood or early adolescence. The median age at which conversion experiences occurred was 11.8 years; 70 percent were "saved" before the age of fourteen.

As we can see in these and other examples that follow, conversion testimonies often begin with talk about the self in its "natural" state—as defiled, faulty, sinful, weak, mortal, or unhappy. Typically, the narrator identifies some sort of tension in the self: perhaps "success in the eyes of the world but misery inside myself," or "failure in my own power, though I had unyielded talents and abilities." Ambivalence regarding God (who is often represented or mediated by parents) signals a pulling-apart of the self as the spirit longs for God, while the flesh resists and fears him.

Suspense then rises to a point of crisis, and resolution comes when the person finally repents, surrenders to God, accepts Christ into her life, and is saved. In the end, the narrator offers some version of the statement, "My life completely turned around," and attempts to illustrate how the Lord changed her and put her life back together, and is now using her to touch the lives of others. Intermittent struggles with the old sinful nature persist, but the person "gets victory" over these with the help of the indwelling Holy Spirit.

Merely to observe that evangelical testimonies of conversion tend to be structured and stylized according to certain conventions of a genre is not to suggest they are somehow disingenuous, or all the same. In fact, they express something that is individualized and very real to these people. Still, there is a kind of recognized *ideal type* of conversion testimony, in relation to which many of these missionaries tell their own stories as variations on a theme. In my view, the reason that conversion retains such significance for them is that it defines the primary axis upon which a culturally demanded separation of sacred and profane,[5] spirit and flesh, can be hinged to personal life stories and thus appropriated by individual identities.

On one level, evangelical believers think of the separation as something that takes place in real time, with a "before and after" for each individual Christian. But in a more mystical sense, they interpret the moments of faith in a Christian's life story as parallel to the moments of divine action in Biblical history: creation, the fall, judgment, death, redemption, resurrection, regeneration. Thus, conversion testimonies help define and maintain the boundaries of the group even as they crystallize individual identities—binding a person's sense of self to a body of fellow believers here and now, and also securing membership in a symbolic spiritual community that transcends history.

For missionaries, in addition, the ability to give an effective personal testimony is of paramount significance because testimonies epitomize their profession. Missionaries need to manage testimonies that work both inside and outside the group. Even before they get to the task of witnessing in a foreign country, evangelical missionary candidates face the challenge of raising funds for their personal support by appealing to churches and individuals at home. To be successful, they must sell themselves as good missionary material by convincing others they are not only talented and well-qualified but—more importantly—totally and humbly yielded to God. They must convey the notion that they are not going out in their own power, but in the power of God, to be used as instruments of redemption. They are not going to the mission field for any personal gain or glory, but only because God has called them to *give up* self-interest for the cause of the gospel.

Clearly then, a dramatic personal testimony of the transforming power of God in one's life becomes valuable currency for missionaries (and missionary candidates). Insiders respond to such testimonies as exemplars of the faith. The story of the sinner saved by grace—a good story well told—at once confirms for the faithful the power of their own beliefs, and promises drawing power on the outside. Thus, one of the missionary's key tasks, in crafting a testimony, is to find rhetorically effective ways of representing the self its preconversion state—as sinful, guilty, and set apart from God—in order to set the stage for personal redemption. But the demand for a testimony that hews to the flesh-and-spirit line of rhetoric, and that lends itself well to a before-and-after style of narration, poses a considerable challenge for people whose entire life experience and development of identity has taken place within the evangelical community. A dramatic conversion experience sometimes is needed to create the watershed moment around which an effective testimony can be built.

Neely's *Come Up to This Mountain* (1982) offers a fine illustration of exactly this dilemma in the life of Clarence Jones, founder of HCJB. Jones had literally grown up around street-corner evangelism, and by age twelve was a regular trombone player in the Salvation Army Band directed by his father. Nevertheless, he found himself in a predicament when his father would call on him to take his turn giving a testimony in public. To the young Jones's "secret humiliation," he could not produce one. In Neely's words, "At this point Clarence had no testimony. He had no personal experience with nor commitment to Jesus Christ. So when his turn drew ominously near, try as he might, he could not manufacture a testimony" (Neely, 1980:21). The ultimate resolution for Jones came at age seventeen, when he left his seat in the band at the Moody Tabernacle and walked to the altar to be saved—in full view of five thousand people who had come to hear the evangelist Paul Rader.

Perhaps for obvious reasons, Neely presents at face value Jones's claim to have had "no personal relationship with nor commitment to Jesus Christ" prior to this moment—despite his having grown up in a family in which prayer, Bible reading, gospel music, and evangelistic activities were a daily diet. But the description that follows puts his conversion experience in perspective: "Back in the inquiry room," Neely writes, "Clarence figured he knew the routine: after all, he'd seen sinners by the dozens at the Salvation Army penitent form. So he dropped to his knees, bowed his head, mouthed a prayer, and within thirty seconds was on his way out the door again." Before he could escape, however, a counselor intercepted him, sat him down, and "led him through Scripture verses till at last Jones could say, 'I know I'm saved because God's word says so.'" (Neely, 1980:22). From that point on, Clarence Jones had a testimony. Through his conversion experience, he came to see that his prior life had been nothing but empty hypocrisy. Neely quotes him: "I thought I was a Christian. But now I know I was just as big a sinner as those bums we've been preaching to on West Madison Street." And as Neely notes, finally, "This experience made a deep impression on Clarence Jones, that all those years he could be making a public profession as a child of God without having the grace of God in his heart and life."

Still the question arises, what does conversion really denote in these missionaries' testimonies? Can their accounts be understood according to any standard sociological or psychological model of conversion? In a well-known treatise in the sociology of knowledge, Peter Berger and Thomas Luckmann (1966:144–145) discussed religious conversion as the prime example of a more general phenomenon they termed "alternation." When alternation occurs, they said, an individual fundamentally changes his or her way of viewing the world and subjectively affects a total transformation of the self. In order for conversion to occur, according to Berger and Luckmann's recipe, certain social and cognitive conditions must be present, to precipitate the convert's "resocialization." In their terms, a new "plausibility structure" must be present and a new group must exert sufficient power over the person to dismantle previous "nomic structures" and to serve as a "laboratory of transformation."

Similarly, Lofland and Stark (1965), Downton (1979) and Stark and Bainbridge (1980) identified converts as individuals who tended to be isolated and distressed as well as ideologically predisposed to accept supernatural beliefs, but also as people who were placed in situations where they could develop social bonds with members of a new group.

More recent studies of conversion by social and behavioral scientists (e.g., Wenegrat, 1990; Kirkpatrick and Shaver, 1990; Dawson, 1990) have tended to focus on the transformation of self as an active process involving some interplay between psychodynamic-motivational and social-exchange kinds of influences. Ullman's *The Transformed Self* (1989) builds on a tradition of theory emphasizing *deprivation* in the developmental experience of persons at risk for conversion. Ullman presents psychological case studies rendering conversion as relief from psychic pain and loneliness; as a "quest for the perfect father"; as a resolution of identity crises; and as a narcissistic merger of self with a transcendent "perfect object." From a more sociological point of view, Neitz's *Charisma and Community* (1987) highlights conversion experiences as "transformative moments" distilled from a socially reflective process of religious commitment, by which individuals actively reconstruct their basic identity, worldview, and values, and come to inhabit a new social reality.

Clearly, if we employ the criteria for conversion implicit in most of these studies, we might tend to minimize the significance of many evangelicals' childhood "born again" experiences because these subjects do not undergo "alternation" in the classic sense. Despite their use of the symbolic language of conversion, most of these people were never "the vilest offender saved by grace," but rather, children who absorbed the interpretive framework of Christianity with their mother's milk.

However, some scholars have suggested—correctly, in my view—that the key to understanding many so-called conversions is to focus on the function of life-historical *narrative*, rather than on the psychological state of the convert or the ideology, structure, and power of a new group or affiliation. Snow and Machalek (1983), for instance, have suggested that what distinguishes religious converts is not so much where they have come from versus where they are now, but the *way they talk* about themselves: retelling their life story, attributing the cause and pattern of human events to a master scheme, and speaking as if their religious beliefs were uniquely true and unlike other beliefs. According to this line of argument, most of what defines the convert as a role or social type reduces to subculturally programmed verbal behavior.[6]

In my view, what is important to note about missionaries' (and many evangelicals') conversion experiences is that, even though great cognitive and behavioral changes may *not* attend them, the moment of accepting Christ is symbolically very meaningful to these people—*as a moment of turning*—because it helps them to organize a testimony that, when verbally recounted, consolidates personal identity and membership within their own group. While we might question the status of these conversion experiences as "alternations" in sociological terms, we must recognize the significance of conversion within the evangelical system of meaning. We have to wonder, what is it that compels a man at age fifty-eight to tell us about the time when he lay in bed and received Christ into his heart at age fifteen? From his point of view, this is the key event that explains how and why he became the person he is today.

Thus, the notion of being converted *from* something *to* something else becomes very significant in a rhetorical sense, even for people raised in Christian homes—as Keith's testimony (given above) clearly illustrates. His preconversion "life in the flesh" is represented primarily by rebellion against his parents' Christianity. He tells us that he only went to their Baptist church because he was forced to, and that being sent to church against his will simply made him angry at God for causing his speech impediment and rejection by others. He never says he didn't believe in God. Clearly, God existed for him, and was powerful and involved in human affairs—enough to give Keith a great deal of trouble as a "non-Christian." But God did not seem very loving and accepting, and Keith did not care to respond to such a God. Keith's conversion represents a change in attitude, if not belief. Another testimony exhibiting this same sort of theme is the following:

> I have known all my life that I would have to make a commitment to Christ. I understood that it meant I would have to give myself over to Christ, and to serve him, not live for myself. But for years I really resisted the call of the gospel. I didn't want to go to Sunday School. I had to go, but I didn't want to.
>
> Then when I was fifteen, I got sick. Very strong flu or something. What it was, I don't know. I was in bed, and that's when the Lord spoke to me. And I told him I would give my life to him. That was the time I made my decision for Christ. I made it completely alone, in my room, in my bed. And I cannot describe the experience of happiness and joy that I had. It was as if Christ had come into my room, and the whole room was full of glory. That's the feeling I had. I'm sure he was there.

About one quarter of the Mission group said that while their families had been affiliated with a Protestant church, they were not "brought up in an evangelical Christian home." These people tend to set the stage for conversion by talking about their parents' tepid, nominal, or backslidden religiosity—which stands in, so to speak, for the unregenerate state of sinful human nature:

> I was raised in a liberal Methodist Episcopal church, where the gospel was never preached. I don't remember ever seeing a missionary in our church. If my dad ever went to church with us, he just slept. And the messages we heard were just very liberal—social gospel. If something important happened in the world and was in the headlines, the preacher might preach on that. And we never had Bible reading or prayer in our home.

> I grew up in a non-Christian home—periodically going to Sunday School or church, but there was no meaning to it. Later I found out that my granddad, on my dad's side, was an evangelistic lay preacher from Tennessee, from a Baptist background. Dad had grown up under that, but somehow his family's Christianity had never touched home for him. That was the problem.

> Now, my aunt had taken us to a Methodist Sunday school, but it was just social gospel, and I hadn't really heard *the* gospel—that Jesus died for me, that he paid for my sins, and that I could accept him as my personal savior. I hadn't heard that.

> Then my family fell away from the church. My father, just having his business problems and—we just fell away from it. I guess we would attend the Baptist church in town every

once in awhile. And every so often my father would get into this spiritual mood where we were all going to get together as a family and read the Bible and pray. But it just did not fit in with our total life.

My father was not a Christian, and my mother, I wouldn't have said she was a practicing Christian. I was confirmed in the Episcopal church. But after the confirmation process, I came out feeling that I was even less a Christian than I thought I was before. I went through it probably out of embarrassment of not wanting to say I was never confirmed. But I did come out with an awareness that I had to work out some sort of relationship with God.

And then, just before I went off to college, my father died—quite suddenly. One day he came home from work, and he was just walking down the road, and he collapsed. That thrust me into leading the family. My mother depended on me a lot. Up until then she had depended upon my father. Now I was the oldest.

I grew up overnight. I went to college, but I was conscious that I was really running away from home, because I desperately wanted to get away from the pressures there. I was scared, yet sort of proud of myself at the same time for being grown up. I was following in my father's footsteps. I was going to study civil engineering. My father was a civil engineer, and that was going to be my life's career.

But through the crisis of my father's death, I determined that I was going to find out, once and for all, whether there was anything to Christianity or not. I didn't really care. I just got fed up with all the battles in my mind. So I said, where's the nearest church? And whatever church it was, I was going to stick there for a semester, and I would see how it went. I decided that if there was anything to it, I would join up within that time. I got involved in this small group, and it was a caring group. There was no heavy witnessing. They just quietly shared what they believed, and they sort of loved me into the kingdom. There was something real to what they were saying. I eventually became a Christian. And I knew, even before I became a Christian, that if I made that decision it would require a complete rethinking of many areas of my life.

The most common pattern I encountered in these testimonies was what might be called "normal conversion," where a child is assisted by adults to receive Christ and be saved almost as a rite of passage. Such testimonies often appropriate the rhetoric of moral crisis and conversion in referring to something that might otherwise be seen as a commonplace developmental benchmark of late childhood or adolescence—a kind of coming of age in the Bible belt.[7] Karen's story, given above, is typical. Others are these:

As a child I went to Sunday School and church. It was a good little community Bible church, very fundamental. We used to have transient preachers come and speak and they would tell you these hellfire and brimstone stories. But I was too scared to go up and make a decision, and too scared to stay in my seat. When I was fourteen, at Bible camp, I finally went forward and accepted the Lord. I was very timid and shy, so it was really quite an experience. I went in the back room to pray, and this lady asked me if I needed any help, but I said, "No." Of course, I wasn't a Christian and I did need help. But instead of having somebody else lead me to the Lord, I just said, "OK, Lord, this is my opportunity," and I accepted the Lord myself. I knew the ropes and everything, so it didn't take much.

My mother taught a Bible class in our house. And I found out the core meaning of Christianity when I was not quite four. She was telling a Bible story using a flannelgraph, and it was Easter week. She was saying that God loved us so much that he had sent his son to die for our sins. Of course, at that age I didn't understand much theology. But I did understand that anybody who loved me that much deserved my life. So I gave my life to the Lord, as a very small child.

I accepted the Lord as savior when I was twelve. Coming to know the Lord really made a change in my life—from a sad child, to a child who had some hope and stability.

When I was thirteen is when I became a Christian. It was in the summer when it happened. It was just at night in bed, and I accepted the Lord. I was thinking about a time when we'd gone on a family vacation and I'd stepped in a water hole—both me and my mother went down. And we would have drowned, but my father pulled us out.

In some testimonies—though not the majority—conversion becomes fraught with ambiguity and anxiety. Particularly for children who experience social rejection because of some personal stigma or disability, threats to the integrity of a developing self may be interpreted as "not being saved." Consider the following testimony (which contains some interesting parallels with Keith's story given above):

As a kid in school, I had an enormous hang-up. I never knew how to read, so I hated school with a passion. I still remember the fear I had of going to school, and not being able to read. The greatest fear I had was of taking an exam and not being able to read the questions. And in Sunday school, when they'd say, "Let's go around in a circle and each read a verse of this Bible chapter"—I'd leave before it came my turn to read. When I graduated from high school, my mother was reading me all my books.

All the time I was growing up, I never did really feel that I was saved. I went forward at least a dozen times, in different churches, to accept the Lord. But I never felt saved. And I don't know why, really. They would always say, "Well, now that you've accepted the Lord, you're going to have to get baptized." But I'd already been baptized, and so I shrunk away from it. Another reason is just that I didn't see any change in my life.

Then I went to Japan, in the service. There was an old missionary there, about sixty-five years old, and he finally led me to the Lord—or led me to the assurance of my salvation. There was a Christian G.I. who took me under his wing. He said, "You've got to learn how to read." He would read one page in this book, *Romans Verse by Verse,* in about two minutes. And I would read the next page in about a half hour. I hated it, but I knew that there was only one way to be a servant of the Lord, and that was to study the Bible. So I had to learn to read, at that age. It was very, very difficult. But I did it. And I did go to Bible school and I graduated, and became a missionary.

In this story, it is hardly difficult to see a link between "never knew how to read" and "never felt saved." On the surface, this testimony is about a child who felt ashamed and isolated because of a learning problem. But on a deeper level, it is the story of a child who got trapped in a group for which Bible reading signified the membership and identity of the saved, so that his inability to apprehend the word of God through his own eyes became internalized as a damning moral defect. Accepting the Lord was supposed to change his life and relieve his anxiety, but it didn't work—until he learned to read.

In such cases, the feeling of fault is typically a lonely, individualized experience. However, some testimonies describe conversion as a group phenomenon, sometimes affecting a whole community that has undergone a form of estrangement or a traumatic dislocation resulting in a spiritual crisis. When this happens among evangelical believers, their children may *all together* come to feel they are not saved. Consider the following missionary story from outside the American experience:

I was born in Siberia. My parents were German Mennonites, and when I was three years old they decided to leave Russia because of communism. My dad already was a prisoner on trial. They called him an antirevolutionary, which was not really true. Every night when he would fall asleep, then the police would come and get him, and he had to answer questions the whole night. After some time—it was just before the winter—he escaped, with a wife and four children. By a miracle, we got out of Russia, over Germany, to Brazil. We settled in a Mennonite colony.

During my first six years of school, I went to German school. I accepted the Lord when I was eight. It was in the grammar school. One day, some children just started crying out, "I am a sinner, I need salvation!" And we came to the teacher, one after the other, to pray with him. . . . Some time later, I found out that the teacher himself had been away from the Lord, and through this he was reconciled with the Lord again.

In sum, in order to grasp the meaning and the importance of conversion for this missionary group, we must attend to both the social and personal functions of Christian testimonies. On the one hand, we have to recognize that testimonies provide a practical definition of membership in the only group that finally matters to evangelicals. But on the other hand, to properly interpret the way in which conversion is appropriated for individual identity construction, we may need to suspend ordinary sociological criteria for defining a convert. We may need to look at it, rather, from the believer's point of view as a spiritual transaction between God and the self.

Self, Other, and God: Ambivalence in the Formation of a Spiritual Identity

The talk of these missionaries about their formative experiences divides pretty clearly into three topical areas, corresponding to three sorts of elements often given in a religious person's reconstructed biography. These are: (1) the inner, moral self (in distinction from the outer self presented to others); (2) the family (parents, in particular); and (3) the sacred (God, spiritual things, faith, ultimate values, and responsibilities).

In a general formula for missionaries' early-stage moral careers, revelatory knowledge of the self and knowledge of God are reciprocally obtained and synthesized: "When I saw myself as I truly was, I realized my need for the Lord/ When I truly came to know the Lord, I saw myself in a new light." As the formula is actually worked out, however, the figure of a parent usually emerges as key to the developing consciousness of both the self (as contingent) and the sacred (as powerful other). The parent occupies a crucial but ambiguous position as a mirror for the child's emerging moral self—reflecting the insufficiency and dependence of a creature, on the one hand, and the transcendence of a creator, on the other.

Profoundly religious parents highlight this pattern. A substantial majority of the Mission members indicated they had been "led to the Lord" by one of their parents. They vividly recall devout fathers and mothers who expressed their own (adult) dependence upon the Lord using the imagery of a trusting child petitioning a parent. In these recollections, parental piety often seems to go hand-in-hand with economic deprivation:

We were a poor family, and we had to make do with very little. My father was a home missionary, totally in faith. He had no salary at all, or mission backing, or anything. So we knew, as kids, what it was like to be without, and to pray and have things arrive at our doorstep. He preached, and ministered in the jails, and in homes, and he was just kind of on the call of the Lord to go at any moment, wherever he was sent. So he traveled a fair amount, when I was growing up, sometimes quite a distance. He would just start out walking, and get rides. His life would make a whole book. He wasn't a public man. His ministry was a lot more private than a lot of ministers'. I can't say I was really close to him, except that we had a lot of respect, in our relationship with him. There was a lot of respect for the way the Lord led him.

My dad showed us how important it is to know God's mind, and to walk in his ways. We knew him. He would never say to us, yes, we could do something, or no, we couldn't—unless he had a strong sense of what the Lord was saying to him. You know, we'd ask him, "Can we go here?"—something we wouldn't think twice about for our own kids—and he would say, "I really need to seek the mind of the Lord about that." He was very strong about praying for things. This left us with little argument. There was never any way to manipulate him, and disobedience was very sternly handled. He was strict in his dealing with us kids. And five of the ten of us have become missionaries.

In this passage, clearly, the father occupies the ambiguous role of this-worldly parent/other-worldly child. Whereas children normally see their parents as material providers, in this family God is seen literally as the provider, while the father is seen, childlike and penniless, trusting in God along with the rest of the family. Whereas children normally live in a world in which parents have ultimate authority, in this family the father possesses no authority of his own but simply expedites the orders of a heavenly father. Years later, when the adult remembers her "respect" for her father, and says, "There was never any way to manipulate him," she is, in a sense, also speaking about God.

In *The Future of an Illusion* and elsewhere, Freud (1927) argued that belief in God is an unconscious projection, or transfer, of people's feelings of admiration and longing for their earthly fathers to an imaginary heavenly father. A discussion of psychoanalytic interpretations of religious experience is beyond our scope here, except to suggest that Freudian views offer one framework within which to observe a primary emotional feature of missionaries' testimonies about themselves, their parents, and God: profound ambivalence.[8]

Sharon:

Sharon's story offers a revealing portrayal of a child's ambivalence toward her parents, and of how such conflict may get bound up in a sense of estrangement and division within the self. Sharon is a young missionary woman whose mother committed suicide, yet her testimony on the surface deals almost entirely with her father. She portrays a man who was strict and demanding, yet weak and inconsistent. She recalls a time when she was thirteen years old and her father lead the family in a profession of faith and joined the Church of God. They all attended for a while, but then her father got involved in a bitter dispute within the church over speaking in tongues and left to start a church of his own. Sharon and her mother and siblings went along with him and attended his new church for about three years. But then, due to some unspecified personal and business problems, her father walked away from the church he started and "fell away from the Lord." On a couple of subsequent occasions, he attempted a revival, but without success. Later he became ill with cancer, was "miraculously healed," vowed to live for the Lord, but then backslid once more. Finally he was bankrupt and, in Sharon's view, morally bereft as well. After all this, we finally hear about Sharon's mother and her tragic death—but only as a brief footnote in her continuing saga of ambivalence regarding her father.

> My mother is no longer living. She committed suicide. It was after my sister had left home, so all the kids were gone. All these things had happened. My father had so many personal problems. I've had to deal with a lot of bitterness since my mom's death. It's very easy to blame my father, because of the type of person he is. But I can honestly say, God has really helped me to forgive him. About a year ago—well, sometimes it still creeps in, and I have to deal with it. But God has helped me, so I can be around him now without looking for all the little innuendoes that make me mad.
>
> It sounds strange, but I always thought my home life was pretty secure. My father was very strict, a very demanding person. During my younger years we were pretty well off. Then as I got older, and really had to deal with my own self-image and form my own relationships, I began to realize how much my home life had affected me badly. Unfortunately, I have some of my father's traits. But my personality is really more like my mother.

What is the significance of the psychological ambivalence reflected in these missionaries' testimonies? In his existential phenomenology of religion, philosopher Merold Westphal (1984) argues (in line with Kierkegaard, Schleiermacher, and others) that the experience of ambivalence lies at the core of what it means to be religious. Westphal's evidence is a delectable sampler of sacred texts and accounts of religious experiences—from Job before Yahweh in the Old Testament, to Arjuna before the transfigured Krishna in the Bhagavad-Gita, to the dramatic conversions cataloged by William James, to Thomas Merton climbing his seven-story mountain. Westphal refers to a kind of universal experience at once simple and profound:

> Perhaps you have watched a toddler in the presence of a large dog who is not part of the family. The child is frightened and fascinated at the same time. . . . Or perhaps you have stood on the Canadian side of Niagara Falls at that point where you can stand so close to the edge of the falls as to be nearly on top of them. Did not the edge, like the edge of any cliff, draw you irresistibly toward it while at the same time it terrified you and made you want to keep at quite a safe distance? (Westphal, 1984:24).

What Westphal concludes is "(1) that human ambivalence before the sacred is grounded in a sense of ontological inadequacy, (2) that this complex and volatile experience comes to expression in the language of paradox, and (3) that the rich variety of such expressions nevertheless arises out of a single experiential core"—perhaps best captured in Rudolf Otto's description of "the numinous" as *mysterium tremendum et fascinans* (Westphal, 1984:37).

Returning to the missionaries, in my view it is this sense of ambivalence before the sacred that underlies many of their accounts of being set apart during early life— perhaps most strikingly in the category of explicitly religious experiences such as conversion or "surrendering" one's life to the Lord. At these spiritual high points, the sense of being in a world radically separated into sacred and profane realms becomes crystallized and culminates in a life-and-death struggle between God and the self. According to Westphal, the self becomes acutely conscious of fault, guilt, inadequacy, and the relativity of its being in the face of the absolute being of God. The self longs for God, yet fears God; one feels simultaneously the need for God's judgment and God's grace. The psychological tension that believers feel leading up to conversion is drawn out by opposing fears—of the consequences of surrendering to God on the one hand, and of failing to surrender on the other hand—compounded by the fear of the freedom to choose between the two.

The result of such crises, for evangelical Christians, is that God—the sacred other—finally wins out over the self. The idea is that by losing one's life in Christ, one's soul is saved for immortality. Complete self-abnegation clears the path for God's grace to bring about a "new creation" in the surrendered life of the believer, and to empower that new life as an instrument for the redemption of others. And yet, even after conversion, the ambiguities of being in the world as both spirit and flesh persist, and the believer continues to struggle with a natural inclination toward the profane "things of this world." Such believers often cite the Apostle Paul's lament, "I do what I don't want to do, and I don't do what I want to do." The alienated self takes on a new form, becoming a self set apart from the world for God—yet must remain within itself and within the world.

In these missionaries' life stories, various manifestations of ambivalence seem to attend not only the spiritual high points, but the whole path of moral-career development leading up to such crises and beyond them—beginning with their earliest judgments of the self in relation to others. The primary "others" mentioned, of course, are parents and parental figures. In the passages below, several variations on the following formula will be illustrated: ambivalence in the child's view of her parents is reflected in the child's view of herself, especially as she confronts the sacred. Estrangement of the child from the parent is then recast as estrangement within the child's self. Such ambivalence builds to a sense of crisis that is moral, emotional, and psychological. Eventually, resolution comes through a spiritual transformation of the self—a surrendering to God—which sets the stage for embracing the missionary vocation.

Yvonne:

When I was born, my parents, for whatever reason, didn't want me. So they put me in an orphanage. I was adopted as an infant—when I was eight or nine months old. I always knew that. So from the very beginning, I suspect there was a certain need for belonging that developed in me. I always had a sense of wanting to belong. I had a feeling of strangeness. We didn't have a lot of structure in our home. I sort of grew up "like Topsy." Both my parents worked, and we were pretty free to do what we wanted. Though I loved my parents, it was just a strange kind of thing—there was something missing there.

The feeling of alienation only intensified when I got to college. I was into drama, and I was elected student body vice president. But I also began drinking a lot, and drinking became a problem for me. One night I went to the home of a friend of mine and I drank enough wine to actually not know what I was doing. Apparently what we did is we went to a football game, and probably raised a ruckus. The next day, the head of the school called together all of the student body officers for an emergency meeting, at which time he said, "I am shocked by what happened at the football game last night. As leaders of this student body, I want you all to set the example of proper behavior." So there I sat, the student body leader, you know, the "example to everybody." And yet I was the very person who had caused the ruckus. He didn't know that—but I knew it.

That was a very telling moment in my life, because I saw myself as I really was. I saw what I had allowed myself to become. So once again, I had this terrible feeling of alienation, and now from my own self. I felt like there were two people, you know, just going through life. And I wasn't a bum. I was succeeding.

So I went home, and I sat in my room and thought, now what am I going to do? How am I going to get my parts together? What is this, that causes me to behave in a way that is exactly contrary to what other people perceive me as being?

I had a grandmother—my mom's mom—who was a real Christian little lady. And she used to come and pray with us, and encourage me to go to Sunday School, and so forth. I thought, "All right. I love my grandmother. And she loves God. So I'll go to church." That's just the way it happened.

I had a little red MG, and I drove around and parked it two blocks away from the church. I went in the church, and sat in the very back row, of course. And it's the classic case. I don't remember what the sermon was about. But the Scripture reading was, "What shall it profit a man if he should gain the whole world and lose his soul?" And at that time I thought, "I do not want to lose my soul." But I had that sense of it slipping away. I left before church was over, so I wouldn't have to talk to anybody. I got in the car and went home. I got down on my hands and knees. I thought, if you talk to God, you've got to show some respect, right? And I just told him what he already knew. I told him that I felt incomplete, that I felt I didn't belong to anybody, and that I would very much like to belong to him. I didn't want to lose my soul, and I wanted to be a complete person in Jesus.

The next day I went to school, and because by nature I am a talker, I told everybody. I told all my friends. Amazingly enough, I never had another problem with drinking, from that time on. I became a believer that night. And I believe God entered my life. I was not responding rationally. I was responding emotionally. So when I went to church and the minister spoke "Jesus," in some vague way I knew that Jesus was the one I needed. I needed to be accepted and to be loved. And that's exactly what he did for me.

This story begins with the key element of ambivalence in the narrator's view of her parents. The natural love Yvonne might have felt toward her biological parents cannot be expressed or reciprocated, because they have abandoned her. She loves her adoptive parents, but they provide an inadequate substitute. The result is an ill-defined feeling of *strangeness*—of not belonging to anyone.

By the time she gets to college, the ambivalence Yvonne felt toward her parents has become internalized, and it reemerges as moral ambivalence in her view of self. She is both good and bad, a success and a failure at the same time. She feels that there are "two people going through life"—one is the acceptable social self, and the other is the unacceptable inner self. This inner self becomes conscious of what Westphal terms "ontological inadequacy" before the sacred, perhaps put more felicitously in Yvonne's words: "I thought, 'I do not want to lose my soul.' But I had that sense of it slipping away."

Her sense of fault and dividedness within herself moves her toward the sacred—but not directly. Her path is mediated by the figure of a moral parent—a grandmother who had prayed with her as a child. The association of the grandmother with the sacred is explicit: "I thought, 'I love my grandmother. And she loves God. So I'll go to church.'" But of course, Yvonne is ambivalent about going to church. She parks two blocks away. She sits in the very back row. She leaves early so she won't have to talk to anybody. She is plainly reluctant to identify herself with religious people and their experience. But when she finally meets God, in the privacy of her own room at home, it is an encounter with the numinous, *mysterium tremendum et fascinans*. She gets down on her hands and knees to "show some respect." She is conscious that God already knows what she is going to say. And in a way, she addresses God as the loving parent she has longed for all of her life.

Finally, Yvonne's inner self is transformed. Her sense of set-apartness does not merely disappear; rather, its locus is shifted outward. In the end she is no longer set apart from her self, but set apart *for God, from the world*. And this is what sets the stage for the missionary impulse. In fact, she immediately becomes a missionary to her friends, boldly telling them about her spiritual rebirth.

Jack:

My parents were missionaries. I was seven years old when they decided to go back to the mission field, and I was left in a mission home. I was one of twenty seven kids living under one roof, and we had three adults to take care of us. From the time I was seven years old until I graduated from high school, I saw my parents just a couple of times, for six months each. I was essentially on my own.

The fact that today I am a missionary at all is still a mystery to a lot of my teachers, and to people who were involved in my upbringing. The two people who were most influential in my formative years said later that of all the kids who went through that mission home who had potential to become something, I was the least likely to make it.

It was a very traumatic, difficult time. I resented it. I rebelled. I was an extrovert, but I felt very insecure and inferior. Usually someone who is loud and boisterous is trying to cover up something he doesn't have by making everyone think he does have it, and that was me. I went around scaring people off, instead of winning friendships. I think that's a syndrome that's very common among missionary kids who are raised away from their parents, because the people who raise them really don't have the ability to love them as we love our own children. Consequently, we are rejected, in that kind of a setting.

Somewhere along the line—though it's not something I take credit for—I turned my life over to God, and God decided to use something that was a diamond in the rough. It was the result of when I finally called out to God, and I came to this whole concept of self-acceptance. The idea that God loves you as you are, so don't be a fool—accept yourself.

Through accepting myself, I began to accept my parents. And I think the basis of acceptance is forgiveness. If I do think they did it wrong, it's forgiven, and it's forgotten that they did it wrong. Now, of course I couldn't do that with my son—leave him in a children's home. Nevertheless, I have to be fair. Now that I have buried my dad, I think more highly of him than I have ever thought of him before. Because I went through his things, I went through his books, and I found poems he had written, found things that he had spent his life doing that have touched me. The man was so much deeper than I ever thought. Why is it that we don't know our parents? Why is it that we don't really understand our parents, until after they are gone? I don't know.

Although Jack's story ends on a questioning note, it is really an account of personal resolution. It is less about the constraining facts of a person's life than about his interpretation and transcendence of those given limitations. Once again, it starts with ambivalence and resentment in a child's view of his parents, which is internalized as guilt, and leads finally to spiritual transformation of an ontologically inadequate self.

From the adult point of view, we might construct Jack's sense of abandonment and personal fault as a variation on the problem of theodicy, as he might contemplate the sacred embodied by his father: Why has my father forsaken me? Is he a bad person? He can't be bad, because he is doing the will of God who is the source of good. The answer must be that *I* am a bad person. I have done wrong and deserve to be punished. For such a child, it is a short step from feeling punished by a father to feeling punished by God. The heroic actions of the missionary father, thousands of miles away, seem to embody goodness, power, and meaning—in an imagined world that comes to seem more real than the small and insignificant world of the child left behind. Thus, through the looking glass of the sacred other, Jack's own self comes to seem somehow less real than that of his father. We see a duplicitous and insufficient self, in Jack's words "trying to cover up something he doesn't have by making everyone think he does have it, and that was me." And then there was the irresistible attraction to the sacred, which was at the same time repelling: "I rebelled. . . . I finally called out to God."

Once again what seems to lie beneath the surface of such a testimony is a feeling of self-estrangement internalized as guilt, something Paul Tillich once described as follows:

> [U]nder the conditions of man's estrangement from himself . . . [a] profound ambiguity between good and evil permeates everything he does, because it permeates his personal being as such. . . . The awareness of this ambiguity is the feeling of guilt. The judge who is oneself and who stands against oneself . . . gives a negative judgment, experienced by us as guilt (Tillich, 1952:52).

In Jack's story, his guilt is resolved through a transcendent act of God's grace, a reconciliation that transforms Jack's inner self as it symbolically reverses his father's act of abandonment. Finally, Jack reciprocates God's grace by a remarkable gesture of unmerited favor toward his own father. Expressing his indebtedness to God, his sense of forgiving and being forgiven, he embraces his father's vocation and becomes a missionary himself.

Rob:

> My parents were missionaries, and I grew up in the jungle, in a house with mud floors, an old wood-burner stove, and an outhouse. My dad would go out alone among the Indians. They were naked people, savages. My dad was a loner. He was a gymnast in school and didn't play a team sport. And when he went to the mission field he was always alone. He would be alone for six months in the jungle, without seeing civilized people. The tribe he worked with was known for killing people. They had killed a missionary just before Dad went in there, and they tried to scare him a few times. I was just a little kid when the five missionaries were killed by the Aucas. I remember it came out in *Life* magazine—big pic-

tures. And I remember looking at those spears, and those dead men, and the Indians. When my dad told me the story, I said, "Could this happen to you?" and he said, "Yes." That didn't bother him. He was so tough. I'm not as tough as he was.

My mother was never a strong person in my life. She was always there, behind the scenes. She was a quiet person, at home, just making sure everything kept running. But she was never the one who molded me. It was my dad who molded me.

When I was twelve, my mother had a heart attack, and the doctor said she could teach only one of her two children. So my sister stayed, and I moved out. I left home and went to a ranch and lived with another family. Then when I was fifteen I was sent to a boarding school in the United States.

I was glad to be away from my mother, because she grated on me. Years later when I go back to see her, she could still grate on me if I let her. But I just smile and let it go, because I've learned to live with it. My dad, I never really missed him, because he was so tough. He was kind of always pushing me to be tough. He never cried in the airport when we would say goodbye—or at the bus station or whatever. My mother would always cry, but he would never cry. As a result, I always figured, well, he doesn't miss me—why should I miss him?

In this first part of Rob's story, we see once again the striking ambivalence of a missionary child toward his parents. Rob intensely admires and tries to emulate his father's toughness, independence, and set-apartness. But at the same time, he fears his father's annihilation and betrays a longing for intimacy, which is prevented by those very qualities he most admires. His father is absent much of the time—both physically and emotionally—yet Rob believes that it was he who "molded" him. His mother, in contrast, is clearly the parent most involved in Rob's life, yet he rejects her as weak and insignificant compared to his heroic father. But as his story continues, the ambivalence and resentment Rob feels toward his parents become internalized, and finally crystallize in a crisis of the self.

The Christian boarding school was very strict, but that was what I needed. While I was there, a lot of things came to a head. That's where I accepted the Lord. I really came to grips with my self and realized that I wasn't saved yet. I also came to grips with my relationships with other people. Because of where I had grown up, I didn't know how to communicate with other North American people. I was very uncouth. I didn't have any manners. I didn't know how to eat my food. I didn't know how to dress. I didn't own a tie. I knew I rubbed people the wrong way, and I didn't really care. I found very little sympathy, because people didn't know how to handle me. They thought, "He's just a wild man." They all just kind of let me go.

But there was one man, a very small man. I used to call him "Pop." He spent a lot of time with me, teaching me how I should slow down when I was eating, how I should handle the silverware, and when somebody asked me to pass the food, how I should pass it. And I found that he really cared. When I found that out, I began to want to please other people, and be nice, and congenial. I had always wanted to play the piano and sing, but I never had. At boarding school I began singing, I began playing the piano, and I enjoyed it. I began to develop into somebody, instead of just being a "wild man."

In boarding school, then, far away from his parents, Rob's sense of insufficiency, fault, and guilt comes to a head. He first comes to accept what he perceives to be others' view of his moral worth. He is a "wild man" and "not saved"—just like the

Indians with whom he has always competed for his father's attention. It is then that a transformation of the self comes about. We see a spiritual component ("I accepted the Lord") and a social component ("I came to grips with my relationships with other people"). Rob acquires a social identity—becoming "somebody, instead of just a 'wild man.'" Perhaps not surprisingly, his remedial socialization occurs at the hands of a surrogate father. "Pop" appears as the antithesis of the narrator's natural father, who is off slaying dragons in the fields of the Lord. Pop is sensitive rather than tough. He is a "very small man," as opposed to his father's symbolic (or maybe even actual) bigness. Pop is involved with those around him, rather than being a loner. And while the father is typically absent from his son's life, Pop "spent a lot of time with me, teaching me." Most importantly, Pop "really cared."

The symbolic climax of Rob's self-transformation is graduation day at the boarding school. On this day, the new social self—now matching the converted, saved inner self—finally emerges for public display. Sadly, his parents are not there.

> It wasn't until I graduated that I was really hurt. My parents didn't make it to graduation. I was being applauded, and I wanted them to be there. I felt that they had made me and they needed to be rewarded for what they had done. It was so hard for me to sit down and write in a letter about what had happened. It was a big "vacio"—a big emptiness. They weren't there for those important moments.

What strikes me about this passage is not Rob's sense of injury at the parents' absence, but his explanation of it: "I felt that they had made me and they needed to be rewarded for what they had done." It is as if Rob suffers not for himself, but for them—for *their* pain at being denied a celebration of *their* labor as parents. But this is such a peculiar expression of grace from a young man who had left home at age twelve and has attributed his "becoming somebody" to God, to his boarding school, to a surrogate "Pop"—in short, to everyone *but* his parents. What really hurt Rob most, it seems, was being denied the opportunity to forgive his parents by his own success. Not to say to them, "Look what you have made me," but "Look what I have become by the grace of God, in spite of what you made me." In a significant way, Rob takes the sins of his father upon himself. He becomes guilty. But he also pays the price for those sins. The "wild man" suffers redemptively and dies. Then, finally, the day of resurrection comes, and the new self stands to declare victory and absolution. But his father is absent.

> My dad only saw me play one soccer game. And it wasn't one of my better games. I had some great games. I got in the record books for some of the goals I made. But there's one game I really wish my dad had seen. We were playing an all-black school, and these guys started beating up on me. And they should have, because I was playing dirty, and the ref wasn't seeing it that way. So they took their fists to me. That's a time when I wish my dad had been there, because I kept my cool. I just let them beat me up, I didn't fight back.

Death and Resurrection in the Moral Career

In all of these missionaries' talk about being set apart in so many ways, it is the face of death that finally emerges as the most psychologically powerful of the images of estrangement characterizing their testimonies. And for a few of them in particular, it is a profound experience with death during childhood or adolescence—usually the loss of a parent[9]—that becomes the key moment in the moral career, the organizing symbol of the mortification of a premissionary self.

Testimonies of parental death are stories of pain, shrouded guilt, and wounded memories. As a number of these make poignantly clear, one of the reasons that parental death in childhood can produce such long-lasting psychic injuries is that it frustrates the resolution of ambivalence toward the parent and forces the stage of resolution inward—covering without healing the wounds of parent-child relationships. The orphaned child faces an enormous psychological challenge of reconciling an assaulted image of self with the ambivalent memory of a dead parent. Relations with the surviving parent can become profoundly conflicted too, as vague attributions of blame in both directions are bound up with refigured needs for intimacy and support. The sense of having caused the parent's death is often harbored by children who suffer at a young age the loss of mother or father. But beyond this volatile fantasy, there are other ways, as we shall see, in which conflicting feelings toward a dead parent—that caregiver whose abandonment is so utterly final and unanswerable—is recast in a deep estrangement from others who survived, and from a self that might have been.

Margaret:

Margaret was a teenager dreaming of going away to college when her father accidentally fired a gun and killed her mother. To Margaret's knowledge her mother had never accepted Christ as Savior, because she had attended a liberal church "where the gospel was never preached." But as Margaret began to leaf through the Bible her mother had left behind, she found that "a lot of salvation verses were underlined." Wistfully, she wondered whether her mother might have been saved after all.

Margaret's grief gradually dissolved into anger toward her father whose careless act had not only killed her mother but shattered her own plans for college. It soon became clear that he expected Margaret to take over her mother's domestic duties, to stay home and care for her younger brother and himself until he could find another wife. Not only was she compelled to manage all the household work, but she had to get an extra job to supplement her father's income. Yet all of Margaret's sacrificial efforts failed to win her father's approval or her brother's gratitude.

Her father remained unmarried for a number of years and then married a woman little older than Margaret. To appease the woman's fundamentalist Christian family, Margaret's father went forward in her church and professed to accept the Lord. But in Margaret's eyes it was a sham. Meanwhile, her ungrateful brother went on to achieve worldly success. He married a beautiful and talented woman, they had lovely children, and Margaret's father lavished upon his son's family all of his attention and pride. When Margaret decided to follow her call to be a missionary, her father offered nothing but scorn. Eventually, he disinherited her.

> According to my father, my brother was so much more successful than I am. For many years he worked for an advertising agency, and he was executive vice president there. His wife used to sing light opera in New York City. She was also a model for Saks Fifth

Avenue. She has a beautiful voice, and now she sings for the very liberal churches. They
pay her two hundred dollars a song.

My dad and stepmother have nothing to do with me now. I got a letter about ten years
ago. He told me that if I did not come home, he was going to cut me out of his will. Of
course I didn't, because that was not in the least in the Lord's plan. So he did it. I got a
letter, informing me that he had cut me out of his will. After that, my brother informed me
he didn't care to see me either. So I have no contact with my family now. I pray for them.
That's the only way I could ever have any contact with him, if he would come to know the
Lord.

Margaret's almost wistful ruminations about her brother's worldly success, and
about the elegant and cultured woman that he married, relate to her own life as a kind
of photographic negative of her missionary sacrifice and set-apartness. As viewed
through her father's eyes, that self-that-might-have-been ceased to exist in real life—
as removed as the memory of her dead mother and the hollow sound of a hymn sung
for money.

Dan:

My mother was a very strong believer, and she led all five of us to the Lord. She took us
to a good independent Bible church. She taught a Bible class in our house. But my father
was an alcoholic during the time I grew up, and I remember that very strongly. Probably
the reason I love to entertain people now is that we were never able to have people over
at our house, because when my father was home he was usually drunk. That was a cause
of shame. Many times we advised my mother to divorce him, but she never did.

My father found the Lord the summer after I graduated from high school. They had
discovered that he had cancer. His stomach was full of it. He asked my mother if they
could start reading the Bible together, so they started reading a chapter of John's gospel
every day. And he found the Lord in the final chapter. He didn't have a lot of opportunity
to live that out, because he died just a month afterwards.

In the first part of Dan's story above, he renders his father as the moral antithesis
of his mother. The tension between the two embodies separation and conflict between
good and evil, sacred and profane, power and weakness. The good parent finally wins
out, yet the resolution is tragically ambiguous. The father is saved by means of the
mother's witness, but only on his deathbed. He never has the chance to fully respond
to God's grace in his life. He gives his soul to the Lord, but the devil claims his body.
Then Dan begins to talk about himself:

I grew up with a group of rough-and-tumble neighborhood boys. I was probably the weakest of all the fellows, and they called me Charles Atlas. I felt that I was a failure much of
the time I was growing up. But in eleventh grade, when my voice finished changing, I
started singing solos in the choir and I was elected Bible club president. Getting into music
gave me a sense of worth, because athletically I had never been able to do anything.

Clearly, two sides, or phases, in the self emerge in this part of the narrative, and
the phases parallel the moral split between Dan's parents. In his weakness and his
feeling of failure, Dan is like his father. In his being elected Bible club president and

in his singing, he is like his mother. As the story goes on, a tension between his pro-fane self and his sacred self is sharpened, and then rises to a point of moral crisis:

> Eventually I got to the point where I was successful musically in a big church. I was also getting some opportunities in acting for the first time. I had always tried out for parts in high school and college and had only gotten one small part in a college drama. But I fi-nally got to play Sky Masterson in "Guys and Dolls," in a local theater production. The trouble was, I played a three-night run of Sky Masterson—Thursday, Friday, and Satur-day—and then on Sunday I sang the role of Christ in the Easter cantata at church. The two directions my life could take suddenly became very clearly focused.
>
> The same weekend I hit upon Romans 12:1 and 2, in Phillips's translation of the New Testament: "With eyes wide open to the mercies of God, I beg you my brothers, as an act of intelligent worship, to give Him your bodies as a living sacrifice. Don't let the world around you squeeze you into its mold, but let God remold your minds from within, that you may prove in practice that the plan of God for you is good, meets all his demands, and moves toward the goal of true maturity." Well, it was so graphic, it just jumped out at me like never before. I decided that the Lord was banging me over the head to make me decide one way or the other, and not try to be serving myself and him at the same time.
>
> I had it in the back of my mind that I might be able to get into some off-Broadway things. The success I was having on the local level was just making me think. But now I realized that the character of Sky Masterson—his purposes were pretty far afield from what mine should have been.

Needless to say, Dan chooses against Sky Masterson and follows Christ. In a symbolic sense, the profane side of his life dies, just as his father died. But unlike his father, Dan is able to go on and live a life of grace, demonstrating the power of God to transform a weak self. In this moral career, then, a father's death provides a par-able for a son's life.

Jenny:

> I grew up in a Christian home in a small town. My parents had eight kids and I was in the middle. But when I was ten, our house burned down. My sister, who was seventeen, and my brother, who was twelve, were killed in the fire. It was really my parents who suffered. I can still—just seeing them, how my parents suffered, and how it aged them. The more I grew up, the more I wondered how they made it through that.
>
> My parents were Christians, and when we were little kids we would pray, all together, before we went to bed. Dad would read us Bible stories. But then that changed, and we never did it any more. Dad is an extremely quiet person, and he doesn't talk about his faith much. I guess we're not a family that really shares, and we're not really close. It kind of faded away.
>
> The fire made me more sensitive to other people, and to death. That was the first time I ever thought of death. At first I thought, you know, how could this happen to us? But then I thought, it can happen to us, and it was just like a revelation. It made me more sen-sitive to people, and it made me want to talk to people, and to share Christ with them. But I was an extremely shy person, and that was really a barrier. I did not want to be a slave to timidity, and I was. I wanted to accept that I was a quiet person, but I did not want that shyness to dictate the rest of my life. I knew God could change me. And he did, and that really made me a missionary.

Jenny's testimony is a complex one to interpret, because it departs from what one expects to hear. It is also a moving human story that rings with a kind of stark honesty and authenticity. Jenny plainly implicates the deaths of her siblings in the loss of intimacy and spiritual wholeness in her family. The inexplicable tragedy irreparably shatters her idyllic childhood image of a Christian family reading the Bible and praying together before bed at night.

If a writer of inspirational religious fiction were telling Jenny's story, it would read differently. What would probably happen instead is that the family would be drawn closer together and to God. Faced with the terrible loss of two children in a fire, the parents would turn to the Lord, to each other, and to their surviving children. The family would grieve deeply, but God's grace would be sufficient for them and in the end their faith would be renewed and strengthened. As Romans 8:28 promises, something good would come of it. The unified Christian family—resolving its tragedy together—would present a powerful, victorious testimony to the power of God.

But this is not what happens. The parents go on living, but apparently at great cost to their faith. Jenny never speaks of her own suffering, but of her parents' suffering and of how it aged them. She does not say she gradually came to understand her parents' resolution of the tragedy, but just the opposite—that the older she got, the more she wondered how they made it. Nevertheless, Jenny's testimony becomes a vehicle for resolution of her own ambivalence regarding her father and the sacred, and for overcoming her self-estrangement. Her father is at first a pious Bible-reading patriarch, but then a quiet person who doesn't talk about his faith. In contrast, Jenny is painfully shy in the beginning, but in the end refuses to allow her timidity to dictate the course of her life. Through the tragedy, she is able finally to do what her father perhaps could not do—to come to terms with real life in a world where children die. She realizes simply that "it can happen to us." The fact of death makes her more sensitive to the living and makes her want to share Christ—to testify boldly to a faith that overcomes death—which is just the capacity that her father lost and could never retrieve.

Anne:

I was the third of six kids. I was born in a small town, and we lived kind of out in the sticks. The first years of my life I remember very well. Money was one of the biggest problems, because we were really poor. The kind of relationship I had with my folks was really poor too. My mom was very high strung and nervous—kind of a psychotic type of person—until she became a Christian, about the same time I did. Then she changed. I'm a lot like my mother, both physically and emotionally. In fact, my dad reminded me quite often that I was a lot like her.

Dad was an agnostic, and became very firm in this, so we couldn't mention God in the house. He was out of work a lot. He was a laborer, and he never made much, which kind of bothered him. He was raised by his sisters because his folks died when he was young. And my mom and dad had to get married because mom was pregnant. My dad had very low self esteem. And he couldn't see anyone else becoming better than him, from his own family. That was really impressed on us—that we were never going to become anything.

I left home and went to Bible school when I was eighteen. Mom was really excited. Dad didn't say much one way or the other. The one thing he did say was that I should have gotten some kind of training. When you graduate from Bible school and they don't have a position for you, what do you do? Nothing. You can't use it for anything. And so I was out of a job when I graduated. And my dad said, "You should have gotten a vocational skill."

Well, I just couldn't get a job. And the Lord knew I was looking. I applied everywhere, you know, all over. I knew I needed experience to get a job, but I needed a job to get experience. And then finally I got a job interview that looked good, and my mom said she would go with me. We set out about six o'clock in the morning, and she was holding my little nephew, who was two. At about seven o'clock we crashed, and my mom was killed, as well as my nephew.

The family took it very difficult. They said it was my fault. My dad moved away, and they went down there to be with him—this brother-in-law and my sister. I don't know what happened down there, but I think all they did was fill his mind with hate and bitterness, because my dad won't have anything to do with me now. One time I went to visit my sister, and he came up to wash his clothes. He found out I was there, and he didn't even want to come inside. I sent him a birthday card once, with a check. I thought, well, maybe he'll open it and cash the check without even thinking, and it will come back to me. But I haven't gotten it. I don't think he would even open any mail from me.

The only thing I could think was the Lord must want me alive for something. After the accident, God just said, "Get going," you know, "You've got to get going now." It was about a month after that I applied to the Mission.

Anne's testimony provides a final example of how a parent's death can provide a metaphor for the annihilation of a premissionary self. In a symbolic sense, the old Anne—the ambivalent child embodying her father's legacy of failure and rejection and her mother's fragile psyche—dissolves in the redemptive suffering of the missionary vocation. In the end, Anne is no longer her father's daughter. But she is a child of God, called to live out the good news of Christ in the uttermost parts of the earth. That calling is the subject of the next chapter.

3

The Missionary Call

I heard a voice, very clearly, saying, "Go, prepare yourself, and serve me." But I was so disappointed in myself. I said, "Lord, how can you go on with me? I have been a Christian for several years now, but such a poor Christian." And the answer was immediately there: "It doesn't matter what *you* are, or what you do. It depends upon my grace. My grace can do it in you." And then I heard it again: "Go, prepare yourself, and serve me." I said, "I understand that, but I have a family. I have two children, and I am an only son. I am responsible for my parents when they get older. Lord, at this moment I cannot leave. Economically there is no way, and I have made commitments." You see, my understanding of missions was that it meant a whole life. I never thought about going for a short time. And then I got the answer: "Whosoever wants to save his life will lose it. But whoever gives it, for my name and the gospel, will save it." I finally accepted that.

This chapter examines the central idea and personal experience that traditionally has launched missionary careers, and upon which evangelicals continue to base their key motivation for a long-term commitment to foreign missions—the notion of an individualized divine call to spread the gospel of Christ throughout the world. As I began my inquiry among HCJB members in Ecuador in the 1980s, I wondered to what extent the nineteenth-century mission movement's ideal of "the call" might resonate in the testimonies of contemporary evangelicals. Would they derive from the Great Commission the same sort of individualized warrant for their spiritual vocation and work in the world? Would they report the same kinds of personal epiphanies and inner voices that inspired the lives of their spiritual forbears?

I discovered that, while not every missionary felt called, most HCJB members gave accounts of personal summonses from God—of experiences whereby they actually "heard" some sort of divine command which they took to be directed at them personally, and which indeed claimed their lives for the cause of Christian missions abroad. As I listened to these narratives and tried to fathom their significance, I approached each account of divine calling in two ways. As with the missionaries' life stories in general, I first attended straighforwardly to their content: What were the typical circumstances, events, and relationships mentioned under the rubric of a missionary call, and what importance did the missionaries themselves attach to these elements of their call stories? Second, I turned a more interpretive eye to the context surrounding these testimonies, to their stylistic and rhetorical features, and to the symbolic connections between the call and the earlier life-historical theme of being set apart. I wondered, how does the language of divine calling get to be appropriated by

66

people who experience various sorts of estrangement? How does the call fit in to their moral careers? Is the call intrinsic to such careers—even today—or is it merely a vestige of missions rhetoric from an earlier century?

The Call, Then and Now

In the summer of 1931, a group of Methodist leaders met in Ohio for a conference on missions entitled "The Significance of Jesus Christ for the Modern World." Fourteen committees had been formed and assigned to report on various problems facing the waning missionary enterprise of mainline denominational Protestantism. One of these tackled the question of missionary motivation—how to sustain Methodist personnel in the foreign field at a time when many were dropping out after one term.

In preparation for his committee's report, Professor C. S. Braden of Northwestern University spent months conducting a statistical survey of 151 Methodist missionaries around the world. One of the key items on his questionnaire addressed the issue of divine calling. In particular, he asked missionaries if they had experienced a "sense of a divine call; that is, some inner compulsion interpreted as a divine impulse, [motivating] direct obedience to the command of Christ" (Fahs, 1933:38). Somewhat surprisingly, only 48 percent of them said yes. But then Braden divided his sample into three subgroups based on the length of time served: first term (0–4 years, N=50); second term (5–9 years, N=56); and third term or beyond (10 or more years, N=45). When he tabulated responses for each group, he found that earlier cohorts of missionaries were much more likely than recent ones to report divine calling: 73 percent of the third-term veterans reported a call, compared to 46 percent of the second-term missionaries, and only 26 percent of the first-term newcomers.

While this finding apparently interested the committee, neither Braden nor the 1933 report of the Laymen's Foreign Mission Inquiry offered much to interpret it. They merely "noted that there is a marked decline [among newer missionaries] in the number of those who mention a distinct call from God" (Fahs, 1933:38). However, one possible explanation was offered by a missions scholar writing fifty years later (Najarian, 1982). In his study of nineteenth-century missionaries, Najarian presented Braden's 1931 finding as evidence for a historical change in missionary motivation. He attributed it to "a shift in missionary policy from an earlier thrust in evangelization to a later strategy in the 1920s [of] social service." In other words, the older, traditional nineteenth-century missionary typically had a divine call; but the new liberal breed was more influenced by a social gospel and motivated by inner-worldly humanitarian concern.

Undeniably, a significant historical shift in missionary policy did occur about this time in the mainline denominations such as the Methodists (see Hutchison, 1987:125–145). But in my view, that shift doesn't necessarily explain Braden's finding. Two other interpretations must be considered, the first of which takes a clue from Braden's reason for conducting the survey in the first place. He, along with the rest of the Laymen's Inquiry committee members, was worried primarily about the number of missionaries who were dropping out. It is certainly plausible that those without a feeling of divine calling were less likely to persist in missionary work, and hence, that relatively fewer of the "uncalled" were around to be counted in the longer-term groups.

A second alternative interpretation would be that over time, the missionaries tended to reconstruct their biographies to include the element of divine calling in the light of subsequent social experience. Probably a good number of the more seasoned apostles, had they been polled as new missionaries, would have betrayed some uncertainty about whether they had a special call. But as their careers got underway and as they spent more time with their colleagues, perhaps they reinterpreted an earlier religious commitment or experience *as* a "missionary call." Consider the following example from my own study:

> You can say it was a call; I'm not sure I was spiritually aware enough at the time to even recognize it as a call, but I was very attracted to the adventure and the active involvement that these missionaries in Ecuador had. It grabbed my attention, and it held my attention. That was the kind of person I wanted to be. And so I came in obedience to his call, which at this point I can interpret as a call. I believe that God specifically said to me, "I want you in Ecuador."

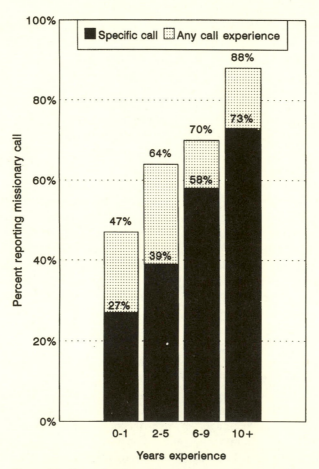

Figure 3.1. General and specific missionary calls reported by HCJB members, by years of experience.

These alternative interpretations of Braden's 1931 findings become more salient in light of my own survey results from 1983, which produced much the same pattern. On the HCJB questionnaire, 129 Mission members were asked if they had felt a definite call to be a missionary: 73 percent said yes in general terms, and 55 percent remembered a specific place, time, and their age at the point they had a special call experience—something akin to what Braden referred to as "a divine impulse." Figure 3.1 portrays the prevalence of such missionary-call experiences among HCJB members with varying amounts of service in the field. Clearly, having a call becomes increasingly common in the groups with more experience in the field. Moreover, there is an increase in the proportion of those with a call who remembered a specific time and place when the call occurred: 83 percent of the ten-year veterans' calls were specified in this way, compared to 57 percent of the newcomers' calls.

In order to render these data directly comparable to the 1931 survey, I also divided the respondents along the lines of five-year terms: 0–4 years (N=41); 5–9 years (N=36); and 10 years or more (N=52). Figure 3.2 compares the two sets of data and

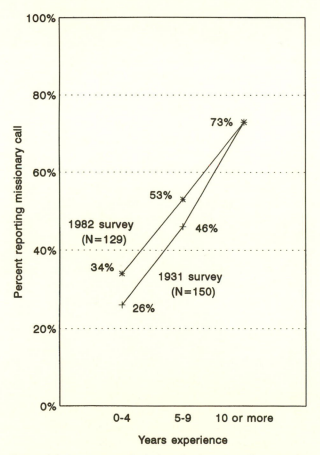

Figure 3.2. Percentage of missionaries in two studies reporting a specific missionary call, by years in the field: 1931 and 1982 surveys.

shows a remarkable similarity in the prevalence of specific calls by years of missionary experience, especially given that the studies were conducted fifty years apart.

Undeniably, denominational missionaries going out in the 1930s were motivated somewhat differently than their counterparts in the late nineteenth century, and a similar shift occurred among evangelicals from the 1940s to the 1980s. Of this latter period, Van Engen (1990:204) observes that "[as] North American Evangelicals experienced new sociocultural strength and confidence, changes in ecumenical theology of mission, and developments in evangelical partner churches in the Third World, they responded with a broadening vision of an evangelical theology of mission that became less reactionary and more holistic."

Van Engen's observation might suggest that the prevalence of personalized "divine call" experiences has declined over time in response to a new ethos of evangelical missions that has emerged—one that deemphasizes the sort of heroic role of individually sent messengers from abroad, in favor of social action in the service of local churches. Nevertheless, I do not think a historical shift in evangelical missions policy and rhetoric can account for the fact that HCJB members arriving in Ecuador in 1980 were significantly more likely to report a divine call than those who arrived only three years later in 1983. Rather, I think these data indicate primarily that individuals who are the most likely to persist in a missionary career (i.e., beyond an initial short-term commitment) are those who come to believe they have been personally called by God to the mission field, and who feel the binding power of that call throughout their lives.

Clearly, the proportion of short-term missionaries has increased overall and now accounts for over 40 percent of all U.S. Protestant missions personnel abroad (Roberts and Siewart, 1989). HCJB is no exception to this trend, which may account for the pattern of data displayed in Figure 3.3. In 1965, a survey of HCJB members conducted by the Christian Service Organization (Bower, 1966) found a much higher prevalence of calls among first-year missionaries than I discovered eighteen years later (71 percent compared to 47 percent). However, for those who had been serving in Ecuador for ten years or more, the 1965 and 1983 survey data were virtually identical; about 90 percent of veteran Mission members in both studies reported divine calling.

Without the benefit of a prospective longitudinal study of the same people over time, I will not hazard a definitive conclusion about what caused these observed effects. Is it that the missionaries who felt no call tended to drop out after a while? Or is it that the ones who stayed more than just a few years tended to *acquire* a sense of calling, and then reinterpreted earlier experience accordingly? Or is it that a new generation of missionaries uses a different idiom to express what their predecessors meant when they spoke of being called? Probably some combination of these factors occurring together accounts for the data. But in any event, these findings do not support the conclusion that the underlying impulse of divine calling has become much less important than it was to previous generations of evangelical missionaries. Rather, I will argue that the experience of God's calling typifies the conceptual (if not chronological) beginning of the missionary's moral career. It continues to function as a primary lens through which long-term missionaries typically view the story of their lives, and a key image that shapes (and reshapes) the narrative of their entire life course.

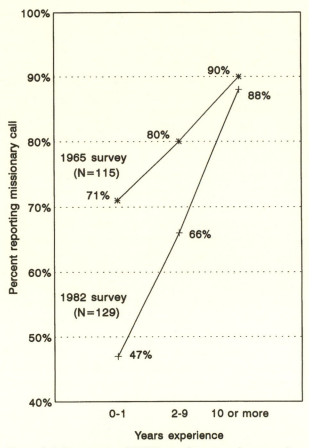

Figure 3.3. Percentage of HCJB members reporting any missionary call, by years in Ecuador: 1965 and 1982 surveys.

Sociological Considerations

When sociologists speak of divine calling, they hearken back to Max Weber. For it was Weber who rendered the call as a crucial idea not only for the sociology of religion, but for the understanding of modern life. He made important observations about two rather different usages of the concept—one having to do with religious authority and the other with inner-worldly vocations. On the surface these may seem unrelated, but both turn out to be helpful in comprehending the missionary calling.

In his historical studies of religious traditions, Weber identified the personal call as a decisive element that distinguishes between two sociological types of religious authorities—the priest and the prophet. The priest "lays claim to authority by virtue of his service in a sacred tradition," Weber said (1922:46). The priest normally comes from a priestly class and dispenses spiritual resources in the power of an office for which he is remunerated. The prophet, on the other hand, is an "individual bearer of charisma" who appears seemingly out of nowhere, proclaiming a message from the gods. His authority has nothing to do with tradition or office, but with personal revelation—that is, a unique divine call. Moreover, the prophet is not paid for his preaching but lives by his own manual labor and by unsolicited alms.

Weber further identified two types of prophets—the ethical and the exemplary. He characterized the first of these as an "instrument for the proclamation of a god and his will," who preaches "as one who has received a commission from a god" and thus "demands obedience as an ethical duty" (Weber, 1922:55). The exemplary prophet, on the other hand, demonstrates the way to salvation by his own moral actions. He appeals to others' self-interest, in effect, by saying that anyone desiring to be saved should follow in the path he has shown.

The missionary ideal has tended to resemble Weber's prophet rather than priest, and to combine elements of both the ethical and exemplary types of prophet. From the evangelical perspective, missionaries both proclaim and exemplify the message of the gospel. As God in Christ became a human stranger in order to redeem the world, so the missionary becomes a stranger in order to spread the news of redemption to the ends of the earth. As Christ sacrificed his life in obedience to God and out of love for the world, so the missionary sacrifices self-interest in response to God's call and out of love for neighbor (Weber, 1922:184). According to this view, Christ's mission was made legitimate not by the priestly tradition of his day, but by the signs and wonders and acts of healing he performed, as well as by the internal authority of his teaching. Likewise, the missionary's authority is not established by tradition, but rather demonstrated by practical efforts to heal and help the poor and oppressed.

At the same time, missionaries display certain characteristics of Weber's priestly type. In particular, rituals of initiation into the missionary career function in much the same way as the ordination of ministers. Traditionally, the missionary was first called by God, but then commissioned by a body of believers who confirmed the individual's call and sent him out as their representative in the harvest of souls.[1] Missionaries were set apart from the church; in one sense, their locus of action was outside its boundaries. But in another sense, they worked within the church's division of labor. They performed a task for which the whole church was responsible—the propagation of the gospel. Moreover, without the material support of the church, missionaries could not fulfill their calling as individuals.

As one senior HCJB member noted, missionaries traditionally have received their church's pledge of support in a formal "commissioning service" with Biblical precedent, organized around the social confirmation of an individual's call:

> In our case and that of many other HCJB missionaries, there was a commissioning service that was meant to replicate the moment in which Jesus sent his disciples out two by two, to preach and to heal, as recorded in Luke's gospel. This was also like Paul's commissioning by the church at Antioch for his missionary task. It was the church's acknowledgment that the missionary is indeed called by God, and it was their pledge of prayer and financial support to the ministry that the missionary feels personally called to.

In a more theoretical vein, Georg Simmel (author of the key essay on *The Stranger* discussed in Chapter 1) observed that ordination for a religious task socially imbues a candidate with a spiritual calling; in a ritual sense, it *"creates . . .* the specific qualification for the task it elects," preparing the candidate's "innermost being" and "making him an adequate bearer" of the call (Simmel, 1906:57). In the case of missionaries, the subjective call experience may already have occurred, but prior to its being examined and confirmed in a social "commissioning" by the faith community, the individual's call does not yet qualify as such. Afterward, others appropriately respond to the ordained (or called) one as a person chosen indeed by God, because it is as if the entire community had witnessed the individual's divine call from the inside. Through the commissioning service, they, too, come to own the missionary's call. And through their investment of support, from that moment forward the entire church stakes a claim to the missionary's subsequent accomplishments in carrying out the call abroad. In Simmel's words, "[by] ordination a spirit, existing in mystical objectivity, is conveyed upon the applicant, making him merely its vessel and representative. . . . [Ordination] defines the subject as if seen from the inside" (Simmel, 1906:57).

Simmel noted that a peculiar tension exists between an individual's subjective call and the social structure that sustains it, within which the call must be worked out. Echoing Weber, he suggested that "in the division of labor there occurs a characteristic synthesis of inner vocation with the limitations from external influences" (Simmel, 1906:56). Simmel's observations, while ostensibly referring to the initiation of religious careers, nevertheless evoke the broader sphere of meaning in which the notion of calling was applied by Weber.

Weber argued that the notion of divine calling historically has borne an important relation not only to religious career development, but to the whole structure of life and work in modern Western society. He conducted an exhaustive study of the origin and fate of the term translated *vocatio* in the Latin Bible, or *calling* in the English, arguing that the idea of vocation never was applied to a line of work "within the world" until after the Reformation—and then only in Protestant countries.

More specifically, Weber traced the modern idea of vocation to Luther's translation of the New Testament. Luther's exegesis of the calling (as an inner-worldly demonstration of grace) had to be understood as a polemic against the world-denying asceticism of the medieval monastic vocation. In this light, Luther gave new meaning to the Pauline exhortation, "Brethren, let each man, wherein he was called, therein abide with God."[2] According to Weber, Luther understood this to mean that a person's highest moral calling was *not* to be set apart from family and life in the world (as the monastic orders were), but to work diligently in the mundane realm of duty—to take up a "vocation" within the world, thereby to support and to serve family and neighbor (Wingren, 1942).

Weber went on to show how this post-Reformation ethic of vocation became ossified in the Calvinist doctrine of double predestination, such that human work in any station became linked to the assurance of salvation in the next world, and not to the pursuit of satisfaction in the present one.[3] The grim Puritans of the seventeenth century provided Weber with the clearest example of life organized around this idea. The crux of his well-known argument is that a distinctly Protestant doctrine of the calling engendered the inner-worldly asceticism and rational conduct of daily life necessary for the conditions of modern capitalism to arise (Weber, 1904).

Weber's ideas illuminate the missionary calling in unexpected ways. In my view, the Protestant missions movement and the moral career of the individual missionary have each depended upon a conception of the missionary vocation as a rational line of work *in the world*—though arguably motivated by other-worldly concerns. The call to missions, as Robert Speer put it in 1901, was not of a "character or quantity different from the call to practice medicine or law, or to lay bricks, in [one's] own country." Clearly, the elements of capitalism and colonialism formed the matrices of Protestant missions throughout the nineteenth century. The gospel that American and British missionaries preached included the blessedness of capitalist civilization; part of the function they served (albeit sometimes unwittingly) was to subordinate the heathen not only to a "modern work ethic" but to the Protestant countries that so prospered by it. At the same time, rational scientific methods[4] and capitalist metaphors of production, investment, competition, and the division of labor were applied to the Western church's "corporate mission" of world evangelism. Coming full circle, as we shall see in the experience of HCJB members, the modern "organization missionary" attempts to resurrect the Reformation's theological meaning of work in an inner-worldly vocation when his or her prophetic spiritual calling dissolves into routine, depersonalized, and bureaucratic labor.

The modern missionary's moral career thus combines the monastic ideal of a spiritual vocation with the Reformers' conception of work in a calling. In the missionary vocation, the rational ethos of inner-worldly duty is applied to the task of world evangelization. While the missionary acts upon a sense of divine summons to a spiritual life, yet his or her work must be done within the world—understood in Biblical terms by the metaphor of economy. The call of the gospel is a great fortune to be invested wisely.

Divine Calling as a Biblical Ideal

To inquire of an evangelical as to the origin or basis of any significant moral idea turns out to be the same, in the end, as to ask, "Where is it written in the Bible?" In fact, the words translated *call* and *calling* occur frequently in both the Old and New Testaments, conveying a number of related meanings. In a broad sense, the call refers to the sum of God's dealings with the human race throughout the Biblical story. In a 1944 essay entitled "The Calling of God," Max Warren emphasized the idea that the present-day missionary calling merely extends the commission given to the Apostolic church, which in turn traces directly back to the call Abraham received many centuries before that. According to Warren, the continuous thread of God's call throughout history consisted of three interwoven strands—grace, faith, and obedience:

> The Apostolic church came into being when God called Abraham out of Ur of the Chaldees and bade him go out into a land he did not know and Abraham obeyed. When the grace of God in choosing Abraham was met by the faith of Abraham in accepting the choice, the Church was born (Warren, 1944:45).

In a more specific sense, evangelicals sometimes construe the call to mean the gospel message of the New Testament—that is, salvation in Christ—as expressed in such Pauline texts as this:

> [T]ake your share of suffering for the gospel in the power of God, who saved us and *called us with a holy calling*; not in virtue of our works but in virtue of his own purpose and the grace he gave us in Christ Jesus (II Timothy 1:8,9).

Still another way in which evangelicals speak of the calling has to do with the spiritual division of labor, or with a person's commitment to fulfill a particular role in the work of the church. For instance, this is what the term is taken to mean in the Apostle's opening signature in the epistle to the Romans: "Paul, a servant of Jesus Christ, *called* to be an apostle, set apart for the gospel of God." Paul is supposedly saying he was not only called, but called to be an apostle rather than some other kind of worker. Here a calling denotes something similar to a spiritual gift, as when Paul writes elsewhere of the specialization of gifts in the body of Christ:

> And his gifts were that some should be apostles, some prophets, some evangelists, some pastors and teachers, for the equipment of the saints, for the work of ministry, for building up the body of Christ (Ephesians 4:11,12).

The call can also refer to any particular experience of divine guidance of one's life along a particular path. Some evangelicals describe such a calling almost as an inner sense of destiny. Others report a moment of crisis, often marked by the perception of miraculous phenomena such as a vision, a voice in the night, or a prophetic dream in which God told them to embark on some course of action. Commonly they compare such experiences to those abounding in the Old Testament: Abraham being divinely told to leave his home and go out to an unknown land; God speaking to Joseph in dreams or to Moses from a burning bush; Samuel hearing the voice of God in the night as a young boy in the house of Eli, and later (as a priest) acting as a channel through which God called David to be king of Israel; and of course, various prophets receiving their call to deliver the Word of Jehovah to a recalcitrant Hebrew people.

From the New Testament comes the archetypal missionary call story, that of the Apostle Paul, to whom many Mission members compare themselves in various ways. According to the Biblical text, following his dramatic conversion on the road to Damascus, Paul was called to preach the gospel to the Gentiles. But his subjective call was first confirmed by a word from the Holy Spirit to the church at Antioch: "Set apart for me Barnabas and Saul for the work to which I have called them" (Acts 13:2). Still later, in the middle of his second missionary journey, Paul received an extraordinary call to take the gospel to Macedonia: "And a vision appeared to Paul in the night: a man of Macedonia was standing beseeching him and saying, 'Come over to Macedonia and help us'" (Acts 16:9).

My point in mentioning all of these Biblical moments is that they provide the essential repertory of images for the expression of divine calling among contemporary evangelical missionaries. As we shall see, when Mission members speak of their own calling they speak in Biblical terms. But they also view their vocation through the prism of a missionary tradition—particularly as it developed in the latter part of the nineteenth century. Let us consider that legacy more specifically.

The Call and the Missionary Legacy

As discussed in Chapter 1, the Protestant missionary movement that began with William Carey in 1795 created a tradition of religious heroism. Among evangelicals—who were culturally dominant in nineteenth-century America—the missionary became almost as significant a mythical figure as was the pioneer on the Western frontier. And a crucial part of that myth was the personal call from God—a mysterious and dramatic sort of epiphany by which the great men of missions heard the voice of God commanding them to go out and claim China, India, or Africa for Christ. They went, as one writer put it in 1895, "fearing neither serpents, savages, cannibals, malaria, starvation, nor death itself" (Jessup, 1901 [1895]:18).

I have already mentioned Samuel Mills, who experience a divine call while plowing his field in Connecticut sometime prior to the famed 1806 "Haystack Prayer Meeting." W. J. Lhamon provided other examples in his 1899 *Heroes of Modern Missions*. A particularly telling story is that of "the great David Livingstone of Africa," whose character God supposedly formed from the humblest beginnings. In Lhamon's recounting, Livingstone as a small child slaved away in a cotton factory from six o'clock in the morning until eight at night. With his first earnings he bought a Latin grammar. Then, at the age of eighteen, Livingstone reported that "the sublime form of Jesus of Nazareth, the Great Physician" arose before him. He determined to follow Christ and to become a medical missionary. The vision was "never to fade away" (Lhamon, 1899:100).

For Protestant churchgoers of the era, the experiences of Livingstone and others who spent their lives in "battle against heathenism on the uncharted frontiers of Christendom" provided inspiring models of the way in which God guided contemporary heroes. At the same time, they maintained an important continuity with the Biblical tradition of divine calling. Toward the end of the century, however, the perceived needs of the mission movement for large numbers of young volunteers demanded that the call be interpreted more broadly and methodically. A series of missionary authorities, most of them connected in some way with the Student Volunteer Movement for Foreign Missions, wrote didactically about the missionary call, successfully challenging thousands of young people to enter the field.

The common wisdom from the early missions movement had been that the call was a necessary, individual "inner experience." For example, missionary spokesman John Lowrie wrote in 1882 that "[if] the call should be from God, by his word, his providence, and his Spirit . . . it will then be heard by the soul of him to whom it is addressed." He insisted that this "inner experience is essential and ordinarily precedes any action." While he suggested that corporate approval of the call was necessary for some people, he nevertheless sanctioned the image of the missionary as a spiritual lone ranger:

> Under the prompting of this inward call, a man might go forth as a missionary without waiting for a commissioning from a missionary board. Some, indeed, have done so. But if his convictions . . . should lead him to desire cooperation with other missionaries in organized relations, and if he requires funds for his support from other followers of Christ, the necessity arises of his call being verified (Lowrie, 1882:25,26).

On the other side, Dr. Jacob Chamberlain, missionary to India, wrote in 1900 to correct the "misapprehension" that each person needed an extraordinary, individual call like those received by the great heroes of missions:

> There is no doubt that in the opening up of the foreign missionary work in this [nineteenth] century, and for entering upon new and untested fields in later years, God has

issued special calls to individuals. He has felt it necessary Himself to select the leaders, the pioneers, in each field. He has sent into their souls such a "call" that they have felt "Woe is unto me if I preach not the gospel" in that particular field. Many of the heroes of missions have been thus "thrust into the harvest," and we have been thrilled by the story of their "call" no less than by the story of their achievements. God may thus call special leaders in the future. But those are the exceptions, not the rule. God does not waste his special Providences, his special calls (Chamberlain, 1901:10).

Chamberlain went on to remind his youthful readers that the Great Commission was given once, to all believers; that it therefore applied already to them individually; and that they had no right to bargain with Christ saying, "Unless you send me a special providence . . . I will not go." Lapsing into King James English he admonished, "Treat not thus the once given command of thy Royal Master, or leanness may shrivel thy soul for thy neglect" (Chamberlain, 1901:11).

Other missionary writers simply emphasized the need—the particular horror of millions of heathen living in squalor and dying in darkness, thousands each day and night passing into God-forsaken eternity for want of someone to go and tell them of Christ. For these writers, the missionary call was the "Macedonian cry."[5] As missionary Joseph Lathern put it in 1884,

The Macedonian cry has become the world's cry. Modern heathenism is fully as dark and debasing, as polluted and miserable as that of Apostolic times. The man of Macedonia represents a perishing world. . . . Masses and millions of people are pleading for succor. . . . Think of him [the Macedonian] as one man; an unsaved Cree or Kaffir, Hindu or Hottentot, Cossack or Tartar. Though rude in speech, degraded to the dust, that man is redeemed by Christ, an heir of immortality. For him there must be a resurrection to eternal life, or to shame and everlasting contempt (Lathern, 1884:20,21).

The relationship between heathenism and Christendom was expressed often in the metaphor of darkness and light. Christ was seen as the ultimate source of light, which missionaries were to absorb into their own lives and then reflect for the illumination of a sin-shrouded world. Another missionary writer of the time, E. S. Baldwin, gave a scientific twist to this Biblical metaphor:

There is a modern astronomer who tells us that this planet of ours consumes only the two-hundred-millionth part of all the rays which issue from the sun. . . . Does the whole church throughout the world consume as much as the two-hundred-millionth part of the fullness that is in Christ? No, by no means. He is the brightness of His Father's Glory and the express image of His Person. In Him dwelleth all the fullness of the Godhead bodily, and all that we can take is but a drop in the ocean of His grace. The super-abundance that we cannot possibly use is for the dying world about us; for the uncounted millions who are sinking on every side, unsaved, unknown, unwept for want of that glorious gospel of which we have not only enough, but abundantly to spare (Baldwin, 1901:23).

Yet another didactic rendering of the missionary call came from the aforementioned missionary leader Robert Speer. Given the perception of massive spiritual need abroad, Speer turned the notion of a call inside out, arguing that a person rather needed a special dispensation to stay home. The Christian in America was like someone standing on a riverbank watching a drowning man. Why should anyone need a special call to go and save him? The awareness of the man's distress and danger should be calling enough; the one on the riverbank would need a very good reason *not* to do something. By analogy, Speer argued that anyone with "an openness of mind to the last command of Christ and to the need of the world" already had a missionary call. Beyond the awareness of great need, the only two constituents of a personal call were to be stated negatively: the lack of personal disqualifications, and the lack of insuperable hindrances. As to which hindrances were insuperable, Speer wrote:

> I think that when once one has gained a vision of the world's need, like Christ's vision, and a love for it like his love, a great many hindrances will no longer appear to be such. . . . The question for us to answer is not, Am I called to the foreign field? but, Can I show sufficient cause for not going? We may be quite sure that if we face in that direction God can much more easily deter us from going, if He so determines, than He can get us out there if we face in the opposite direction (Speer, 1901a:5,6).

In sum, Speer's recipe for a missionary call was simply that young Christians proceed on the assumption that they were going to the mission field. If any obstacle should prevent them from going, this was then to be seen as divine deterrence and hence a calling to stay home. Similarly, George Wilson exhorted the young readers of *The Student Volunteer* in 1897 that "Christ has no uncalled servants, and his servants have no self-chosen spheres. . . . The parting of the ways of your life is with the Lord, and be quite sure that you stay at home only under direct orders from the Master." Accordingly, Wilson presented only two essential components of the "attitude in which you can hear, understand, and obey Christ's call to the office of a missionary." The first was conversion ("that you are scripturally, radically, and consciously converted"), and the second was surrender ("that you are absolutely surrendered to the will of Christ") (Wilson, 1901:7).

Wilson further suggested that such an attitude of receptiveness toward Christ's call was easiest to attain early in life. Thus he urged his student readers to settle their missionary call with Christ immediately, at whatever stage of education they happened to be. If they would receive a call in youth, he said, the Spirit would then bring all the rest of their schooling to bear on the life work to which the Lord calls them (Wilson, 1901:9).

The inspirational figures in the early missions movement did not hesitate to enumerate the specific talents, abilities, and skills useful on the mission field—languages, teaching, medicine, physical strength, and so forth. But these were always subordinated to the qualities of spiritual surrender and self-abnegation. The idea was that God called and used especially the weakest and humblest human vessels, in order to manifest his power. The aforementioned M. S. Baldwin, reporting to the 1898 Student Volunteer Convention in Cleveland, cited the Biblical example of Moses. Well-educated and brought up in the court of Pharoah, Moses at first proceeded in his own human strength toward liberating Israel from the Egyptians—only to fail and be forced to flee the country for his very life. However, as Baldwin explained:

> God's plans were deeper far. He sends [Moses] to school for forty years . . . to learn God's power and his own nothingness . . . At last the time for action [comes], and

as he is tending his flock he sees a strange and unprecedented sight—a thorn bush and fire. The fire was within the bush, and the bush was not consumed. Two antithetical truths were here before his eyes. The bush was to represent the weakness of man, the fire the omnipotence of God. The bush itself was the dry acacia of the wilderness, almost valueless, but a fit figure of Moses—a fit figure indeed of every man that God intends for service. Only a poor thorn bush in a dry and desert world. On the other side, there is the fire, emblem of consuming power and disintegrating might. . . . God, the omnipotent One, was about to dwell in the poor thorn bush Moses, and make him efficient for his holy work. . . . Now, fire has many qualities. In the darkness it will illuminate, in cold will warm, in contamination purify and in might consume. . . . [But when God finally spoke to him from the bush, Moses] offered no less than seven objections to prove his own unfitness. Certainly he was wrong in making any objections when God gave the command, but the facts prove the lowly estimate Moses had of himself and the high regard in which he was held by God (Baldwin, 1901:26–28).

Further expounding upon the humility of the missionary calling, Baldwin employed the image of a legal witness, as distinct from an advocate. He asserted that missionaries are not called to be advocates of the gospel, but witnesses. "An advocate," he explained, "is a much higher being than a mere witness; an advocate has to be one learned in the law, but a witness may be a poor, unlettered man. He has not to explain the law; he has to witness to a fact. Now God says: "Ye are My witnesses" (Baldwin, 1901:31).

A key emphasis in these writings about the call was the notion of simple obedience to the will of God. This idea of going out and acting on divine orders was often expressed in the metaphor of foreign service to an earthly sovereign—either as a soldier or diplomatic envoy. For example, consider a lecture delivered at the Missionary Training School in 1905 by E. R. Hendrix. Asserting that the first qualification essential for a missionary was a "supreme sense of the glory of God," he went on to illustrate:

No ambassador is sent forth by a European monarch who does not go forth after a personal interview with his king. He goes forth as his personal representative, and must everywhere be received as such. He must therefore be impressed with the power and dignity of the royal throne, and know the will of his sovereign. He is always a representative, an ambassador, one who is sent. The moment he forgets his representative capacity he becomes disqualified. The more fully he represents the august power that sent him, the better foreign minister he becomes. . . . So it is always with the ambassadors of our Lord. We must never for one moment forget who sent us, and whose will we are commissioned to carry out, and whose power is pledged to sustain us so long as we are seeking to make known and to do that will (Hendrix, 1905:8).

The metaphor of military service was even more predominant. Chamberlain, for instance, referred to Christ as "our Commander-in-Chief" who has given an "order to the front in the foreign missionary enterprise [and who] says to all believers, 'Go ye, evangelize all nations.'" Chamberlain admitted that not all can go—even as many able-bodied conscripts reporting to service are not sent to war—because of "physical defects . . . certain mental ailments . . . certain filial or family duties, certain social or professional obligations." But he added a warning for spiritual draft-dodgers:

"Woe to those who in this case give a false excuse, for He knows the inmost soul" (Chamberlain, 1901:10–11).

Besides conveying God's sovereignty in human life, the military metaphor proved to be an apt one for expressing other themes in the missionary calling. One of these was the notion of heroic conflict—the idea that missionaries were going forth to do battle with the forces of evil. Inspiration came from knowing that the Lord was on the missionaries' side, and hence that victory was assured. Consider this theme as expressed in 1895 by Henry Jessup, missionary to Syria, in an article entitled "Who Ought Not to Go as Foreign Missionaries." He mentioned such disqualifying factors as having infirm health or unsettled religious views; being afraid of torrid climates and hard languages; being too old, intractable, impatient, or intellectually ill-prepared; and lacking common sense or long-term commitment. But he especially cautioned against persons who lack a taste for victory, who are pessimists, and who suspect that the missionary campaign might fail. As if fearing such persons would lower troop morale, he wrote:

> We want hopeful men in this glorious aggressive warfare. Our King and Captain is going forth "conquering and to conquer." It is a winning cause. Expect to succeed. Omnipotence is on your side. . . . Is the voice of Christ still ringing with the command, "Go and teach all nations"? Are the heathen still crying, "Come and help us?" If I am a Christian should I not be like Christ? If I am a soldier should I not obey marching orders? (Jessup, 1901 [1895]:15,21).

Personal sacrifice was another characteristic seen as common both to military and missionary service. As Robert Speer expressed it, a crucial qualification for the missionary was "the spirit of willing sacrifice, in the sense of endurance, of hardiness *as a good soldier*, and of surrender of all devotion to comfort and ease" (Speer, 1901b:44).

Jessup wrote more specifically about the sacrifice to be made. The missionary—like a career soldier—he said, must be set apart from family, friends, and home:

> The thought of a life separation from home and friends and country, from father and mother, brothers and sisters will cost you many a pang. And the thought of what *they* will suffer will be more bitter than any anxiety about yourself. You may have cherished ambitions, even in the thought of Christian ministry at home. These must be set aside. Am I willing to give all up for Christ? (Jessup, 1901 [1895]:22).

As I have already suggested, the imitation of Christ emerged a central theme connecting various ideas about the missionary calling that were espoused by leaders of the late nineteenth-century missions movement. The missionary was like Christ, sent by God as a stranger into the world; like Christ obedient unto death, sacrificing his life as a ransom for many; like Christ representing God, bearing witness to the truth; and in the end, like Christ the conqueror. Moreover, Christ's incarnation and continuing presence in the human heart was a key metaphor of sacrifice in the traditional missionary calling. Consider the way in which Jessup expressed the higher meaning of missionary "condescension" to the heathen:

> There are tribes of half-naked, filthy and imbruted children of nature from whom a civilized man involuntarily shrinks. Yet they are men for whom Christ died. Can you go and live among such men and women? Do you say, I am not called to such degradation, this is too great a sacrifice, too exacting a condescension? Think of what

Christ has done for you. . . . [quoting missionary Dr. W. Goodell writing in 1854] "When your whole nature revolts from contact with degraded and naked savages, and you feel that you cannot bear to associate with them, remember what a demand you make every day, when you ask the pure and sinless Spirit of the Eternal God to come not to sojourn but to *abide* in your vile, sinful heart!" (Jessup, 1901 [1895]:19).

The image of Christ's death and resurrection was used to express the death of the "old self" necessary for missionaries to properly represent the gospel. Baldwin, for example, portrayed the "essential spiritual qualification" of the missionary in the following way:

[W]hen St. John [in his vision of the apocalypse] saw our Lord, He bore the marks of death. He not only looked like a "Lamb," but as one that had been slain and was risen to life again. To be like Christ, therefore, is to look like one who has died, been buried and raised to life again in the image of His resurrection. . . . What the world sees [too often] is the old unslain natural life, and unsatisfied they turn away and say: "Is this Christianity?" . . . If you are to do the work of the Lord, live much in His presence, bury yourself in His infinite fullness and there stay until when at last you go forth on His errand, people will say: "These men look like those who have died forever to sin and risen again unto righteousness—look like the Lord Jesus Christ" (Baldwin, 1901:29,30).

In sum, the legacy of the nineteenth-century Protestant missionary calling unfolded in two phases. In its early phase, testimonies of calling provided evangelicals with powerful models of Christian heroism while maintaining a dramatic continuity with the Biblical tradition of divine summonses. In its later phase, the missions movement set forth the foreign missionary vocation as an image of the way every true Christian must live within the world by the power of God. Its metaphorical link to the incarnation of Christ—being set apart and sent into an estranged world on a divine mission of redemption—mandated that every serious follower of Christ should aspire, in a symbolic sense at least, to be a missionary.

The effects of this dual legacy persisted, and were clearly to be seen in midtwentieth-century American evangelicalism—the milieu in which many of the long-term HCJB missionaries in my study received their calling. On the one hand, later missionary writers continued to produce didactic statements on the call: what it was, how one was called, how to prepare for the missionary vocation, and so forth (Adeney, 1955; Houghton, 1956; Kane, 1975, 1980). On the other hand, missionary heroes continued to inspire youthful commitment, and to carry on the Biblical tradition of individual divine calls. Missionary David Adeney, for example, wrote in 1955:

The uniqueness of the missionary vocation lies in the fact that the Holy Spirit brings to certain members of the Church a compelling conviction that they have been set apart as apostles and commissioned to give their whole lives to the gospel and to build the Church of the Lord Jesus Christ (Adeney, 1955:79).

At about the same time, A. T. Houghton advanced the notion that God could use the life of an individual in one of two ways, and that both required a calling. Some were called to be full-time witnesses—to evangelize, preach, and build up the church; but an equally valid calling might be to stay and work in a secular occupation, and thus provide materially for *others* to go as missionaries. And in Houghton's view, this latter calling still entailed a "missionary" task, insofar as every Christian was obligated to "seize every opportunity of making known and commending the gospel in [his or her] particular environment." In whatever circumstance, Houghton exhorted his reader, "You have been entrusted with a part of the fulfillment of the Great Commission. . . . The Lord who called you out of the darkness into His marvelous light has a purpose and plan for your life" (Houghton, 1956:10).

Having noted that stay-at-home Christians could still play a role in fulfilling the Great Commission, Houghton went on to reiterate many of the same themes that had characterized late nineteenth-century writings on the missionary calling. He cited such Biblical models as Abraham, Moses, Samuel, Jeremiah, and Isaiah, noting their initial human unfitness and unworthiness to perform the task God had in mind. He defined the call as the mere conviction of need, plus opportunity. He asserted that the only necessary qualifications for a missionary calling were spiritual: a deep personal experience of conversion, and a life wholly yielded to God (daily dying to the old sinful self). "Apart from true spiritual enduement," Houghton wrote, "all other qualifications will ultimately prove inadequate for the missionary's task" (Houghton, 1956:33).

Houghton also suggested (as others had before him), that "the missionary call must come in youth if it is to be implemented" (Houghton, 1956:35). He urged young Christians to study the Bible, but also the biographies of great missionary pioneers who had responded to God's call early in life. He challenged them likewise to commit their lives to the goal of a career on the mission field, and to persevere:

> [B]egin to test all life and conduct by the question, "Will this bring me nearer my goal? Will this help the life to be lived?" . . . You were set apart for this purpose, and "no man, having put his hand to the plow, and looking back, is fit for the kingdom of God" (Luke 9:62). Can you imagine Paul going back on his call? When he heard God's voice saying, "I have appeared unto thee for this purpose, to make thee a minister (to) . . . the Gentiles, unto whom now I send thee" (Acts 26:16,17), there could be only one response: "I was not disobedient to the heavenly vision" (Acts 26:19) (Houghton, 1956:32,91).

Also around this same time, mission board member Mel Larson of the Evangelical Free Church of America compiled and edited an influential book of the personal testimonies of contemporary missionaries, titled *117 Ways to the Mission Field* (1957). Most of these narratives included stories of conversion early in life, followed by experiences of God's leading to the mission field. Some of Larson's respondents connected their calling quite explicitly with conversion, such as in this account offered by Mrs. Evelyn Clingingsmith, missionary to Venezuela:

> The way God called me to be a missionary is simple, even as was my conversion. I knew He wanted me to be His servant because that was why He had saved me. Almost immediately I told people I was going to be a missionary. When I chose my subjects in high school it was with this in mind. It was all settled when I was saved.
>
> I was 12 years old when one night, after I had gone to bed, I began to tremble and become rigid. Although it was winter and we slept in bedrooms which were not too well heated, the trembling was not from the cold. I seemed to hear a voice telling me to go talk to my mother. . . . When I told her I couldn't go to sleep and had been

trembling, she said to me, "I think that the Lord has been talking to you. Don't you want to give your heart to Him?" . . . Mother and Dad got up and we went to the living room and knelt by the big chair to pray. The trembling stopped and peace and happiness came (Larson, 1957:295–296).

Others related call experiences such as the following dialogue with God:

Then, as she was working, she seemed to hear a voice say, "Naomi, aren't you willing to go to the foreign field?"

Mrs. Naomi Olson Skoglund turned, saw no one. Again the voice came.

"Naomi, aren't you willing to go for My sake?"

She could only say in her heart, "Lord, is it Thou that is speaking to me?"

She felt uneasy. It was noon and in a moment the group headed for lunch. Usually very talkative, she said little this noon, but only smiled. She went back to work until 2 p.m., then headed for her room. . . . She got her Bible, slipped to her knees and started talking to God.

"Lord, if it is Thou that is speaking to me, show me in Thy Word."

Her Bible opened to Matthew 28:19-20, "Go ye therefore, and teach all nations, baptizing them in the Name of the Father, and of the Son, and of the Holy Ghost: teaching them to observe all things whatsoever I have commanded you: and, lo, I am with you alway, even unto the end of the world. Amen."

God said to her, "Naomi, are you not willing to go to the foreign field and tell others of Me that they, too, might have everlasting life, even as you have?"

She replied, "Lord, I have no talents or gifts as others have."

He asked again, "I am not looking for talents. Are you willing?"

She yielded and as she said, "Yes, Lord, here am I, send me," joy filled her soul.

She next said, "Lord, I'm willing to go to India."

He countered, "Not India, Naomi. I want to send you to Africa."

After a period came her answer, "Lord, I'm willing to go even to Africa . . . or wherever You lead me" (Larson, 1957:121–122).

The writings of Elisabeth Elliot provided some of the most influential exemplars of missionary calling in modern times. In *Through Gates of Splendor*, a book that became a classic of its kind, Elliot chronicled the lives of five young Americans who, in 1956, set out to reach the isolated Auca tribe with the Christian gospel—only to be speared to death in their first attempt on the banks of the Curaray River deep in the Ecuadorian rain forest (Elliot, 1957). One of the slain missionaries was Jim Elliot, Elisabeth's husband. In a second book, entitled *Shadow of the Almighty* (1958), she penned his biography in the genre of a heroic spiritual pilgrimage.

The story of what happened to Jim Elliot, Roger Youderian, Pete Fleming, Ed McCully, and Nate Saint—and especially the way in which that story reverberated through a generation of young evangelicals in post-war America—stands as an important chapter in the saga of twentieth-century missions. But the "Auca massacre" bears an extraordinary significance for the missionaries in my study, because it happened in Ecuador. Numerous HCJB members trace their missionary call directly or indirectly to that 1956 incident, and to the spiritual influence of the Auca martyrs' testimonies. Jim Elliot's story in particular provides a sort of anatomy of a call, and thus bears special scrutiny. Near the beginning of *Shadow of the Almighty* we find this description of his family, in which Elisabeth Eliot uses the word call in its general New Testament sense to mean a decision to follow Christ:

Fred Elliot read the Scriptures daily to his children, seeking to show them the glory of Christ above all else. . . . And each of the children at an early age heard the call of Jesus and set his face to follow (Elliot, 1958:25).

Later we learn that Jim felt precisely the sort of divine calling about which Robert Speer had written at the turn of the century in *The Student Volunteer*—that is, the absence of a call to stay home. Elliot's widow wrote, "In view of the unequivocal command of Christ, coupled with these staggering facts [about the unconverted], Jim believed that if he stayed in the U.S. the burden of proof would lie with him to show that he was justified in so doing" (Elliot, 1958:44–45). Passages from Jim Elliot's journals confirm this notion:

[quoting Paul] "Some have not the knowledge of God—I speak this to your shame." And they must hear. The Lord is bearing hard upon me the need of the unreached millions. . . . Why does not the church awake? What a high calling is offered any who will pray, "Send me" (Elliot, 1958:54).

I dare not stay home while the Quichuas perish. What if the well-filled church in the homeland needs stirring? They have the Scriptures, Moses, and the prophets, and a whole lot more. Their condemnation is written on their bank books and in the dust of their Bible covers (Elliot, 1957:19–20).

To anyone who reads Jim Elliot's story—told largely in the pages of his own diaries—it is obvious that he believed his missionary vocation to be the culmination of a prior spiritual journey that had set him radically apart from "the world." In short, for Elliot, following the missionary call meant seeking strangerhood with a passion. The following passages from his personal Bible study notes, correspondence, and daily journal are telling:

Genesis 23—Abraham calls himself a stranger and sojourner in a land he believed God was going to give to him. . . . Lord, show me that I must be a stranger, unconcerned and unconnected with affairs below. . . . Oh to be known as Israel, a prince with God; no longer as Jacob of the carnal mind (Elliot, 1958:51).

The Lord has given me a hunger for righteousness and piety that can alone be of Himself. Such hungering He alone can satisfy, yet Satan would delude and cast up all sorts of other baubles, social life, a name renowned, a position of importance, scholastic attainment. What are these but objects of the "desire of the Gentiles" whose cravings are warped and perverted. Surely they can mean nothing to the soul who has seen the beauty of Jesus Christ (Elliot, 1957:17).

Coming home we stopped for a bite to eat, and ran into a confused waitress. Had a heart-rending time trying to speak the Words of Life to her, and as I think of all this country now, many just as confused, and more so, I realized that the 39th Street bus is as much a mission field as Africa ever was (Elliot, 1958:44).

Even Billy Graham's *alma mater* Wheaton College, with its insular evangelical environment, smacked of worldliness to Jim Elliot. Insofar as college life represented intellectual pursuits that might distract attention from matters of the soul, Elliot considered it "dangerous" for a Christian—a threat to spiritual sensibilities:

"Culture," philosophy, disputes, drama in its weaker forms, concerts and opera, politics—anything that can occupy the intellect seems to turn aside the hearts of many here on campus from a humble life in the steps of the Master, though we sing about this most delicately! No, education is dangerous, and personally, I am beginning to question its value in a Christian's life. I do not disparage wisdom— that comes from God, not from Ph.D.s (Elliot, 1958:41).

On a journey by rail, Elliot sat amongst unsaved earthlings, reading the biography of a great missionary. The train became, for him, a kind of metaphor for the infernal destination of the human race without Christ:

> I write on board the train, having just finished *The Growth of a Soul*, the life of Hudson Taylor. . . . Boarded at Billings about 5:30 a.m. and slept fitfully till nine. Woke with the realization that I am in Satan's realm still. One woman near me seemed to encourage the red-eyed imp Desire, and oh, how base and hateful I think of myself now having prayed and read some of the Word. What *will* Hell be like, enraged by unslaked Lust and made seven times hotter with the vengeance of an outraged God? Oh to think of these men and women, these happy boys and girls going there. Father, save them, I pray. . . . When will the Spirit's power make me a witness of the things which I have seen and heard? (Elliot, 1958:61).

Gradually but unmistakably, Jim felt God answering his prayer for a calling to a specific field. In Elisabeth Elliot's rendering, "He met a former missionary from Ecuador who told him of the needs in that field, and mentioned the great challenge of the dread Aucas. This was the climax to several years of seeking direction from God. Jim devoted ten days largely to prayer to make sure that this was indeed what God intended for him" (Elliot, 1957:19). A diary entry captured the earnestness of that season of prayer:

> Father, if Thou wilt let me go to South America to labor with Thee and to die, I pray that Thou wilt let me go soon. Nevertheless, not my will (Elliot, 1958:72).

Finally, the resolution came:

> My going to Ecuador is God's counsel. . . . And how do I know it is His counsel? "Yea, my heart instructeth me in the night seasons." Oh, how good! For I have known my heart is speaking to me for God! (Elliot, 1957:14).

Roger Youderian, another of the five missionaries slain by the Aucas, was a paratrooper in World War II, surviving the Rhine jump and the Battle of the Bulge. In 1944 he had a deep conversion experience (though he had been brought up in an evangelical home). In 1945, from Berlin, Youderian wrote these words to his mother:

> Ever since I accepted Christ as my personal Savior last fall . . . I've felt the call to either missionary, social or ministerial work after my release from the service. Can't say now what the calling will be but I want to be a witness for Him and follow Him every second of my life (Elliot, 1957:75).

Then there was Pete Fleming, an earnest student who had obtained a master's degree in literature, submitting a thesis on Melville's *The Confidence Man*. Elisabeth Elliot describes his spiritual beginnings: "Converted at the age of thirteen after hearing the testimony of a blind evangelist, Pete, like Enoch, 'walked with God' in a way that set him apart in the eyes of fellow high school students" (Elliot, 1957:21–22). Steeped in the Bible, Fleming described his own spiritual impulses toward service in Ecuador in a letter he wrote to a senior missionary there:

My thinking, both in and outside of the Scriptures, was directed toward the strin-
gency of Christ's words to His disciples, when he sent them forth: "I send you forth
as sheep among wolves . . ." "He that loveth father or mother more than me is not
worthy of me . . ." "He that taketh not up his cross and followeth after me is not
worthy of me . . ." "He that findeth his life shall lose it: and he that loseth his life for
My sake shall find it." It has seemed that the severe requirements of a difficult field
like Ecuador are matched on a spiritual level by the severe requirements placed on
real disciples. Ecuador, as it seems, is a God-given opportunity to place God's principles and promises to the extreme test (Elliot, 1957:23).

In her telling of the fourth of the five martyrs' stories, Elisabeth Elliot emphasized, once again, the theme of sacrifice in the missionary calling:

The following year Ed McCully, having turned his thinking toward the bar, entered
the law school at Marquette University. . . . But God, who ordains men of His own
choosing and moves in them to the accomplishment of His eternal purposes, had
other plans. Ed told his Wheaton classmate Jim about it in a letter dated September 22, 1950 [beginning his second year of law school]: "On the way home
yesterday morning I took a long walk and came to a decision which I know is of
the Lord. . . . I have one desire now—to live a life of reckless abandon for the
Lord, putting all my energy and strength into it. Maybe He'll send me someplace
where the name of Jesus Christ is unknown. . . . Well, that's it. Two days ago I was
a law student. Today I'm an untitled nobody" (Elliot, 1957:50–51).

Finally, there was Nate Saint, who piloted the small aircraft that carried the men
into the jungle on their fateful mission. The aptly named Saint described his own
missionary call experience as follows:

Now, you've heard about people being spoken to by God. I don't know about the
other fellow, but that night I saw things differently. . . . Just as though a different
Kodachrome slide had been tossed onto the screen between my ears. . . . A joy, such
as I had never known since the night I accepted Jesus' forgiveness for my sins,
seemed to leave me almost weak with gratitude. It was the first time that I had ever
really heard that verse: "Follow me, and I will make you to become fishers of men."
The old life of chasing things that are of a temporal sort seemed absolutely insane
(Elliot, 1957:68).

Some time after he arrived in Ecuador, Saint delivered a brief sermon over Radio
Station HCJB. The memory of World War II was still fresh, and he employed the familiar military metaphor to convey the idea of missionary expendability—evoking
the supreme sacrifice that he himself would make not long afterward:

During the last war we were taught to recognize that, in order to obtain our objective, we had to be willing to be expendable. . . . We know there is only one answer
to our country's demand that we share in the price of freedom. Yet, when the Lord
Jesus asks us to pay the price for world evangelization, we often answer without a
word. We cannot go. We say it costs too much. . . . Missionaries constantly face expendability. Jesus said, "There is no man that hath left house, or brethren, or sisters,
or mother, or wife, or children, or lands for my sake and the Gospel's but shall receive an hundred fold now in this time and in the world to come eternal life" (Elliot,
1957:60).

In sum, these martyrs' testimonies reveal strong thematic links to the nineteenth-century missionary movement, as well as to the Biblical story that evangelicals believe inspired that movement. These themes include the ideals of strangerhood, sacrifice, heroism, and the imitation of Christ. Such testimonies significantly enhance the script, stage setting, and tradition of performances through which new missionary recruits continue to apprehend their own dramatic experiences of divine calling. Let us now attend more fully to these experiences in the lives of HCJB Mission members.

Patterns of Calling among HCJB Missionaries

Carol and I sat there in the church until 9:30 that night, listening to the music, watching this slide series about HCJB, called "The Heavens are Telling." And something just burned in my heart. All those preteen years, all those teenage years, all those college years of missionary commitment—all this history—it just burned through my heart and mind that night. I just sat there quietly. It was a cold November evening, a little snow falling outside. I just sat there watching this thing happen. And then the Lord said to me, "Go by the literature table. Pick up the literature so you can have the address." Then afterward I found out that the whole time during that meeting, the Lord was whispering to Carol, too, "You're going to work at HCJB in Quito, Ecuador. You're going to work there. That's where you're going." Well, we went home, and I wrestled with this thing for a couple of days—maybe a week or two—and I got to the place where I just couldn't work. You may call it "under conviction," but I could not work. And finally, the Lord said, "When are you going to write that letter?" So I finally said, "OK, Lord, I'll put everything aside." And I put a piece of paper in my typewriter and I wrote to HCJB in Miami, Florida.

A missionary, in the true sense, is any person who obeys the command of Jesus, "Go and make disciples of all nations, baptizing them in the name of the Father, Son and Holy Spirit." Some people need to feel a special "call" because maybe they grow up in a church where you're called. So then you get called. But if you don't, then God works some other way—to nudge you to the fact that *we are* his witnesses.

Two kinds of narratives that dealt with missionary calls emerged from my interviews with missionaries. First, my respondents often had a good deal to say about missionary calls as a general topic for discussion—how a call ought to be defined, why it is important or not, whether it is necessary and valid. Second, most Mission members offered a personal tale relating their own divine call, some more eventfully than others. A mere catalog of these missionaries' experiences of (and opinions about) such divine calling might be interesting in itself; but to understand this material sociologically and historically, we need to examine it with a number of specific questions in mind: How is the traditional imagery of the missionary calling manifested here? What is the relation between the call and a previous moral career? How does the call transform personal identity or reshape expectations and images of a future self?

In my interpretation, what emerges from these testimonies is the powerful yet ambiguous myth of the missionary vocation in evangelical culture. People tell of recoiling in fear from the calling, yet feeling irresistibly attracted to it. Historically important themes and metaphors—military conflict, sacrifice, heroism, strangerhood, the imitation of Christ—are clearly illustrated in these contemporary narratives. Yet we also find considerable innovation, improvisation, even denial of the traditional missionary call.

For instance, one man who is a second-generation missionary at first tells us that going into his father's profession was simply the natural thing for him to do—much like a farmer's son becoming a farmer. But then he admits there is something extraordinary—something set apart—about the missionary calling. After all, he finds a clear Biblical precedent for it in the Book of Acts:

> There's this impression that you've got to be called to be a missionary. You've got to have a call. So you've got all these people wandering around waiting for God to call them. I don't buy that. My coming to the mission field . . . was just as natural as some other guys I knew who went into milking cows. And I think their calling was just as natural to them as my coming to Ecuador was to me. People in missions conferences and churches try to make this big deal about the call, and I find it more of a natural thing. I find that people who come unnaturally to the mission field usually don't last. I believe we're all, in a sense, missionaries—as we show Christlikeness.
>
> Now, it is true that in Acts, people were separated—were called apart; they laid hands upon them, and they went out as missionaries from that particular church. I do believe in that. I believe in the missionary with a "big M," so to speak. There is a confirmation from a church that, yes, this man is missionary material and we commend him to the gospel and we promise to support him in our prayers, and financially, and in every way. But missionary with a "little m" means that every Christian is a missionary, whether they want to be or not. They are an example of Christlikeness. It's like the God with a "big G" and gods with a "little g." We are the gods with a "small g" and the God who created us is the God with a "big G."

This narrator portrays two ideas that form a primary tension in the missionary vocation. On the one hand, it is an ordinary line of work in the world, like other lines of work, for which some people have an inherited affinity. But on the other hand, missionaries are spiritually set apart, commissioned by God and by a body of believers as divine instruments in the worldwide harvest of souls. He also expresses the notion that the missionary ideal of imitating Christ is actually the ideal of every true believer; and in that sense, every Christian is a missionary. But then, almost as an aside, this son of missionaries makes a remarkable statement:

> I don't think there's a normal person here. I think you've got to be weird to be a missionary. I've never met a normal missionary. And that's why missionary kids have such a hard time adjusting when they go back to the States. They have this combination of a different personality they've inherited from their parents, and a different cultural experience.

Another respondent reacts against the idea that "every Christian is a missionary." She feels she is a missionary, in a special sense, because she was *called* to be one. But then she adds something interesting. She doesn't like to use the word "missionary" to refer to herself. Moreover, somewhat curiously, she justifies a kind of undercover approach to missionary identity as an imitation of Christ:

> I think it makes language meaningless to say, "We're all missionaries," because I don't think we are. I do think of myself as a missionary. It's a *calling* I responded to, and I always

see my work in light of *being a missionary,* in light of being sent here for that purpose, of seeing the gospel go forward in another culture. But at the same time, I don't like to use the word "missionary." The way I think of it is, when Jesus Christ came into the world he was the son of God— but he didn't go around calling himself "the son of God." In the same way, when I introduce myself to Ecuadorians I'm not going to say, "I'm a missionary."

In testimonies about the calling, many Mission members include reminiscences about their childhood perceptions of missionaries, their earliest understanding of what the vocation meant, and their first images of what it might be like to be a missionary. When we consider how these people as children viewed the missionary calling—in the context of the culture they were growing up in—both the power and ambiguity of the myth become more sharply focused. On the positive side, the missionary vocation was accorded exceptional prestige, of a spiritual sort, in the homes and churches most of them came from. It was considered to be a heroic adventure and a high calling; those chosen by God were to be admired and respected:

My dad was a farmer and we lived in a very small community, so not too many missionaries came to our church. But from the few that did, I got very interested in missions. A missionary was someone to be honored. It was a very special vocation, really. I never saw a missionary looked down upon, ever. I never saw a missionary made fun of. Nowadays, you know, I'm surprised at a lot of people who think that you're a missionary because you can't do anything else. I always had a very high view of missionaries.

My father was a pastor in a small evangelical church. Of course, growing up in a pastor's home you get to see a lot of missionaries. We had quite of number of them stay with us. Also, my aunt and uncle were missionaries in the Far East. I always thought of missionary life as very exotic, and I guess I put missionaries up on a pedestal, spiritually. We lived in a rural area. It was a very ingrown community, and so was our church. I hardly ever traveled outside of a hundred mile radius from home. My world was very small, but somehow I knew it could be bigger. When I was around ten years old I decided I would like to be a missionary, and that the Lord wanted me to serve him on a foreign field.

In our home, from my earliest memories, missionary work was something that just was honored and promoted as one of the highest, most privileged vocations one could aspire to. My mother would take time out to read missionary biographies to us, as part of our childhood devotion time each night. Also, our church had extensive missionary conventions. When I was quite small, they had two conferences a year, that ran for two weeks nightly. These were the hallmark events of the whole church year. There was nothing more important, or that took more energy and promotion than these conferences. They were well attended, and I was very much influenced by them. My parents were careful to see that we got to those meetings, and we got to all of them. It wasn't a matter of being forced to, either, because they were very interesting for a child. There were pictures and even movies and stories about mission work. It was there that I began to get my first taste and desire, and the idea that I would like to be a missionary someday.

Quite commonly, respondents who recalled such early-life positive impressions of missions also went on to report a significant missionary call experience of their own. Often, these experiences echoed the primary themes of the late nineteenth-century Student Volunteer Movement—the metaphor of military service, the needs of a lost world, the absence of a "call to stay home," and obedience to the Great Commission and to God's personal command:

Out of this early experience came my sense of personal obligation to the people around the world—to carry the gospel witness to them. It was a lost world, without Christ. I define my own call as a growing conviction that I really could do nothing else. That is, I could do nothing else and be true to my conscience, and true to what I sensed as my obligation to the world. I did see that I could be a witness at home, but I also got the impression that not enough people were going into overseas mission work. *I saw God as a general in the army, working with a group of volunteers and shorthanded for his foreign campaign.* I thought that if I volunteered for foreign service, I would probably be accepted just on the basis of his apportionment of resources. So I expected that God would ask me to be a missionary. There would have to be a very good reason for me *not* to be one, given the shortage.

Two key ingredients in the recipe for early call experiences seem to be a "missions minded" church background and parents who promoted the idea of Christian service. A penchant for extraordinary piety, often combined with fantasies of adventure and spiritual heroism, tended to characterize the early-life narratives of those who said they had aspired to the missionary vocation since childhood:

> Our church was very missions-minded. Our church always had a missions conference, every year, about a week in length. Quite frequently there were other missionaries who would come by and would be in our services. And so I was always exposed to missionary life around the world. What I observed in missionaries, even at an early age, was just cor-roboration for what I heard my parents saying to me about Christian commitment, period—that I had a responsibility to make a knowledgeable, careful commitment to the Lord. And I suppose some of the missionary adventure and—you know, some of that—kind of captured me. But I can never remember a time when I did not consciously desire to be a missionary. As early as first grade, I had it in my mind.

> The idea that I would be a missionary occurred to me pretty strongly even in grade school. By the time I was in high school, I had a good idea that this is what the Lord was going to ask me to do. Toward the end of college, it was very clear. The only question was, what professional preparation should I seek?

Beyond abstract teaching in the church and home about responsibility and Christian commitment, Mission members quite commonly note the early influence of missionaries themselves—attractive, heroic models for their young lives. Specifically, a number of HCJB missionaries relate their sense of calling directly or indirectly to the story of the Auca martyrs killed in 1956:

> In our home church, I was always taught that a missionary was a person to be highly re-spected and admired. But also, Mom and Dad made sure we saw all kinds of missionaries. We had missionaries in our home. There was always a glow about their lives. They had a very present concern, and that was to win lost souls for Jesus Christ. They all said it in dif-ferent ways. Some were very earnest. In particular, there was Nate Saint. I never forgot about him. His wife would write prayer letters back, telling about where he was flying, and what he was doing. And I could imagine I was right there with him, doing his thing for the Lord, supplying the missionaries in the jungle with food and medical supplies. When he was killed by the Aucas years later, it made a tremendous impression on me. Ecuador, and the jungle, and flying just captivated my imagination. I thought it would be great to be a jungle aviator.

It was during my early high school years that five men decided it was important to let some savage Indians in Ecuador know about the gospel, and wound up giving their lives for that cause. I became very much aware of this. I read everything about it that I could get my hands on, some published and some not published, and basically felt a kinship with these missionaries. In my later high school years I decided I wanted to be a missionary pilot, through the influence of the stories of Nate Saint and Jim Elliot. And so I made application to Missionary Aviation Fellowship as well as to Moody Institute of Aviation, believing that was the direction God was taking me. As it turned out, the doors to becoming a pilot and being in missionary aviation were closed. But the country of Ecuador began to play a very predominant part in my thinking. I was aware of HCJB from the time I was seven years old, because my dad used to listen to HCJB. Now I didn't have any thoughts of being anything but a pilot. But God used that goal to keep my eyes on Ecuador. All of this was in God's providence, though he had something else in mind. Much later, when a couple of guys from HCJB visited our college, I became interested in the opportunities that HCJB had, and ended up coming to Ecuador. Even though I could not fly around Ecuador, I had a feeling that God was calling me to this country.

But there was also a darker, disquieting side to the myth. Missionaries were admired for their courage and other-worldly dedication; yet they were seen by some as strange, peculiar souls—disturbingly set apart from the commonplaces of life:

Missionaries were strange, odd people to me. When I was growing up, that was the last thing I wanted to be. I thought, how horrible to have to go far away from home and—being a very shy and timid person—to think of going and talking to people about the Lord. I admired them because they could do that, but I thought, that could never be me. And I was scared to death that that's what the Lord was going to call me to do. I didn't want to have anything to do with missionaries. I was not one of these kids who was really interested in all the junk they put out on their tables. I didn't like missionary conferences at all.

The missions conferences at our church made a big impression on me as a child. There was this great sense of sending people out with the gospel to faraway places. Still, in my early years, I thought missionaries were kind of odd. The artifacts they brought back seemed very strange to me. It was just a hard thing to understand, as a child. I wasn't attracted by missionary life then. I can remember being given biographies of missionaries by my grandmother, and I don't think I ever read them. It was not so much that missionaries *themselves* were odd, but that their situation had made them odd. I thought, they couldn't help it that their clothes were so out of date. Their kids didn't seem to fit in, but they couldn't help that. It was just kind of a situation that bred that.

The themes of sacrifice and strangerhood emerge prominently in a number of these reminiscences, some of which could have been taken directly from the biographies of nineteenth-century missionary heroes. But the tone in which they speak hardly expresses the pious joy of suffering for the gospel. Rather, it seems to betray the memory of a child's very real fear—that somehow God would banish her to an unbelievably dismal life, far away from anything lovely and familiar:

In my mind, the image that I got of being a missionary was that you had a mud hut, and you were right in the middle of Africa, with nothing around you, and you were sitting around your firepot boiling your water—and reading the Scriptures to people. The idea was that you had to really suffer, physically. A dirt floor. No electricity. No appliances. Now, that would just drive me nuts, but that was my image—somewhere in the darkest of Africa, preaching to the natives. Very poor circumstances. I had no inkling that I would grow up to be a missionary.

But then, after my mom died it began to seem that it was going to come true. I just got a nebulous feeling, or sense that I wasn't going to be here in my home town for the rest of my life. And one day I was walking past a shop, and I remember thinking a dreadful thought: You know, maybe the Lord wants me to go overseas—but not the Congo! I couldn't bear it.

Well, I started to think, is this really true, or am I just dreaming? I used to go to what was called a missionary camp every year. And you know, I just said to the Lord, "If this is really it, you've got to show me. I can't do anything until . . ." Well, I was listening to a guy speak about Brazil, and about a missionary there. And as I thought about him, my mind started to go in a hundred different directions. I thought of a couple I knew—and it's funny, because this couple is now in Zaire, what was then the Congo, where I didn't want to go. But at that time they had been inquiring about some other country. And I thought, what was the country they were interested in? And it was Ecuador! They had been writing to a missionary in Ecuador. When that came into my mind it was as if the Lord said, "That's it." And you know, I got scared! I didn't hear another word this guy said about Brazil—I just felt like the Lord was saying, "Ecuador, Ecuador, Ecuador."

How do we interpret such ambivalence in these missionaries' early perceptions of the vocation they eventually sought? It seems almost as if there are two kinds of missionaries—those who always felt attracted to the missionary calling, and those who were always repelled by it but somehow drawn by a destiny to fulfill their worst fears. This is at least partly true; but more significantly, these two kinds of responses represent a profound tension inherent in the missionary vocation itself. What both kinds of experience have in common is the thought of missionary work occurring to a young person often and forcefully enough to form a kind of fixation—and for some, almost an obsessive thought. In the end, most of these people approached the calling in the same way they encountered other manifestations of the sacred, and that is with marked emotional ambivalence. Hence, getting a call to the mission field is much like being converted; one is repelled but irresistibly attracted at the same time:

> When I was a student at Moody, every year they had a missionary conference. And I was always afraid of those, because a lot of times they would ask people to go forward and give their lives for missionary service. I was always afraid to do it, because that meant I really would have to be a missionary, and I was scared to. But the last year I was there, they had that service and it was just like a magnet drawing me to the front. And I knew I *had* to go. I thought, "As of right now, I am willing to go, and as the Lord directs, I would do it."

The question arises, what exactly is it about the missionary call that frightens people? Two aspects stand out: one is the call's association with the sacred, as discussed in Chapter 2. The evangelical belief in an all-powerful, all-knowing, and righteous God arranging the course of an individual's life can be terrifying, especially when this notion is confounded with a sense of guilt and isolation of the self before the Almighty. The other frightening aspect of the call is the way it evokes the unknown, the strange and unfamiliar. Indeed, the missionary vocation may become a

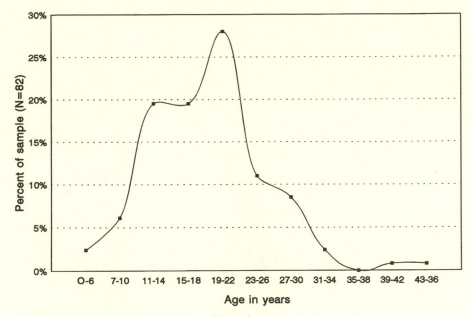

Figure 3.4. Age at time of missionary call experience.

sort of symbolic antithesis of a conventional, secure, and desirable life. And perhaps missionary work is most scary to those who think they may be inevitably drawn to it against their own desires.

The missionary call is almost always a young person's experience. It occurs most often before marriage and preparation for a specific line of work—in late adolescence or earlier, and only rarely after age thirty. Figure 3.4 shows that of the 82 HCJB missionaries who remembered how old they were when they had a specific call experience, almost half had the experience before age nineteen, and seventy-five percent before age twenty-three. The median age reported was 19.5.

Though it is possible to think of the missionary call as a unitary phenomenon that is stylized in general ways by culture, nevertheless different patterns of experience characterize the life stories of various people who come to feel called. Some felt called in a general way, gradually, over a period of time. Others had a dramatic experience at a moment in time—hearing God's call as inner voice, in a dream or vision, or the like.[6] Among HCJB mission members, the second pattern was more common, accounting for three-quarters of those who said they had a calling.

Those who had a special call tended to be slightly younger when they first had a conversion experience, (average age 11 vs. 13); younger when they first seriously considered being a missionary (average age 17 vs. 20); and younger when they arrived on the mission field (average age 29 vs. 31). Beyond this, few differences characterize the two groups—except for one background variable. Interestingly, those who reported a special call experience such as an "inner voice" were much more likely to have had one or both parents active in religious work. Specifically, of those who reported a special call experience, 62 percent had at least one parent active in religious work. Of those who reported only a general or gradual sense of calling, only

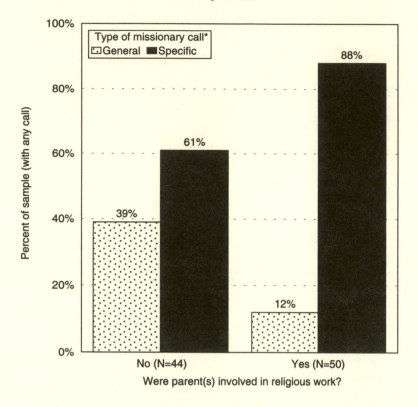

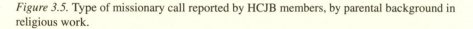

* *General* sense of calling acquired gradually vs. *specific* experience (e.g., inner voice, vision) occurring at a given time, place, and age rememberd by the subject. Prevalence of type of call by parents' background was statistically significant at p<0.01.

Figure 3.5. Type of missionary call reported by HCJB members, by parental background in religious work.

26 percent had a parent who was a religious worker. Figure 3.5 displays the prevalence of specific vs. general calls among missionaries with and without parents who were themselves Christian workers.

Another sort of distinction among call experiences has already been mentioned, but bears further scrutiny. On the one hand, there were those respondents who said they had wanted to be a missionary since childhood or adolescence, and who received a call quite naturally in an ordinary kind of church setting—almost as a matter of course given their background. A woman whose father was a missionary provides an example of this sort of call:

> I think the call was very, very clear at the age of thirteen. I was at a meeting—a missionary meeting—when they asked for people to stand up who would be willing to commit their lives to God in missionary service. And I responded. I was very young, but it did mean a lot to me, and I feel that the call was from God. After that it was just a matter of the steps of preparation. I never really doubted, all through those years, that God would have me do missionary work.

On the other hand, there are those who say they never expected to be a missionary and who tended to receive a call as the result of a crisis—such as the death of a parent. The stories of Sarah and Anne from Chapter 2 stand as clear examples.[7] In this pattern, a young person is thrust into the portal of adulthood in a moment filled with pain and confusion. Up until that point, she may have been imagining the rest of her life stretching out in a conventional way. Perhaps she would have attended college, married and had a family, worked at a job, bought a house. Now everything is changed and she realizes that her ideal was not a courageous and worthy choice, but rather a taken-for-granted life determined by others' expectations. It is then that the alternative, unfamiliar, and sacrificial life scenario of the mission field comes into focus. It appears as the antithesis of the ordinary social blueprint for her life; and it comes to be seen, rather, as *God's* blueprint. It is the divinely chosen way of self-denial and heroic difficulty. The imagery for this radically different life course is provided by the missionary myth in evangelical culture. The sense of crisis is generated by the perceived opposition of two wills—God's sovereign will, and the person's own self-interested will: "Am I willing to give up living for myself, in order to be set apart for God?"

When we look over the range of call experiences reported by HCJB missionaries, we see that the primary social occasion for such a challenge is a religious meeting or retreat—a church missions conference, a student rally for missions or evangelism, or a church youth camp. The typical catalyst in this kind of experience is a missionary speaker—someone who has gone out and then returned to stand over against the banalities of everyday life and challenge those inside the fold.

The common motivational theme in these missionary calls paradoxically combines self-abnegating commitment with spiritual and physical adventure; there is the challenge of the unknown, and the image of striking blows to the forces of darkness and evil with the sword of the gospel. The traditional missionary, returning with exotic tales, tribal trophies, and color slides from the shadowy jungles of Africa, New Guinea, or South America is cast in the role of mythic hero. The missionary is the one who has gone forth from the regions of his or her birth, from the mundane realm where ordinary mortals live, and has met the challenge of fantastic forces in a far country. The missionary is also the one who has returned, with an aura of special power, to challenge and to instruct younger pilgrims in the ways of spiritual warfare.

Most respondents who say they felt God calling them before age nineteen in such a meeting do not say they were called specifically to HCJB in Ecuador—nor to any real place, for that matter. Rather, they were called to *be* (or to become) somebody for God—a missionary like the heroes of their Sunday school periodicals. The focus was not on specific places and tasks, but on being one of those willing to go out to win the world for Christ:

> The one conference I really remember was when the missionary speaker gave a tremendous challenge, of who was willing to really obey God, even to the point of going somewhere far away and doing a hard thing. That really pulled at me. It was at a point in my life where I just needed to know that I would be willing to do anything, even something very difficult. He gave an invitation, and you had to stand up and face the audience. And that was very hard for me, because in my younger years I was very shy. But I stood up. It was a real relief to me, to be able to think of something very difficult, and be will-

ing—and I did not have any great desire to go to an exotic place and be a missionary. That seemed really hard, to me.

The juxtaposition of two life scenarios—the previously taken-for-granted way vs. the sacrificial, negative image of the missionary vocation—is clearly seen in the following account:

When I was fifteen, in the summer, I went with the youth group from our church to a camp. I went to this camp, and there was a week-long series of meetings. The whole thrust of the preaching was that God has a blueprint for your life, and if you ask him, he will tell you what it is. But don't dare ask him unless you are willing to do *anything,* because he might ask you to be a missionary.

Well, this became a consuming thing for me, that I should ask God to show me, directly, the next step in my life. I began praying—and then I began to think, "Oh, horrors! What if I should be asked to be a missionary?" It was certainly a negative thing, but I recognized the value in praying this total kind of prayer—to be willing. But I was certainly hoping that the answer from God would be, "I want you to be a Christian person right here at home." I wanted to be a kind of rich, influential Christian, so that I could give to other people.

That was a long struggle, that week. It just became something I couldn't stop thinking about. I didn't know what I wanted to be or do, but I had wanted to go to an important school, like a prestigious school. I'm sure that was part of it. I had certainly wanted to raise my standard up somewhere. And now I thought, I'll have to be a missionary, and I'll have to ask the Lord where to go, and probably have to go to some kind of a Bible school. Finally, I said yes to the Lord, I would go wherever he wanted me to go. And to me, it was the lowest possible thing, a complete emptying of pride, to go and prepare to be a missionary—even to tell somebody you were going to be a missionary.

Then I had to think, "Lord, what country would you like me to live in?" I had wanted to live someplace beautiful in the United States. I had no knowledge of the world—its geography—and to me, anyplace outside the United States had to be undesirable. I was thinking probably it would be Africa, in a gray, mud-hut village. It was a real struggle. "Are you willing to go to any country?" I kept praying, and finally I said, "Yes, Lord. I will go to whatever country." Finally I could see myself there, as the only white person in this African village, never to be seen or heard of again. I was willing to do that.

Then it was, "What about marriage?" And I was definitely a girl who liked boys. I had a boyfriend then, in my town. He was seventeen, and I was fifteen. I liked him quite well. But it was a problem for me just to get him to become a Christian and come to our youth fellowship. It was unthinkable that a boy like him would be a missionary. So I had to think, would I be willing never to be married? And it was just such a shocking thought to me. I had never thought that I would not be married. And I prayed, and wept over that, and finally said, "Yes, Lord. I'm willing never to be married. I will be single all of my life."

Even after that, there was still something else. There was a dream I had of having a house, and it was going to be a beautiful house, with a spiral staircase. And finally I said, "Yes, Lord, I am willing never to have a house." The verse that came to mind was Matthew 6:33, "Seek ye first the kingdom of God and his righteousness, and all these things will be added unto you." But I never heard the last part. It was just "Seek ye first the kingdom."

As it first emerges, then, the call usually means something quite different than finding the right line of work. It is a spiritual experience, and it implies a culturally stylized image of a life to be lived, and of work to be done. One is going out to preach the gospel in the uttermost parts of the earth, to those who have never heard it. It is only after the initial decision that the practical implications are worked out.

Consider once again the emotional context of a student-oriented missionary meeting. The impression is given that "the needs of the world are crying to be met," and "God is calling you now," and "the missions out there are dying for lack of committed volunteers." A young person hears this as the voice of God, and responds with great passion and commitment. She may see this as the ultimate challenge that has burned beneath the surface of every other moral dilemma: "Am I willing to be set apart for God? Would I be willing to set everything aside and go wherever God wants me to go?"

This experience is often reconstructed as a great inner struggle, or even as an argument with God. As in the story of Jonah, the young person feels a certain urge to get on a ship going the opposite direction from Ninevah—even as she knows deep inside that the call will finally be irresistible. Quite a few respondents tell of a first commitment to God in which they said, "Yes, God, I'll do anything you want—but just don't make me a missionary." Somehow they feared that surrendering to God's will virtually ensured that he would send them alone to the "darkest jungle of Africa"—there to languish amid insects and deadly snakes and great pestilence, returning on brief furloughs every few years to wear out-of-style clothing among their former friends. But then they go on to tell how they struggled and "wrestled with the Lord," and became willing even to be a missionary—usually phrased as "willing to give up everything in order to follow God's will for my life."

Other than a church missionary conference, a Christian college or Bible school provides the most common institutional setting within which these subjects received a missionary call. In fact, it was so common in some of the schools they attended that a person who *didn't* hear a call might experience a good deal of confusion and cognitive dissonance:

> While I was at Bible college I was exposed to missions. But I went through a real crisis about "the call." It was that a lot of the kids would get up in chapel and say, "The Lord called me to India." And I'd go up to them and say, "How did the Lord call you? I'm not feeling any call from God. How do you know?" And nobody could give me an answer. They didn't say what type of ministry they were going to do; they just said, "I'm going to be a missionary." And I had all these big questions in my mind, because I didn't know what they were saying when they said, "God called me."
>
> But then there was a man who came through the Bible college, and he just gave a short message. He dealt on this theme. He said, "Do you want to know God's will for your life? Do you want to know God's calling? God made you a distinct person, and you have distinct abilities. The Lord has given you a gift. You find out, before the Lord, what that gift is. Develop that gift. Then you will be walking right in the Lord's will. And at that time, he will show you *where* to go—when you develop your gift." My, that just clarified everything. Today, that is what I hang my hat on.

This narrator's notion of a call clearly resembles Luther's concept of vocation. A calling can be any line of work in the world for which one has an affinity, and within which one can demonstrate God's gift of grace. Being sent out to a specific place is merely superimposed on the core notion of calling as a gift or talent to be developed and rendered in Christian service. Another Mission member expresses a similar idea:

> The way I see a missionary is he does what he's best at doing—I guess what I'm best at doing is maintaining technical equipment—but I'm doing it for the expansion of the

gospel. That's the way I see a missionary. He doesn't have to be in a foreign country. You can be a missionary in the States—but I don't think I have enough discipline to do that. I look back on my old job. I used to work for a company. I had a great opportunity. I went to all different people's homes. I could have been a great witness. There were many opportunities where I could have said something about Christ, but I didn't, because I didn't know what to say. So a missionary, I think, is someone who does his work for the furtherance of the gospel. And you can be a missionary even in the States, if you just get your line together, and say, "I'm going to do something for the Lord, today." Just be a witness.

This idea leads to a somewhat distinct pattern of experience by which some people feel called to the mission field at a later stage in life. That is, they initially settle into some profession or line of work, and then receive a call to go out and employ their talent and training in some specific manner or place. For some of them, there is no shift in motivation, but rather the call is the climax of a whole life of preparation. For example, one respondent tells us that he undertook medical training solely as missionary preparation. He then entered medical practice to gain further experience for the mission field, as he continued to seek information about various medical missions. One night, the call finally came:

And then, in my third year of medical practice I had an experience, one evening. It was a very divine, transcendental kind of experience—one like I had never had before, and I don't think I've had anything quite like it since. I was driving along in the car, on my way to a Christian Medical Society retreat. I just felt that the time had come for an answer, when God was going to indicate to us what we should do. And this is what happened.

I was praying about three or four opportunities, in various parts of the world where physicians were needed. I had actually corresponded with missions working in these areas. I was singing a little song, "On the darkest side of the road, where the sick and wounded lie." And each time I came back to Ecuador in my circle of praying, I was very strongly reminded of the verse from Isaiah which says, "You shall hear a voice behind you, saying, 'This is the way! Walk ye in it!'"

Well, I sort of tried to disregard the idea, thinking it might have just been a trick of my own mind, to remember that verse. But each time I went back and prayed about Ecuador, the insistence of that word, in my own mind, was something far out of proportion—I don't even know how to describe it. It was the kind of insistence that I simply could not put out of my mind. Nor could I disregard it as some sort of fabrication. It was almost like somebody was shouting it at me, within my own consciousness.

As I prayed about other places, all of a sudden there was a complete sense of release. I had gotten to the point where I felt personally responsible for lost people around the world, and there was no particular location I didn't feel responsible for. But as this focus came on Ecuador, there was a very interesting, strange sense of release from my responsibility to other places. It wasn't that I was no longer concerned for those other places, but I no longer felt a sense of personal duty or responsibility there. I became convinced that my responsibility was in Ecuador. This to me became a personal call—to a specific location. It was a very divine experience.

Compare this with the experience of his colleague, for whom the missionary calling represented a dramatic shift in motivation:

Probably the basic motivation for getting the training I had was a good job, good money. I mean, let's face it—I could have been making $150,000 in a few years. But somewhere along the line, that whole appeal just left. It just seemed so empty. And it was then that we started to attend a missions-minded church. And you know how the Lord uses different people and different things. Well, through the messages of the pastor, we were just challenged over and over again to make a commitment, especially to mission work. It was at that time that some HCJB missionaries came on furlough, and presented the work. And I was very intrigued. Well, the more we prayed, the more we realized it was the right thing to do. The more we considered it, Quito just seemed to be it. And we had said that regardless of what anybody else says, we in our own selves had to *know*—Is it or isn't it God's will? And then we got the assurance, yes, this was it.

For other HCJB members, the call came about not so much as an experience of being drawn to the mission field, but grew out of a sense of dissatisfaction or being trapped by one's present circumstances and life trajectory. As one narrator put it, he felt trapped by his own security:

Being a tenured teacher is a desired plum. It is just a nice thing. I had that. We had bought a house, and furnished it. We had bought a brand new car. It was an air-conditioned station wagon. And one day, I was driving down the freeway in this insulated, air-conditioned tin can, and I just felt trapped. Trapped by financial responsibilities. Trapped by the classroom situation—I was set up to teach the same thing forever. The security became a trap, to prevent me from ever leaving and being free to do what I wanted to do. And I started to see that in our home, and our home furnishings—which we were buying on time—we were just parroting what everyone else was doing. We bought a new car because everyone else our age was buying a new car. And I could see we were just fitting in to a cultural thing that was just a dead end. I'm so glad I'm out of the trap. I'm a little worried about retirement, but there's a God out there who cares. He's taken care of me up until now, and he's not going to stop when I turn sixty-five.

I was having a lot of trouble at the job I was at. I didn't make a whole lot of money, and things were tight. And we were just more or less existing. I mean the job was down, everything was down, and I wanted to improve myself. So finally I said, "All right, I surrender." So I applied to HCJB.

One problem with describing patterns of *individual* calling is that many people don't make important decisions as isolated individual actors, but as couples or families or members of extended social networks. In the case of husbands and wives, ideally both must feel called to the same place. For some Mission couples, the potential conflict over a call (or the lack of it) was apparently resolved by the ideology of "the husband being head of the wife." The wife was assumed to have a kind of derivative call through her marriage to a missionary:

I feel if the Lord leads your husband to do something, he's leading you, too. I don't think he would call one without the other. He wouldn't lead him to Venezuela, and you to Chile.

I'm not playing games or anything. The truth is I married a man who wanted to be a missionary. I never knew that the highest calling was being a missionary. I just fell in love with a man who was going to be one.

We were married there, we settled down, and we started a dairy farm. We had children. I think it was four or five years later, Frank got a call—very clear—that the Lord wanted him into mission work. And I, of course, went along with him.

But a number of Mission women were far less sanguine about appropriating their husband's call. Sometimes a call had to be negotiated between the two of them over a period of years—both before and after they had come to work in Ecuador. One missionary wife described such a process:

> I think that it takes a certain amount of guts to be a missionary. It takes a certain amount of independence to stick with it. But in my case, it wasn't guts, it wasn't independence. It was obedience to what I thought the Bible taught me about my husband. I'm not, I have not been a particularly independent person. I did it because I thought it was right. I don't feel I did it because of any great spiritual call.
>
> When my husband got this idea, we had already bought a house. I had really wanted to redecorate, and so one of my really good friends and I, we just made a project of that. We did the living room, and went out and bought furniture, and paneled walls and that kind of stuff. I had never done anything like that, and it was a very exciting thing for me, because it was an expression of *me*. And I had probably had that done for about ten months when Andy really brought it up strongly about coming to Ecuador. I think that was one thing that really bothered me—that I had just gotten a chance to express myself, and I was going to have to get rid of it all, and throw away everything that showed what was "me." That bothered me. Another thing was that I come from such a strong family. I had had a real close relationship with my grandparents, my aunts and uncles, and that has been such an important thing in the formation of my life, in my character. I wanted my kids to have the same thing, and I knew if we came to Ecuador they would never have that chance. That was hard for me.
>
> But he kept talking about it, and kept talking about it, and so because I am an analytical person and he was talking about these feelings, I said, you know, "What's the motive? What's your motive here?" I questioned his motives very seriously. He's a man who likes adventure. He likes to do different things. He likes to meet new people. So I sat him down, and I said, "All right, you tell me, besides the fact that it's fun, and you like the mountains, and you like another culture, and you like travel —you tell me how you think God has really led you, in your life." And he had never had to do that. He had never done that. That really made him start thinking. He started to think back to his grandmother, and how his parents always helped other people, how they helped the missionaries, and how he had wanted to be a missionary pilot when he'd heard about the five missionaries killed by the Auca Indians. That was good for him to have to recount all that, because he had never really thought it through that way. It was all just kind of like a big adventure. And I wasn't ready to come to Ecuador just for a big adventure. So once he really outlined it for me, I said, "All right, I'll go with you. I can see that there have been ways in which God has been leading your interest to Ecuador specifically. Not just to missions, but to Ecuador. Once he was able to outline it, I said, "All right, I'll go." But it was horrible.

Another quite common pattern of calling was a sort of two-stage call. In this pattern, the first stage is typically an early, generalized "commitment to full-time Christian service," sometimes occurring in conjunction with a conversion experience. The second stage involves a response to circumstances presenting the actual opportunity of coming to Ecuador with HCJB. From that later point of view, the first commitment tends to take on new significance and specificity, and is then recognized and labeled as a missionary call. The same sort of reconstruction process may characterize what happens in the lives of missionaries who gradually grow into an awareness of a calling, after coming to the mission field. In retrospect, such a person can look back and reframe earlier experiences in terms of "God working out his calling." From case to case, the content as well as the structure of what eventually gets defined as a missionary call varies considerably, albeit within the outlines of general patterns.

Second-generation missionaries tend to report experiences of calling that don't neatly fall into the more general patterns, but may combine elements of more than one. Some missionary kids report feeling an early and definite call to do just what their parents are doing. Others reject their parents' vocation—for a while—then end up doing something very similar anyway. Some flounder on the foreign shores of what was their parents' country of origin, then see the missionary career as a way of returning home. Others never feel that they have a homeland, because they have grown up feeling set apart and different, both internally and externally. But sometimes they are able to turn a handicap into an advantage, insofar as their rootlessness makes them more autonomous and more adaptable to a third or fourth culture.

In the preceding discussion, I have attempted to sketch the various formations of a personal and social landscape over against which a missionary call normally occurs. But given that something does occur in these people (whether suddenly and dramatically, or gradually through ordinary circumstances), an important question remains. What effect does the call have on a them—that is, in relation to the moral career? What is it that is transformed as a "missionary self" begins to emerge?

The Call as Transformation: Preparation and Passage

To begin with, the call tends to alter the way a person views the future—both the future of the world, and his or her own destiny within it. Events that lie ahead seem to confront the called one with a new sense of urgency and immediacy, rendered in the apocalyptic images of global spiritual conflict and the rescue of dying souls. In the moment of the call, the future no longer appears as an indefinite extension, development through time, or even a cyclical repetition of past and present realities. The future emerges, rather, as the last act in a moral drama played out on the final stage of human history—not a drama to be watched, but one to be engaged in and brought about. That stage encompasses the whole world, pictured as a vast mission field. As the called one begins to anticipate a life of moral confrontation in the mission arena, the future takes on transcendent personal significance. All other specific issues regarding one's life direction (what to study, whom to marry, whether to have children, and so forth) become subordinated to the question, "How must I prepare to fulfill my call to the mission field?"

The call also changes the way a person views his or her past. As with the conversion experience, the missionary candidate begins to reinterpret key biographical influences in the light of a new awareness of destiny. She may perceive God's agency in a fresh way, as if it had been there guiding her life all along, though not properly noticed or understood until now: "Finally I could see that God had this planned for me all of my life." Experiences that previously may have appeared as distressing liabilities—growing up in a poor family, suffering the loss of a parent, even the disappointment of unrequited love—now become assets. They fall into place like puzzle pieces.

In addition to changing a person's perspective on the past and future, the call also shifts her view of the world at large, and of relationships with people in it. In one sense, the world gets larger. The aspiring missionary's scope of interest expands beyond the narrower boundaries of her family, friends, church, town, and nation. She becomes newly, acutely concerned with "the world." But in another sense, the called one's global view seems to become constricted and oversimplified, bifurcating human cultures and communities into two realms: (1) all those historically saturated with the evangelical message; (2) everyplace else—collectively, "the mission field." The evangelical world in the home country also gets divided into two classes: (1) those set-apart ones called to the foreign field; (2) all the ordinary Christians who must stay home to support the missionaries.

When Mission members look back and reconstruct their missionary call, they often portray it as a singular and rather crystallized event—though the experience may involve a process such as an "argument with God." But really, the period surrounding a decision to embark on a missionary career often entails many complex events, circumstances, and personal influences stretching out over a number of years. Moreover, the interlude between the call and final arrival in Ecuador is crucial for understanding how a person who feels called begins to shift her identity toward a new reference group, and gradually takes on the mantle of the missionary.

One narrator provides a fine illustration of this process. The story of her calling culminates in the experience of attending, with her college boyfriend, a week-long missionary conference sponsored by Inter-Varsity Christian Fellowship (successor of the Student Volunteer Movement for Foreign Missions) on the campus of the University of Illinois at Urbana. At the conference the two are challenged by prominent missionary speakers, including Elisabeth Elliot. Both of them sense God's call and make a commitment to become foreign missionaries. However, this spiritual high point only initiates a long process that will eventually lead them to Ecuador:

> We went back from Urbana, and there were years in between. We got married, we finished school, and all that. And finally we got to that point where it was, "Now what are we going to do?" We decided to go to Trinity School of Missions, and I view that as a very strategic decision. Because once we pulled up roots and went there, it was like we were going in a different direction from then on. We made some deep, long-lasting friendships with other missions-minded people. And there was just kind of an excitement. Up until then, all of our friends thought we were oddballs, really. I mean, they had heard of missionaries, but to really be considering something like that was strange. But once we got to Trinity and got with people who were discussing missions in the world today, and trends, and that sort of thing—it was exciting. A lot of our friends were talking about Asia. You know, there was a lot of talk about peoples in Asia that just have no witness at all. There was a kind of restlessness. We were only twenty-four and twenty-five—not that old when I think back now—but we felt a sense of urgency. We felt that we had wasted a lot of time. We had been married two or three years, and we felt that we needed to find out what God had for us. We felt that "pulling" again, that call to missionary work.

Overall, HCJB members received missionary calls at a median age of 19.5 years, but did not actually arrive in Ecuador until a median age of 28.8 years. On the average, then, there was almost a ten-year interlude that occurred in most of their lives—coinciding with a profoundly significant time in the life cycle with respect to adult identity formation, establishing independence, the search for intimacy, acquiring job skills, professional socialization, and so forth. In their larger culture of origin, the years between the ages of twenty and thirty tend to be promoted as a period of youthful hedonism. These are the years to "find yourself," and have fun doing so. Most major decisions—where to go to college, what to study, whether and whom to marry, what sort of work to do, when and where to travel, where to live— are subordinated to the question, "What do I want out of life?" The data on Mission members suggest, however, that most of them pass through these young-adult years asking themselves a different question. While surrounded by the same youth culture and confronting the same dilemmas and decisions as their peers, the question they continue to pose is: "How will this help or hinder my preparation to serve God as a missionary?"

Consider, for example, that most missionaries felt the call before they were married. As we have seen, complications can arise when a would-be missionary marries someone with no similar calling. But the fact is that almost all of them chose mates with an equally fervent interest in, or call to mission service. The following account is typical:

> It was during that time that I first noticed my wife-to-be. She, too, was the kind of a person that was sort of set apart, even at a Christian college—very intense and a dedicated type of person, wanting to follow the Lord. Both of us had strong feelings about missions. I was part of the Foreign Missions Fellowship all through college, and so was she.

A good number of missionaries told of rejecting, or being rejected by, a potential mate for the given reason that the other did not feel called to missionary service. Sometimes this reason was not clearly perceived until afterward, but it was nevertheless given great importance.

Consider, also, that most HCJB members felt the call before they would ordinarily have decided what major to pursue in college. This helps to explain why about 75 percent chose religious studies—Bible, theology, missions, or Christian education— as either a first or a second major field in college. The decision about what to major in was not always easy:

> I had some real difficulties learning how to study in a college setting and that all came to a crisis near the end of the first semester of my sophomore year. I pretty much knew that I was failing miserably. It was an awful, awful feeling. I had five subjects, and there was only one subject in which I had a C or above. The whole world was crushing in on me. And then I remember going to my room one day—my roommate wasn't there—and just falling on my knees, crushed before the Lord. I just said, "Lord, I don't know what it's all about. What's going on? I don't know where I've failed—if I've failed you, or who I've failed. But at this point in my life, I just have to know your direction. What do you want of me? You know that I have not been rebellious against you. I have not been rebellious against my parents. But Lord, I am not making it. I am academically crushed." And that day, I remember the Lord saying, "OK, what I want you to do is to give the rest of your college life here to the study of my Word." And I said, "Lord, what is it you mean? Do you mean I'm supposed to make Bible my major?" And I clearly remember the Lord indicating to me in my heart that that was the thing—that if I made that decision, very clearly, and began to practice it, my whole life results would change. And so I got up off my knees, dried my eyes, and said, "This is what it's going to be. I'm going to be a Bible major, and

I'll add a few of these other things, skills and so on, as I can." Well, every semester from there on was "up."

The second most frequent college major chosen was premedical science or nursing. Clearly, HCJB selects a disproportionately large number of missionaries from health-related fields to staff its hospitals and clinics. But what is interesting is that among those who entered the formal study of health-related fields, most said they did so with the specific intent to use this technical knowledge in the service of a missionary vocation. For example:

> I went to medical school with missions specifically in mind. I had no other plans. Medi-
> cine was just a tool I was going to bring along. There was never any question, throughout
> medical school, about whether I would be a missionary—although there was a question
> about whether I would become a doctor! When I got out of medical school, the only ques-
> tion was when and where.

The extended period between the missionary call experience and actual departure for the foreign field is a time during which the called one's social identity and inner sense of self gradually shift—away from the home group, and toward the missionary world. During this time of anticipation, many of them attend missionary conferences and get involved in student missions groups, make numerous inquiries to missionaries and mission boards (often with initially disappointing results). Not uncommonly, the young, idealistic, recently-called, would-be missionary experiences a huge gap between his or her own excitement to embark on a missionary career and the perceived eagerness of an established mission organization to bring him or her to the field. One such couple, now with HCJB, felt a call and soon afterward applied to the China Inland Mission:

> By then we had three children. And China Inland Mission wrote back and said the lan-
> guage study was very difficult, and with three children they didn't think we should even
> try to go to the mission field. J. Hudson Taylor would turn over in his grave! So the Lord
> closed that door.

A fair number of the Mission members recalled similar disappointments in the aftermath of a personal call experience. Typical of these accounts is a student or young professional who "says yes to God" in a burst of idealistic passion and emotional release. She tells people about it—friends, family, her pastor—but gets mixed results. Others try to temper her excitement. Her parents say she has gone a bit too far, and suggest that "God can use you here at home." Upon reflection, these reactions make sense to the would-be missionary because, after all, a call is supposed to entail sacrifice. It means putting God first before loved ones. It means being set apart. Still, she imagines that a mission organization will understand and respond with enthusiasm. So she writes to the Mission, and months pass with no answer. Finally, she receive application forms. She finalizes her decision to apply to HCJB, fills out the forms, gathers letters of recommendation, makes plans, and announces her intentions to family, friends, and church contacts. Then again she hears nothing from the Mission—sometimes for a period of several months. As one Mission member recalls:

If I had not been convinced in my heart that God wanted me to go to Ecuador with HCJB, I would have given up at that point. But God was preparing me, testing my commitment and patience. I had to learn to wait for him to give me instructions.

Finally, after being formally accepted into Mission membership, the candidate enters the great wilderness of "raising support"—garnering financial pledges from churches and friends to cover her salary and a piece of the Mission's administrative overhead. Here, again, is a crucial stage in the process of becoming a missionary. For the first time, the called one is publicly set apart and labeled a missionary. Others begin to see and treat her differently, as the candidate must learn how to appropriately solicit, receive, and acknowledge "offerings for God's work." Moreover, raising support tends to be construed as the final test of one's calling, on the premise that if God has genuinely selected someone for missionary service abroad, then he will supply the support. Otherwise, perhaps the candidate's calling was not genuine—or else further preparation, spiritual tempering, and molding of character are required. Some people attempt to make the test more difficult for God (while preserving a modicum of self respect) by never actually asking for money. Of course, it is well understood in evangelical churches that when a missionary candidate presents herself and the work to which she feels called, she is—in so doing—asking for donations. But the etiquette of raising support in some churches demands that the would-be supporters inquire, unsolicited, about the missionary's needs before the candidate herself is forced to mention her need for money.

Other benchmarks must be passed in the process of becoming a missionary. For HCJB recruits, formal candidate orientation sessions are required. And, as mentioned earlier, in many churches a rite of passage known as a commissioning service is conducted, during which the home congregation officially confirms the candidate's missionary call, promises support through prayers and financial gifts, and then sends him or her out as the church's representative in the harvest of souls abroad. After such an official setting-apart, the missionary's relation to the home community is never quite the same again.

Finally, there comes a great equalizer—a kind of purgatory known as language school. Most HCJB members attended language school in San Jose, Costa Rica, although a number of recent cohorts have done their stint in Texas. Language school is not quite the mission field, but it is a long way from home. Symbolically and actually, it is a place half-way down. In language school, neophyte missionaries from diverse professional backgrounds come together to learn what young children will take for granted in the host country: how to speak and understand what others say. It is often a period of mortification, of feeling stripped of the props that have sustained one's identity as a socially competent adult. Language school is the most crucial preparation of all, but it can appear to render all other preparations useless. Finally, the old familiar set-apartness is submerged, and a new kind of strangerhood—symbolized by foreign words and phrases mispronounced and barely understood—emerges.

In this chapter, I have focused on how the missionary call converges with the theme of being set apart that runs through various layers of the social, psychological, and religious experience in missionaries' earlier lives. Before someone can be called as a missionary, he or she has to be conscious of what it means to be called—not only in dynamic personal terms, but in cultural terms. That is to say, in order for a religious experience to be interpreted as a call, a specific social and cultural-historical context must be present within which a call to missionary strangerhood may sensibly occur. Typically, the evangelical subculture provides this context through a mythology of missionary heroes and through opportunities to know contemporary missionaries personally, hear their testimonies, form impressions of the lives they lead, of how they were called, of the kind of people they are, and so forth. Sometimes a call seems to emerge naturally out of an individual's deep-seated motivational structure—a religious drive or a developed sense of duty, an obligation, a destiny, a parent's footsteps. Sometimes extraordinary circumstances precipitate a call—traumatic events such as a parent's death—which seem to foreshorten the future, heighten the significance of transcendent values, and strike the psychological resonances of guilt and sacrifice.

In any event, the call shifts a person's interpretive frame away from the patterns and possibilities of a conventional, taken-for-granted world. As the called one gradually becomes part of the missionaries' set-apart world, the call is redefined and elaborated in the new group's terms. The experience that first sets a person apart will become, in the new context, a virtual criterion for full and permanent membership in the missionary group. And as we shall see, the sense of a call becomes a key to the missionary's interpretation of her subsequent experience in the foreign field. Significantly, missionaries who feel called are more likely to persist in the face of disappointment, more likely to embrace their multifaceted strangerhood as an enduring identity. The next chapter of this study is about living out a calling—in the company of apostles and other strangers—on the mission field itself.

4

Living Out the Call on the Mission Field

It's obvious that missionaries are set apart. But if missionaries are chosen by God, it's not because they're more capable, it's just that they're more available. They're more open to going where God wants them to go—open to going out and being vulnerable and helpless.

For a non-Christian, it can be devastating to be a foreigner. For Christians no, because the Lord has asked us to be foreigners. We are passing through, by definition. . . . We are called out, and we are different, right from our calling.

This chapter examines the elaboration of moral careers on the mission field. As we have seen in their narratives of early life, missionaries often see themselves as having been set apart in moral and psychological terms, before they leave home. On foreign soil they tend to assume a cultural posture that dramatizes their prior strangerhood in several dimensions. First, they approach the host culture as an abstract matrix of *otherness* in which to develop a personal mission. Second, they look back on their home country from an expatriate's remove. Third, these missionaries become members of an ambiguous community—an enclave whose character derives from a shared sense of cultural and moral set-apartness, even while its identity is bound up with the ideal of a mission that is to breach all barriers, transcend all boundaries, with the gospel of Christ. As we shall see, HCJB missionaries often appropriate the rhetoric of strangerhood to interpret the development of their calling in Ecuador. As they do so, the personal meaning of their call is enhanced, but also changed in unexpected ways. Themes of divine calling and strangerhood continue to organize the new (and often dissonant) facts of their experience, but are in turn profoundly reshaped by them.

The pages to follow will show how the missionary-as-stranger develops in the compound of *language* and *membership*.[1] Missionary talk will be understood as a form of symbolic mapping of social and cultural territories, as it domesticates problematic new experience and manages the conditions of *otherness* that arise from the missionary's ambiguous membership and conflicting interests in various communities. In order to interpret conversation as social mapping in this way, we must see how it employs images that demarcate a group's external boundaries as well as its internal structure; how it locates the speaker's own (often shifting) positions with respect to audiences in groups of interest to him.[2] The stranger's conversation thus produces a personal cognitive map that not only represents the social terrain he confronts, but also reflects the scheme of his own identity (Schutz, 1944).

To be clear, my focus on social membership and language does not imply adherence to a specific theory of identity, its nature and development. My goal is not to present the missionary data as evidence for a more general accounting of social and psychological reality, neither to construct nor deconstruct a particular version of the missionary self. Rather the idea of personal identity, as I shall apply it to these evangelical missionaries and to their self-understanding, may be fruitfully interpreted from different perspectives that coalesce around key metaphors of the self. These metaphors include such notions as marginality and rebirth, but also: dramaturgy, the mirror, the story, the journey.

Dramaturgical accounts[3] of identity, in particular, tend to highlight the performances and processes by which a self emerges in a given relationship at a given moment. In this view, identity is plastic and dependent upon audience, context, and interests. A person's own ideas about himself or herself are "mental predicates," about which Kenneth Gergen, expounding on Wittgenstein (1958) and Austin (1962), makes a provocative point:

> [M]ental talk is largely performative—that is, it does not mirror or map an independent reality but is a functioning element in the social process itself. In the case of mental predicates one is thus invited to look not for their referents but for their consequences in social life. . . . [The] mental world becomes elaborated as various interest groups within the culture seek to warrant or justify their accounts of the world. In effect, our vocabulary of self shifts as pragmatic exigencies dictate (Gergen, 1990:71–72).

In phenomenological terms, it could be said that missionaries manage multiple selves: There is a self confined to a given social sphere of interest in the present; another haunts the memory as a self that was; still another inhabits the imagination as a self that might have been—or one that could yet become. Testimonies of religious conversion offer prime examples of warranted social performances made possible through the pragmatic management of these separate—even radically discontinuous—versions of the self. The same paradigm applies, in many ways, to the transformations of missionary identity in the foreign setting.

And yet, for evangelical missionaries especially, the construct of a *transcendent* self becomes an ideological and narrative necessity. The plausibility of their religious vocation rests, after all, on the notion of the individual person—a *moral being* who stands alone unmasked and responsible, a core self who moves through the transitions of life and persists in the hereafter. For related reasons, some sociologists of religion reject the Goffmanesque view of identity-as-performance, as it seems to obscure the significant ways in which religion delineates both the framework of a persistent self and the boundaries of social groups in which the self is nurtured throughout life. Along these lines, Mol (1978) argues that if religion is to be understood as an integrating force in the life of a person, then identity is best viewed as a "stable niche" in a social ecology. Ultimate values, beliefs, and faith are foundations—not projections—of identity.[4]

As an alternative to the symbolic-interactionist account, life-course narrative theories offer a more integrative general approach to identity and development—one that leads to a different (but finally complementary) sort of insight into the lives of missionaries. Here, personal identity emerges as a tale to be told, rather than a repertoire to be enacted (see Rosenwald and Ochberg, 1992; Cohler, 1988; MacAdams, 1985; Kotre, 1984). The story of one's life is always being rewritten in the light of new associations and new experiences. Unexpected events, ironic reversals of character, twists and turns of plot all produce discontinuities in the life narrative. These vicissitudes often turn out to be even more significant for understanding the story than its large underlying themes. Nevertheless, the story moves according to its own *telos*—toward coherence, meaning, integrity, aesthetic sensibility, and intelligibility. In short, the primary locus of identity is the *text*, rather than the *context*, of the emergent self. Still, the self is never free from context; life-as-story implies a form in which the person exists simultaneously as narrator, internal audience, and primary character.

These alternative notions of personal identity raise a number of questions about missionaries and the significance of their life work. Is there room here for missionaries to be seen as authentic persons who make choices in good faith, and who own responsibility for their choices in relation to other human beings? Are missionaries to be unmasked as conscious manipulators of impressions, advancing their own moral-entrepreneurial interests while reducing other people to objects that merely sustain the artifice of missionaries' own identity? Or could it be that missionaries remain basically unaware of the real program of their lives, as it follows some larger logic of social evolution through hegemonic relations and cultural conflict? Does the moral career of the missionary—with its guiding personal myths and symbolic architecture of identity—finally dissolve into false consciousness?

These are provocative questions that are carried along in the subtext of the entire discussion to follow; while I hope that my observations speak to these questions, I have no definite answers to them. Missionaries are a complex and diverse lot; my goal cannot be to discover their "true motivation." Like other social actors, they at various times respond to different motives, some more conscious than others, any one of which might appear sufficient to explain their actions (Schlesinger, 1974).[5] Rather, I have two agendas in mind. First, I examine missionaries' spoken and written words from the point of view of their several audiences—including the internal audience of a reflective self—in order to understand the complex meaning of *being a missionary*, both for these individuals and for the evangelical community in which they are suspended. Second, I treat these materials as fragments of a story—with linkages to older stories both large and small—whose driving purpose is to achieve an internally coherent telling of a human life.

Ideals of Redemption and the Redemption of Ideals

New HCJB missionaries tend to arrive in the field with an overlay of idealistic notions about the work they will be doing. In subtle ways of which they are not always aware, their expectations are bound up with images given in the evangelical subculture and made personally relevant by the earlier sequence of their own moral careers. These images may be situated historically, but they continue to be reinforced by media portrayals—of both secular and evangelical varieties.

An excellent example of contemporary missionary myth-making by a major instrument of popular culture may be found in a 1982 *Time* magazine cover story entitled *The New Missionary*, written by Richard Ostling. While in many ways informative and balanced, the story includes passages that embrace the missionary worldview in its own terms. We read that missionaries "are seeking to spread the good news of Christ . . . where the demons worshiped by animistic tribes are almost a palpable presence" (Ostling, 1982:44). The missionary adventure as a mythic form stands out especially in the way Ostling tells the story of Ray and Helen Elliott, Wycliffe Bible translators sent to the Ixil tribe in Guatemala. We imagine the Elliotts as they leave home in Independence, Kansas, and arrive in Guatemala to settle "with their three children into a two-room dirt-floor sharecropper's cabin" (Ostling, 1982:47). For two years they try to befriend their Ixil neighbors, but are met with "stony rejection." Then a crisis occurs. Two local boys are horribly burned in a fire, and Helen comes to their aid. After trying to undo a "ghastly native treatment" (neighbors had smeared the wounds with a paste of lime, wood ash, and motor oil), she wraps the children in sterilized sheets and gives them pain killers and antibiotics. The story rises to a climax:

> When Helen returned after putting her own children to bed, she discovered that a witch doctor had ripped off the bandages and was rubbing hot pepper on the wounds, invoking Christian saints and Mayan deities, all the while drinking rum. In a scene reminiscent of Elijah confronting the prophets of Baal, Helen told the parents that they must choose between her treatment and the witch doctor's.
>
> The parents chose Helen. As the boys hovered near death, she prayed as never before. "This was the chance for people to experience the living Gospel," she recalls. But she adds, "my family's lives were at stake." The boys survived and Helen was so besieged by the sick that she soon became the village's practical nurse, delivering hundreds of babies, suturing hundreds of wounds. The Ixils began to accept the Elliotts as prophets of a loving god (Ostling, 1982:47).

This is very much the sort of background imagery that sets an internal stage against which HCJB members initially view their own work and attempt to construct a missionary *persona*. The story contains key elements of traditional missionary strangerhood: sacrifice, set-apartness and rejection, other-worldly conflict in an exotic cultural arena, analogy to a Biblical adventure, danger, sickness and sin, healing and redemption. In its moral bifurcation of the world, the story even implicates demon rum—a rhetorical flourish reminiscent of American sawdust-trail revivalism. As missionary rhetoric, in fact, this passage stands as an exemplary genre piece. It could almost be lifted verbatim from the pages of *Time* and set into an evangelical missionary prayer letter. Probably only three changes would be necessary: The witch doctor should be invoking "Catholic" not "Christian" saints; the Ixils should accept the Elliotts as "messengers" not "prophets"; and "a loving god" should be "the loving God."

With this sort of imagery in mind, it is easy to see how HCJB missionaries' narratives about their own success (or the lack of it) in their calling derive meaning from cultural as well as personal symbolism attached to missionary work. On its face, doing missionary work is a means to the end of world evangelization. But in psychological terms, the mission field is also an end in itself—a mythical place and inner destiny to which a previous life of set-apartness has led. In the lives of many missionaries, that place is forever elusive; the story does not always turn out as it did for the Elliotts in Guatemala.

James Clifford (1982) offers an outstanding historical example of such underpinnings in the life of Maurice Leenhardt (1878–1954), missionary and ethnographer of Melanesia in the early part of this century.[6] Leenhardt's childhood was marked by the pain of a brilliant and imaginative mind that failed in school due to a physical impairment, a substantial loss of hearing following an acute illness. In the early pages of the story, we find the young Maurice in Christian boarding school, feeling utterly abandoned by his parents, staring out his window at "dark and sad" buildings set close together on narrow streets. His letters convey a yearning for fresh air, "a whole sky, to see trees, expanse" (Clifford, 1982:20). In answer to these longings, Clifford says, the missionary vocation began to take shape in Leenhardt's adolescent mind:

> [Maurice] had listened with fascination to accounts by a visiting Moravian evangelist of work among the Eskimos of Labrador and the islanders of the Pacific. During the years that followed, the boy's "dreams wandered over white ice and blue ocean . . . ," an immaculate vision of opening horizons and freedom. Prior to his boarding school experience, the idea of evangelical work was linked to adventure and escape. This was the heyday of Livingstone, Stanley, Brazza, and the romance of exploration. But during this first long separation from his family, Maurice identified the mission career with a personal, religious need. It sanctified the pathos of separation and transmuted a general desire for adventure into an image of approved work in the service of Christ. It was through the idea of missions, Leenhardt said, that he came to love God. The idea provided a clear spiritual direction for his unruly, adolescent energies (Clifford, 1982:17–18).

In 1902, Leenhardt was ordained as a missionary to New Caledonia. At his commissioning ceremony, he rhapsodized that "the Christian church seems nowhere so pure as in missions," and reveled in anticipation of his "privilege of sowing in a virgin land rather than incessantly pruning sprouts from sick roots."

> The Leenhardts departed with hearts full of faith. Their aim was to participate in the life of a faraway land. . . . Perhaps they hoped, half consciously, for a clean slate, the pure, open spaces Maurice Leenhardt dreamed of as a schoolboy. Many missionaries have desired such a place, a spiritual clearing where religious life can be simple and authentic, where the Christian evangelist can lay the foundation of a noble edifice. Such dreams receive rough treatment on contact with a culture possessing its own prior historical and religious traditions. Nor do such dreams leave much space for a very clear idea of the colonial milieu and the agonies of culture contact (Clifford, 1982:29).

After a quarter-century of service, Maurice Leenhardt left his mission work and returned to France in a state of melancholy. He had discovered only that the missionary movement—and indirectly he, himself—was at the core of the "colonial problem." Years later, a student at the Sorbonne asked him skeptically, "How many people did you *really* convert during all that time out there?" Leenhardt pondered for a moment and replied, "Maybe one." And to be sure his readers understand, the biographer adds, "There could be little doubt that the 'one' in question was himself" (Clifford, 1982:1).

This vignette makes two very significant points about the moral careers of missionaries—even those bearing little resemblance to it on the surface. First, missionaries' life stories begin with an inner sojourn long preceding their actual foreign encounter, and this shapes their intensely personal point of view. Second, though missionaries set out to transform other souls in the outer regions of the world, in the end they are often the ones who must undergo transformation—in the inner regions of the self. For Leenhardt, his own "conversion" came about when the "pure open spaces" of his young missionary dreams confronted a Melanesian world defiled by the colonial Christendom of which he was inevitably a part. Where HCJB missionaries are concerned, a different, but no less significant alteration occurs. From the vantage point of a personal myth, mundane work in the Mission corporation often appears disconnected from their original ideals of soul-winning and world-redemption. Ironically, work in the Mission may loom as a barrier to becoming a *real missionary* in the manner once envisioned:

> All those years of wanting to be a missionary—I imagined it would be wearing a pith helmet, carrying a big Bible under my arm, living in a hut with a grass roof and no floor, no telephone, no electricity. That's what I visualized a missionary would be. I didn't realize what I would be doing down here, even after I learned about HCJB. I still thought I would be a church planter. They put me in the business office. I said, "I'm not a very good business man, but I'll sure try it." What I'm doing here isn't really that much different than what I was doing back home. But you know, I do try to help people. I give out Bibles. I do the best I can do.

> During my first term, the job I was doing was just not my idea of being a true missionary. I could not see any spiritual results from it. I finally decided there was no point to it and I was going to resign from the Mission. Then at the last minute we had a church meeting at our house, during the weekend right when I was getting ready to present my resignation. In fact, I already had some drafts of it written. And this fellow from the countryside— whom I had never seen before and never saw again—just stood and spoke. He told how the Lord had drawn him and his whole family to himself through HCJB radio programming. And suddenly, all the things I had been saying—about how it's not worth it—just fell apart. In fact, I was so moved that I had to rush out of the room and go back to the bedroom and just sob for about an hour. I couldn't even say goodbye to the people. It was the Lord very gently saying, "This is my business, and I'll take care of the results. Just hang in there." I did get into a different job in the Mission. The Lord caught me in time, and it would have been very foolish and very reactionary to leave at that point. But the Lord is very loving and gentle in the way he brings us through things like that.

> I spent four months in Texas trying to learn Spanish. But I get down here, and everything I do is in English! That is a great frustration to me. It's more than a frustration, it's embarrassing. I mean, you meet people and they say, "How long have you been in Ecuador?" and you say, "Six years"—and you can barely even say it Spanish. I feel that if for any reason I would leave here and go back to the States, that would be the reason— if I just couldn't handle it any more, living here and not speaking Spanish. It's a great barrier. There are things that I cannot get done that I need to get done in this country. If I had Spanish, I would probably be meeting with the President of Ecuador, and with cabinet officers. I would make sure that socially I was in that circle. I know I could do that, because I have those skills. I know how to do that, but I don't have the language. And whenever I go to a Spanish church, I feel like a first-class hypocrite. I sit there and act like

I'm enjoying it and I don't know one thing the guy's talking about. And then they'll call on me to pray because I'm a missionary. I get so embarrassed. I've got a prayer written on a card that I give. I can read it. But I just feel bad most of the time.

I think HCJB has been a very good mission. But we are on the verge of leaving the status of *mission* and becoming something else—maybe a business corporation, maybe a machine, maybe a monster.

Accounts of arrival and beginning work with HCJB in Ecuador often follow a theme of initial disillusionment, leading up to a renegotiation of the calling and a rebuilding of the missionary image. As part of this development, the new member typically learns to appreciate elder colleagues and gradually fuses his missionary *persona* with the identity of the Mission community as it comes to exist for him. The Mission organization assists individuals in this process in several ways, beginning with its use of rhetoric in orientation documents. Consider a passage from the HCJB *Worker's Manual*:

EXHORTATION TO NEW MISSIONARIES . . . to be read and meditated upon as they begin their ministry with our mission.

Dear Colleague:

You are now entering into actual service in a missionary fellowship. As missionaries of the Cross of Christ, we follow in the train of such stalwarts as William Carey, David Livingstone, Hudson Taylor, Adoniram Judson, J. G. Paton, Jonathan Goforth and a great host of others who through their consecrated zeal, passion for lost souls, willingness to endure hardship and tireless concentration on the job to be done have given us examples that should inspire us to 'give every ounce of energy, every moment of our time and every atom of our being' to the fulfillment of the Great Commission of our Lord and Savior Jesus Christ. May we who serve the Lord as missionaries in this latter part of the 20th century be endowed with the same noble characteristics that those outstanding missionary predecessors manifested in other generations. . . .

God has given you a glorious privilege in choosing you to be one of His ambassadors to the 'regions beyond'. . . . Be sure to keep your heart constantly open to the Spirit's leading; be sure to keep your passion for lost souls ever aglow; pray constantly that your personality, disposition, influence and daily life before all men (nationals, fellow-missionaries, etc.) will always make others praise God for you.

This exhortation makes it clear, perhaps even more by its idiom than by its content, that the Mission recognizes how important it is for individuals to develop a distinctively *missionary* identity in line with traditional imagery. It also recognizes how essential it is for the organization to establish continuity between the missions movement of "other generations" (i.e., nineteenth-century missions heroes) and the current endeavors of HCJB. Through the use of special language, the Mission leadership attempts to harness the individual ideal of *being a missionary* to motivate routine work as a member of the organization. The rhetoric of personal missionary vocation thus serves an important function for the Mission group.

As if anticipating the problem that new missionaries sometimes feel their job does not sufficiently distinguish them from the people they left back home, the manual goes on to incorporate the people at home as significant, too, insofar as they contribute to the Mission's efforts through prayer and financial gifts. In effect, all activity linked to the organization is infused with spiritual meaning and urgency. As the metaphor shifts from colonial diplomacy to military conflict, we learn that the "ambassadors to the regions beyond" are supported by "prayer warriors in this battle against the prince of the power of the air":

> A missionary work like ours is a combination of the efforts of many people on the field and at home. . . . The routine work in office, studio, hospital and laboratory must have the strength and inspiration of a host of faithful prayer warriors in this battle against the 'prince of the power of the air.' The outstanding element in the personnel comprising our organization should be that of deep devotion and sacrificial effort in the greatest cause entrusted to man.

Ostensibly, the Mission provides corporate roles that channel individuals' subjective sense of calling. However, some roles are by nature less conducive than others to the performance of a personal missionary repertoire, especially when the performance requires a foreign culture as its audience. For example, in some sectors of the Mission, work is conducted almost exclusively in English so that members interact with Ecuadorians only rarely and superficially in the course of their jobs.

> Because of my work situation and the responsibilities I have in the Mission, I don't think I will ever come to the point of really being able to communicate in Spanish on an intimate level. I realize now that the only way I could ever do that would be to dissociate myself from my responsibilities with HCJB and to involve myself in the culture of Ecuador, in the church of Ecuador. Then I would really get to know them, live with them, and really communicate with them. But here I am, in a professionally oriented organization with a specific job assignment. And for me to fulfill all that is required of me, I really can't do both.

This narrator's dilemma suggests a significant problem for the Mission at large. How does the organization motivate these inner-directed missionaries—each pursuing his own personal heroic myths—to fill slots in a Mission corporation? The problem is compounded by the tenuous state of "human authority" in this company of missionaries with its ethos of subjective spiritual guidance. The legitimacy of the Mission's authority over its members remains always conditioned upon individuals' perceptions of whether human agents are acting in God's will or not. While the HCJB organizational charts show hierarchical structures and chains of command, there is an alternative sense in which every member holds equal status as a "person called by God," with equal claim to discern God's will.

Many decisions in the Mission are in fact made democratically by a vote of the membership. Yet HCJB members often mention "theocracy" as the ideal form of government, evoking Biblical and Puritan images of a Christian community in which leaders and followers are all responsible individually to God, so that God literally commands the community. But what they also mean by theocracy is that the performance of their own personal mission should be *unmediated*; when God directs them to do something, they do not want resistance from the Mission. The challenge for an organization composed of people who believe this is, of course, that individuals can earnestly disagree about what the Lord has in mind.

If at any point I felt the authorities of this Mission conflicted with what I thought the Lord wanted, that would be the time to resign. I'm willing to do what I'm told as long as it doesn't violate something the Lord has said clearly. I don't think democracy is necessarily the Lord's way, either. In the Bible it's a theocracy.

I would never feel that I have to justify what I'm doing to the mission executives of HCJB. It's to God. In my inner sense of calling, I have to feel that I'm doing what God has given me to do. I have to feel that my life is being used, by my own finding of what my spiritual gifts are, to build the Kingdom of God.

When asked how he discerns God's will in the decisions of daily life, a senior HCJB member responds with a sermon illustration about a ship approaching harbor on a dark night, guided by the alignment of three lights on the shore. (A sociologist might hope that at least one of these three lights would reflect the common wisdom of a surrounding human community, but alas, this is not to be.)

There are three basic lights. There is the light of God's Word. There is the light of the inner witness of the Holy Spirit—that *inner voice* that I guess I've referred to a few times. And there is God's control of circumstances. So how do you know you're going to get into the harbor safe, and be in God's will? Well, you examine the thing, the problem, from those three points of view. And when those three points of view line up and say the same thing, then you go on in, home safe, and with confidence.

This is indeed a highly subjective, individualized concept of divine guidance. It comes by the individual's own reading of Scripture, is confirmed by an inner voice that no one else can hear, and is manifested by God's control of the circumstances impinging on an individual life. Not surprisingly, the Mission's abstract corporate goals often fail to resonate with the self-image and ideals of missionaries who employ this sort of inner map to guide their actions and interpret their experiences. Yet the Mission leadership has long understood this very phenomenon, at least pragmatically. One administrator casts it as a problem of motivation:

It comes down to what makes a missionary go. I think that to be a missionary in the first place you've got to be some kind of a mustang—somebody to break out of the herd and take a risk. There's got to be a separate driving force. So one of the problems we have here is that we do have a lot of wild mustangs, and how to motivate them to work with the team is a real challenge. How do you reward them? For the most part, they're not in it for money, prestige, climbing the ladder of success, or belonging to an organization. As a supervisor you can try the routine of, "I'm your boss, so you have to do this." Well, it just doesn't work with missionaries. We're not motivated by the things people are motivated by in a normal job.

When HCJB founder and past-president Clarence Jones enumerated the "greatest needs" of the Mission in the 1960s (Jones, 1966 [1962]), he called for "less insistence on ultra-democratic proceedings on the part of our staff, along with more acceptance by them of God-appointed leadership." But he also advocated a more decentralized management structure that would "free our President for the higher aspects of his office to plan, think, pray, and work toward the greatest realization of God's destiny for the WRMF."

Clarence Jones acknowledged that the Mission he had founded in a sheep shed in 1921—which had grown to encompass international radio, TV production, hospitals, publishing, and so on—now required an increasingly complex and bureaucratic structure. In his opinion, the Mission's "organizational setup" was "not keeping pace with the growth demands being thrust upon [HCJB] in these recent years." But at the same time, he sensed that the core strength of the Mission had to do with its spiritual ethos, its "heritage . . . [of] God-inspired origins, God-called men and women, God-provided sustenance, God-given message." He believed that this "sense of divine intervention and divine direction" prevailed among most HCJB workers, but cautioned that "it is something we can lose if we do not guard it well. To preserve our spiritual heritage, we must make sure all the present staff maintain their vision clearly and that all newcomers . . . are properly and thoroughly oriented to our particular ministry, under God." He added that "each section of our ministry must yield its full measure of fruit spiritually. The hospital cannot be allowed to become just another hospital; it must be a *Christian* hospital in its fullest sense."

Significantly, Jones understood that, no matter what their job assignment, HCJB members had to be *missionaries* first—for their own sense of fulfillment, but also to maintain the strength and character of the Mission organization itself. In his view, "more of a sense of privilege to be on the mission field [needed] to be instilled in some workers." In part, this is what prompted him to propose that HCJB missionaries focus on their Ecuadorian employees as prime targets for evangelism. There was real missionary work to be done right inside the compound, and every member could do it. Specifically, Jones listed as a top priority his "concern over the lost condition of the unconverted nationals among us, and a definite plan to reach them individually."[7] He suggested assigning each unconverted employee to an individual missionary as a personal evangelistic project. The same general dilemma surrounding the fulfillment of individual callings persists in HCJB today, though it tends to be cast in different terms. Here is where the *work of ideology* is required, in effect, to produce an *ideology of work*—one that will enable the individual member to fulfill and interpret his or her own sense of mission while contributing to the group, and thus to sustain the identity of both in the process. A telling illustration is seen in the way the Mission implements its policy on local evangelism. While HCJB includes an official Department of Evangelism, it anticipates that individual members throughout the Mission will initiate their own evangelistic endeavors in Ecuador. Far from discouraging these personal initiatives and unofficial campaigns, Mission policy states simply that efforts involving other staff members "should be carried out in consultation with the Director of the Department of Evangelism." Short of openly sponsoring them, the Mission accommodates, or at least tolerates independent forays for converts and disciples.

> I have an official job at the Mission, but besides that, I usually get out a couple of times a month—out among the Indians. Sometimes it's wet and miserable out there, but I enjoy it. It gives me a chance to preach. When I go out, maybe for a whole week of Bible teaching, I am not sponsored by the Mission. I like it that way very much. I am an individualist and a loner. I go where I feel the Lord wants me to go, and teach what he wants me to teach.

By not requiring that such endeavors have official sponsorship with its overlay of legitimation and bureaucratic authority, the Mission thus enables individuals to live out their personal missionary myths. At the same time, HCJB provides its own official, structured opportunity for members to experience "real missionary work" in small doses. Regardless of regular job assignment, any missionary can request to spend several days on a medical caravan as part of a health-evangelism team that travels to remote areas of Ecuador:

> Sometimes you do think, am I really doing missionary work? Am I really fulfilled? And it's good to ask yourself that. But we have a unique situation here at HCJB. If I don't feel fulfilled, I can say to the personnel director, "Frank, I want to go out on a caravan." And for three days or seven days, I can go out there and be on the front lines, so to speak. Then I get over that feeling. I've done those caravans. Not as much recently, because I really do feel fulfilled in this job. The way I feel about it is, if I don't do it somebody else is going to have to. It's important, and I'm filling some shoes so somebody else can be the front-line man. But I'll have to confess, I get envious of the doctors who go out on the medical caravans and heal the sick and give them the gospel at the same time. But it really doesn't bother me enough to pitch the whole thing and go back to the States.

This open policy on medical caravans serves the organization in several ways, some more obvious than others. Its manifest purpose is to increase the staff pool for health-evangelism teams that are supposed to meet local needs, demonstrate and attract people to the gospel message, and build a positive public image for HCJB and the evangelical church in Ecuador. Beyond that, however, these collaborative caravans enhance group solidarity and the sense of teamwork in different quarters of the Mission membership. They provide heroic, humanitarian images around which to motivate more routine work—images that can then be used to solicit financial support for individuals with unexciting jobs, as well as for the Mission's abstract agenda of global proselytization. For new members especially, perhaps the most significant reason for going out on a caravan is to effect a temporary cure for the lack of fulfillment in one's regular assigned position.

> I think the younger missionaries, we're caught in a transition period where the role of the missionary is changing. That's been difficult. We all came down with expectations and we're not seeing them fulfilled the way we thought. You know, we thought we would be the missionaries out evangelizing the world. I think that the older missionaries, they were the ones who really were out there—you know, they were the ones really going out and reaping the harvest. But we're in the transition where the missionary is not called to do that so much any more—the David Livingstone type of thing. And that's frustrating. But God still wants us to go beyond our boundaries. The Great Commission is still a command, just as relevant today as it was a hundred years ago with Hudson Taylor.

It is important not to misconstrue the underlying cause of disenchantment among many young missionaries. With few exceptions, HCJB members do not come to Ecuador actually intending to invade a primitive tribe with the gospel and penicillin, only to get stuck at a word processor in a third floor office in Quito. In fact, most of the newer recruits are technicians who say they chose HCJB specifically as an organization that could employ their skills in a modern, corporate effort to Christianize *the world* at large. And yet certain mythic aspects of their calling and spiritual sojourn continue to play out against the quotidian realities of their labor in the Mission organization. Beyond everyday cognitive schemes, concrete actions, purposes and expectations, the moral career of the missionary is a life made up largely of the *imagination*.

Paul Ricoeur, in his *Lectures on Ideology and Utopia*, suggests that imagination works in two important ways. On the one hand, imagination can preserve a social order by staging a process of identification that mirrors the order, says Ricoeur. On the other hand, it can be "an imagining of something else, the elsewhere." Ideology represents the first kind of imagination, a conservative preservation of identity. Utopia represents the second kind of imagination, a "glance from nowhere" (Ricoeur, 1966:265–266). For HCJB missionaries, imagination must work in both of these ways. Along the border between the inner self and the evangelical culture of origin, a personal mission must be fashioned that is somehow morally heroic—a sacrificial adventure to rescue strangers, denizens of a place in the mind that is radically *other*. This is *utopia*, in Ricoeur's sense.[8] At the same time, the missionary must imaginatively reconcile this inner sense of heroic vocation with the routine tasks of a job at HCJB. This is *ideology*.

For many of these individuals, the calling to personal evangelism lies at the core of the missionary vocation around which their identities are built. Proselytizing encounters with people *of the world* are thus necessary to buttress these missionaries' basic sense of self. As Shaffir (1978) has observed, while it might appear that witnessing or proselytizing would threaten the believer's identity through exposure to challenges from outsiders, witnessing actually consolidates identity. Thus, it is through conversation with nonbelievers, in a context controlled by the believer, that the missionary articulates and thereby continues to validate a set of core religious beliefs—one of which is that Christians possess a spiritual identity that sets them apart from a rejecting world.[9]

> You have to take a risk. You really have to go out on a limb. You have to be so convinced that the human race is in a terrible plight, that you have discovered something so marvelous about the God of creation and what he can do for people, that it's worth your bearing the onus of being an "intolerant" person, to tell others. You have to have a compassionate, overriding commitment. When you identify with people in their pain, some will come out of their pain, but there are going to be other people who would like to send you back where you came from. But those few people who respond are worth bearing the onus of being thought intolerant or a fanatic or a religious bigot. You bear that for the love of Jesus Christ, who came even though he was not asked to come, but rescued many.

> I can never sit on a plane next to a man or a woman, regardless of where they're from, without striking up a conversation and trying to find an open door to be able to share the person who means more to me than anything in the world, and that's Christ. A missionary is someone who lives constantly as an example of what Christ has done in your own life, to be able to share that with whoever you come in contact with.

> When I find myself talking with a non-Christian, I try to get as much gospel in as possible before he changes the subject. I recall one young man who asked me, "What in the world do missionaries do?" Well, this gave me an opportunity to really lambaste him with the gospel, and today he is a born-again believer.

> I am a missionary in Ecuador because I believe that the Lord Jesus died for our sins and there *is no hope* apart from accepting him and following him. People say, "Well, religion

is a private thing." But you can't just keep it to yourself, when it's vital for everyone else. It's like watching people driving over a cliff, and you want to say, "Stop!"

The corporate nature of work in the Mission organization, coupled with the insular character of the mission enclave, may actually deprive such people of their primary calling—in ways that produce large ironies. Through conversation, new interpretations of problematic experiences must then be formed, and adjustments made in the sphere of action to bring it in line with overarching schemes as much as possible:

> Some missionaries are down here as part of a group that is sending the gospel out to the world, and they feel content in that. I do not. I like to look someone in the eye, and tell them personally about Jesus Christ and have them respond. This has even gotten me in trouble with the Mission at times. When I was assigned to the hydro construction, one of the things I did was preach to the work crew out there, and we had many of these men accept the Lord. But after a while I was told by one of my bosses in engineering that I could not hold services for the men on the project. The rationale was that they were out there to work, not go to church services. We weren't paying them to go to church. Well, we were taking an extra hour at lunch time and having sessions about the Christian life, and we were teaching them from the Word. And the head of engineering was definitely against that, because we were paying them to work. Well, the consensus of the Mission was, after it was talked over, if we are building a hydroelectric power station to get the gospel out to the ends of the earth, why shouldn't we start with the job site where these local men are working?

Thus, in its official rhetoric HCJB reminds its new members that they "follow in the train" of William Carey, David Livingstone, and Hudson Taylor, and exhorts them to keep their "passion for lost souls alive." Yet their assigned jobs often make this difficult. Moreover, the structure of social life in the missionary group separates them from the immediate surround of lost souls in Ecuador.

Perhaps the most extraordinary manifestation of missionary separateness is the existence of English Fellowship Church, a place of worship operated by HCJB for its own members and other English-speaking evangelicals in Quito. English Fellowship turns out to be one of the largest gatherings of Protestant believers anywhere in the city of Quito, claiming an attendance of about 800 persons during three services on Sunday[10]. Yet its use of English excludes, in effect, most of the people in the surrounding Spanish-speaking community, to whom the Mission directs many of its other ministries.

Here, again, is where the work of ideology becomes necessary—to bridge the gap between images and reality. A kind of remapping of the landscape takes place on several fronts simultaneously, resulting in several distinct variations on arguments drawing from the same stock of missionary rhetoric. Thus, in an official statement the Mission can evoke the Great Commission to legitimize a social institution that in seems, on the surface, to contradict the ideals of the missionary vocation: English Fellowship Church is necessary for the "nurturing and edification of God's people so that they can better go forth into their Jerusalems, Judeas, and uttermost parts of the world with the gospel message." At the same time, a Mission manager employs the rhetoric of the individual missionary call to justify attendance at English church:

Our mission is an international mission. There are people here who are not called to Ecuador, never received a call to Ecuador. Their call may be to communicate the gospel to the people of the world, and it just so happens that we are here in Ecuador to do it by radio. They're not called to start new churches here. For the most part, they just want to be together, to worship together. So we're going to have to be tolerant of each other's different callings, and quit comparing callings. That's the old, "I'm of Apollos" and "I'm of Paul" routine.[11] You know, "I'm called to get down and mix with the people, why aren't you?"

Another senior HCJB member advances the argument that English Fellowship Church can better demonstrate the New Testament ideals of "body life Christianity" precisely because it is isolated "from the materialism and worldly influences that churches back in the States have to deal with." (This almost evokes John Winthrop's seventeenth-century idea that the people of God were to be a model of Christian charity in the virgin wilderness of New England, set apart from the corruption of religion back home across the Atlantic.) Still other reasons given for attending English church are based on the priorities of Christian family life, and a defensive retreat from perceived opposition to the presence of missionaries in some Ecuadorian churches:

When we started out, we went to Spanish church. But the pastor was strongly anti-missionary. And our kids would come home from Sunday school almost every week crying, saying that the teacher was mean to them, or the other kids were mean. I finally had to make a decision. I asked myself, am I responsible for the spiritual welfare of my family or not? Is it more important for me to put on a good front and be in a Spanish church, or take them somewhere that when they come home from church they feel great, like they've worshiped the Lord and they are learning something about the Scriptures. And so, it may be the nationals who have driven people to English Fellowship Church.

We did attend a Spanish church for quite a while. We stopped when our child totally rejected the Ecuadorians because of the experience. He quit speaking Spanish. He would not play with the children. He would have nothing to do with Ecuadorians, or with anything related to Ecuador. We were able to figure out that he was made fun of in Sunday school. So we started going to English church.

I can remember being on a panel during annual meeting, talking about church ministries and just raking people over the coals for going to English Fellowship Church, saying they were useless missionaries. Maturity is finding that a lot of these judgments we make are simplistic. I wasn't considering the over-all family scene. For instance, now that I have teenage children in the Alliance Academy,[12] I realize the pressures to be a part of the English-speaking group.

As we shall see, HCJB missionaries who continue in their careers never completely abandon their original calling. Yet only some of them fulfill their original images and ideas of missionary work through their own personal ministries. Many other missionaries manage to redefine or redeem their ideals through common strategies of rationalization. A number of these strategies make use of the call itself. In one variation, the missionary convinces herself at the outset that God has personally called her and brought her to the field through a whole series of divine arrangements. Given this as a fact of experience, then *whatever* reality she subsequently encounters can also be seen as part of a transcendent plan. The sense that God's ways are inscrutable can liberate such a person from the cognitive need to reconcile human expectations with reality.

> When we came here to Ecuador, we knew that the Lord had brought us here. And it was very good to know that—very good to know that whatever happened, we were here because the Lord wanted us here. There was no doubt in my mind that I had been called to be a missionary, and that's probably the thing that's kept me in Ecuador all these years. The real constraining thing is the sense of vocation, the call to it.
>
> I did have a hard time feeling fulfilled in my job assignment, because that's not what I came here to do. It was very difficult. But I'd keep thinking back to how I got here. It was like the pegs in Chinese checkers, when you go from hole to hole. Well, I'd go back and I'd remember all those moves. And I knew they weren't accidents. I knew they were all part of God's plan. And so I'd keep thinking back, and I'd say, He's got me here for some reason.

In another variation, the call is pushed through a hoop of circular logic: I was called to be a missionary; I am a missionary as member of HCJB; I am assigned to do X and Y as a member of the Mission; I was therefore called to do X and Y; I am doing what I was called to do. Here the call is renegotiated by shifting its meaning from personally carrying out the Great Commission to being a good worker at one's station in life—just what Luther meant by *vocatio* (at least in Weber's view).[13] The missionary call thus dissolves into the notion of *gifts*—doing whatever one is good at, or whatever convention demands. A woman with conservative views of marriage, family, and gender roles discovers her missionary calling to stay at home and build a nest. Her husband, a man with mechanical abilities, discovers his gift to stay in the background and help to equip the "front line" troops.

> Here I am, a missionary living in this neighborhood. What have I done to reach the people on my street? I've done virtually nothing. But you know, it comes back to the question: What are my gifts? Not, what should I be doing in Ecuador to reach people, but what are my gifts and what am I doing with my gifts in light of eternity? Mainly, it's caring for my children and being supportive of my husband so he can be out doing the things in line with his abilities. And so I realize that *I am working in my call*. For both of us, the call has been the utilization of what he has given us, what he's prepared us for, within the framework of opportunity that exists.
>
> I see myself not as a preacher or an orator, but a person of flexible abilities in working with my hands—whether it comes to carpentry, mechanics, you name it. That's where I see my gifts. I'm not someone on the front lines, but someone who is satisfied being in the background and helping those and supporting those who are on the front lines.

While these individuals apply cognitive strategies of rationalization in unique ways, they tend to draw them from a given repertoire of evangelical interpretations attributed to the Bible. A common example is provided by a nurse who worked a set shift in the Mission hospital, who felt too busy even to talk to patients (to say nothing of "witnessing"), and thus felt frustrated in her missionary vocation. In order for her to fulfill a personal calling in light of the Great Commission, she says, "something had to change." However, what did change over time was not the job itself, but the symbolic frame within which she saw it as meaningful. Gradually she adopted a

new Biblical interpretation, a new cognitive map that relocated her missionary position within a wider scheme of significance. Thereafter, her work in the hospital was
no longer just an avenue for personal evangelism, but an activity to be valued intrin-
sically as *service to others for the glory of God*:

> Now I feel very strongly that, like the Bible verse says, if we give a cup of water in God's
> name, we are doing it as unto him. And when I work as a missionary nurse, I really am
> doing it *all* in the name of God and for his glory.

However, this particular reformulation of missionary work and identity must
withstand challenges from colleagues in other quarters of the Mission, who often use
the Bible to support narrower perspectives. Medical work, in particular, becomes a
crucible for arguments about the social vs. spiritual, local vs. global goals of HCJB,
and whether these goals and activities compromise the true nature of the missionary
enterprise:

> If it turns out that all we're doing is trying to heal the sick, then we might as well close up
> the hospital. Because what is our ultimate goal in this mission? Is it to heal the sick, feed
> the hungry, to house the homeless, put clothes on people? Or is it to win them to Jesus
> Christ and to build them up in the faith? The Great Commission comes in here, and if
> we're not doing this with the idea of winning those people for Christ, then I say forget it.
> I know people have social needs, too. But I am against the "social gospel" that does noth-
> ing but feed, clothe, heal, house people. It doesn't do anything but prolong their life a little
> longer so they can go to hell.

In one sense, this argument should be set in its historical context as a variation
on a central ideological theme of Protestant missions since the seventeenth century,
namely the primacy of "pure evangelism" over the "civilizing" of primitive tribes.
As William Hutchison (1987) points out, the legacy of missions as a civilizing enterprise emerged in the early twentieth century as the "social gospel" which
fundamentalists vigorously opposed as a liberal watering-down of the true message
of salvation. Thereafter, the missionary impulse of mainline Protestantism either declined drastically or else sort of dissolved eventually into the Peace Corps, depending
on one's point of view. On the other hand, contemporary nondenominational fundamentalist and evangelical missionaries still define their primary purpose in terms of
pure evangelism, and in so doing lay claim as rightful heirs to the early Protestant
denominational missions. Evangelical groups such as the Wycliffe Bible Translators
now defend themselves against accusations of imperialism by stating that their goal
(and indeed, the effect of the gospel itself) is not to destroy or even change native
cultures materially, but "only" to bring about the spiritual transformation of human
lives (Stoll, 1982).[14]

The important point here, though, is that such arguments amount to more than
merely theoretical debates for missionaries, more than ordinary attempts to justify
one over another professional approach. Rather, they bear profound implications both
for the master identity of the missionary—whose inner self becomes fused with the
sense of mission, and for the core identity of the Mission organization—whose membership becomes a community held together in a field of ideological discourse. The

opposing forces in that field form a tension that is both internal to the missionary's self-understanding and projected outward into the social arena of lived relations. Hence, the common ways in which missionaries imbue their own lives with meaning, i.e., through conversation surrounding objects of mission, are also the ways in which they delineate the boundaries of their own community of strangers, i.e., *in relation to* those objects.[15] In this manner, new strategies for rationalization of the calling take their place, along with the Biblical rhetoric and cultural mythology of early Protestant missions, as social texts of identity for HCJB members.

The Work of Ideology in Discourse among Insiders

Staff meetings among HCJB members offer a revealing look—from a broader angle—at the sort of rhetorical process through which missionaries develop ideological categories that advance their own personal interests while reinforcing the solidarity of the Mission group. Group conversation illustrates how the sources of ambivalence in the personal missionary calling are projected into the group as conflict between factions. The resolution of such conflict for missionaries—whether at the individual or social level—involves negotiating between competing interests by reinterpreting the motives of each side on the common rhetorical ground of membership in a spiritual community with a shared calling.

To illustrate such matters, what follows is a selected portion of a Mission staff meeting.[16] As a form of data, recorded dialogue among insiders offers some advantages that significantly enhance our interpretation of personal interview narratives. First, while the private "backstage" setting of the individual interviews was an artifice of research, the mission staff meeting was a naturally occurring event in the public life of the group. Second, a transcript of such an event allows us to hear multiple voices speaking among each other and to the group, rather than to an interviewer as primary audience. It allows us to understand missionaries' talk in its ordinary dialogic context and to follow its actual effect on group process.

The discussion to be heard was focused largely on a mundane economic issue of concern to missionaries themselves: the Mission's policy on housing allowance as a component of the salary support that HCJB members must raise from donors in their home country. I selected this discussion deliberately because it shows the missionaries' facile movement between two levels of relevance in the Mission ethos—the mundane and the spiritual—and demonstrates how rhetoric is borrowed from the latter to advance interests and solve problems in the former.

A bit more background is perhaps necessary to set the stage. The Mission designates a portion of missionaries' salary as a housing allowance prorated to family size. However, individual missionaries who spend less than the allowance on rent can use the balance for other expenses. A controversy had arisen surrounding a proposal by the Field Council (the Mission's governing body in Ecuador) to roll back the dollar allowance for missionary housing in response to the severe devaluation of Ecuadorian currency. The missionaries were receiving monthly support in U.S. dollars, while many were paying rent to local landlords in *sucres*; as a result, quite a few of them had seen their actual housing costs nearly cut in half over the preceding two years as the *sucre* exchange against the dollar skyrocketed, far outpacing inflation. There were, however, two groups of missionaries who had not benefited in kind from this windfall: (1) those who had purchased homes with U.S. mortgages and were paying for them in dollars, and (2) those whose landlord was the Mission itself, whose rent was being paid in dollars at a rate increased 15 percent per year over the previous two years. A movement had arisen among this second group, the Mission tenants—including a number of prominent, senior members—to get the rent on Mission properties rolled back by 30 percent.

The Field Council responded with a surprising proposal that affected the entire body of HCJB: (1) decrease the dollar housing allowance for everyone, since missionaries renting in *sucres* no longer needed as much for rent; (2) lower Mission rents accordingly, to create equity across the membership. The resulting surplus in support could not be used to cover everyday living costs, but only for Mission-approved projects and special expenses such as travel and equipment. This would present mission members with a dilemma. Would they tell their donors straightforwardly that they no longer needed as much money to live in the field? Would they seek Mission approval to use the money for charity in Ecuador? Or, rather, would they allow the money to accumulate in a personal account to be used for special, Mission-approved projects and expenses? In any case, the change would mean a significant decrease in most missionaries' discretionary income.

The proposal was being considered for ratification by the Board of Trustees, the Mission's corporate directors based in the United States who were in Quito for the annual meeting of the membership. In the discussion to follow, each speaker was given a maximum of two minutes to speak. All names that appear are pseudonyms.

George Lomax [Mission tenant]: If the Mission rent were lowered, we would have a little bit more money in our support accounts, for which we would be responsible before the Lord and before the Mission of HCJB. We could give this money to HCJB ministries, or have something to help those who are in great need—more than just words.

Phil Schmidt [outside tenant]: The issue here is simply whether HCJB rents are too high or not. How we as outside renters got dragged into this—and we are being penalized because of it—is beyond my understanding. We get our allowance every month and we spend it as we feel the Lord would have us do. Every family has their own financial priorities, and ours doesn't happen to be housing. We count on using that extra we have saved on rent, in other areas where our priorities are higher. For one thing, we have made a commitment to each other as a family to put so much away monthly for our future and the future of our children. If we get a cut in our housing allowance, we will not suffer in housing until our landlady raises our rent, but we will suffer in other areas where our priorities are higher.

Helen Freeman: Bob and I are against the decrease in housing allowance. And I would just like to ask the question—probably sounds ignorant—but I would like to ask whoever decided that it should be decreased, what was their reason?

Carl Gelb [moderator]: I believe that the question should be answered. We'll ask a representative of the Field Council to speak to that please. [*recognizes Nellie Palacios*] Thank you, Nellie. Jack, would you come and translate in English please? She wants to do it in Spanish.

[laughter from group]

Nellie Palacios [in Spanish, with serial translation by Jack Gaston]: We decided, basically, that the housing allowance could be decreased because we are receiving more than we need to live. We made some calculations about the effect of the devaluation of the sucre on missionaries' actual cost of living here. From my point of view as a Latin from the Third World, missionaries have a standard of living much higher than the average person, much higher than most of our employees. I don't think a single one of us would suffer to a great degree if our income for housing were reduced thirty percent, as the Field Council recommends.

Derrick Petersen: We would like your prayers that we can find a place, if this goes through. We are looking for an apartment right now and we have not had any success yet, within a reasonable distance from the station. Because of the work hours that I have, my wife being pregnant and our two kids needing to go to the school here, we need a place nearby. Our rental allowance, with the 30 percent decrease, would limit us even further. So just pray for us that we'll be able to find something, if the decrease does go through. Thank you.

Dave Ritchie: Personally, I have rather mixed feelings about the whole thing. On the one hand, we would very much like to give our supporters a break. They have been so faithful, and they are up against some tough times themselves. On the other hand, after fourteen years on the field, we personally have almost no savings. In the next two years, we face two kids going to college, and I don't know how I'm going to do it.

Henry Nordstrom: The feeling of a lot of supporters is that missionaries are supposed to just make ends meet. We've lived here for ten years and that's the way we've been living. Now it's just nice to have a little extra money that you can put into things, start a savings program, and help some needy Ecuadorian when he comes along. So I would like to see the allowance stay the same.

J.B. Garner: I myself am glad to see the reduction in rents and in housing allowance, to give a break to my supporters. I have lots of them that are not rich and therefore do sacrifice to keep me on the mission field.

Barbara McCormick: When you talk about giving the supporters a break, would we actually be writing back to our supporters and telling them that we need less money?

Carl Gelb [moderator]: That would be your own individual decision. You could use those funds to build your undistributed balance, wipe out a deficit, transfer those funds to some other fund, or write to your supporters and tell them to give you a little less every month.

Rick Baumann: I was told the other day that three out of the six people on committee who decided to make this change in our rent allowance are in the red. So that would affect them in a very positive way if we went ahead with this.

Kyle Carpenter: I've been debating about whether I should say what I have to say, but I think in view of the spirit of what we've heard here today, I'd like to. This morning I had my devotions and I asked the Lord for something, and this is what he gave me. "If I had the gift of being able to speak in other languages without learning them, and could speak every language there is in all the earth and didn't love others, I would only be making noise. If I had the gift of prophecy and knew all about the exchange of the dollar and what it will do in the future . . . but didn't love my fellow missionary, I am nothing. Even if I had the gift of faith, so that I could say to the exchange, 'Don't move!' I would still be

worth nothing at all without love. If I were to give everything extra that I had gained because of the rising value of the dollar to the poor people in my neighborhood, and if I were
to be burned alive for preaching the gospel to them, but didn't love my brother who dif-
fers with me on this particular issue, it would be of no avail. Love is patient and kind,
never jealous or envious of the guy who has a lower rent, never boastful or cocky or self-
ish or arrogant about the fact that I pay less rent than the next guy, love is not touchy or
irritable when Field Council recommends something that will cut my money. Love does
not hold grudges when after it is all over the Board makes a decision that's not what I
want. And as a matter of fact, love hardly even notices when others do it wrong. Neither
is it glad when the decision which is popular to me—[*time called*]

[laughter]

Sy Pendergast: One of the problems we have in this organization is the desire to make
all people be equal. I don't think that can be done. If we could take the 250 people of this
group and put us in the United States, I don't think we could all be equal. So I don't think
there's any particular advantage in trying to do that here either.

Clayton Anderson: I'll use my two minutes to finish off what Kyle started. I felt kind of
bad that we had to cut him off.

Bill Reuss: That's illegal!

Clayton Anderson: No, I'm using my own two minutes, and you just used up ten seconds of it. [*Reads Kyle Carpenter's statement*] ". . . Neither is it glad when the decision is
popular to me, but unpopular to others. If you love someone you'll be loyal to him no
matter what the cost. You'll always believe in him, always expect the best of him, and
always stand your ground in defending him. All the special gifts will someday come to an
end, but love goes on forever."

Mark Blakeney: In the twelve years we've been with the mission, Marla and I have noticed that the lead up to annual meeting seems to be a catalyst to problems that are of a
personal nature to missionaries. Now people get talking about it, and pretty soon we have
a group of people excited about their point of view of what's happening, and whether or
not they will be heard. And I'm not so sure that what, many times we forget the reason we
came here to Ecuador. It wasn't to fight for allowances and things that involve money.

Roger Alness [board member]: You know, we are staying with Kyle and Charlene Carpenter, and this morning we all had these devotions that Kyle mentioned. He had them
individually, and then he brought them to the table. And you know, it hurt me deeply when
I heard people laugh at Kyle. This is not a laughing matter, folks. Stop and think about
what the word says, I Corinthians 13. Sure, Kyle added some current language to it, but
there is a real meaning. And it hurt me when some of you laughed and made fun of him.
I think that was wrong.

Mark Blakeney: Mr. Alness, may I address that statement? I was one who laughed, and
I personally was laughing because of the creativity that Kyle expressed. That was all. I
agree with it, and I accept it.

Roger Alness: We must not lose sight of the fact that without love, any decisions that we
make, any business we have, any faith that we have, is nothing. I'm preaching to myself
as much as to any one.

Carl Gelb [moderator]: You're preaching to all of us.

Morgan Muhler [board member]: As a Board member I think I have not only heard your thoughts, but I have felt them. A lot of you have spoken not just from your minds, you've spoken from your hearts, gently, in loving ways. I know our Board is committed to listening, and we want to make a decision that will be honoring and glorifying to our Lord Jesus Christ, which will also be glorifying to each one of us members of the body of Jesus Christ. And I think after listening to this, our desire is that of the Apostle Paul as he spoke to the Thessalonian people, that in his deliberations with them he would come in the gentleness of a nursing mother, and with the compassion of a father to a son.

Audience and Identity in the Moral Career

The work of missionary ideology is carried out through conversation with several kinds of others, each a different sort of audience for the performance of a personal mission. As these audiences reflect components of the missionary self, they provide sources of meaning and belonging.

The First Audience: God and the Other-Worldly Self

Proceeding from the core to the periphery of missionary identity, one could say that the first audience is God, who exists for the individual as an internalized *Other* along with the ideal self that is formed in God's image (or vice versa, depending on one's theological vs. psychodynamic point of view). Thus, the missionary's continuing evaluation of self is carried out as an internal dialogue with God. Self-knowledge and self-guidance arise from knowledge of God, which becomes an exercise of a sort of inner-directed listening.

> God and I have a pretty solid relationship. I view him as the guide of my life. He's harder on me than most people are, and he'll let me know if I've done well. So I've built a system of evaluating my success that's all internal. I have my own system, and I know when I've done a good job and when I've done a bad job. I could preach a great sermon, and nobody say a word to me, and it wouldn't make any difference. I could preach a crummy sermon and people could say it was great, and that wouldn't make any difference. I know when I've done something well, and when I haven't. I don't rely on people's responses or even apparent results.

> The thing that keeps me going is just knowing God. I mean really knowing him, knowing how to listen to him. When I can't express myself to another human being, I go to him. I am learning more and more to listen to God, and to obey him. Then he uses me to influence and help other people. I get my fulfillment from God himself. I don't get it from what's going on around me.

> I take my signals from the Lord every day. I try to have a very close walk with God, and that means I have to be candid with God. Even if it's, "Lord, this morning I do not feel like being a missionary—I feel like going out and raising hell." I am open that way with God, and he has never let me down yet. I don't expect he ever will.

If God is a key figure in the imagination and inner conversation of these missionaries, so is Satan. In fact, the other-worldly dimension of their ethos, worldview, and identity may be seen nowhere more clearly than in the rhetoric of military conflict that they apply to the moral sphere, evoking a sort of Manichaean universe where the unseen forces of God and Satan wage war in the arena of human life:

> I see the job we have of getting the gospel out to the world as warfare. And I think Satan is at work in our midst so desperately, and sometimes we fail to see it. In these little things, where we have personal problems, and difficulties with one another, I think the Devil must sit back with glee and laugh at us. He is out there as a roaring lion, trying to devour us! And sometimes we go innocently on our way, and let him do it. And we forget that we have the most powerful force in the universe—the power of the Lord Jesus Christ, bought by his blood on the cross—available to us in these daily situations.

> We're involved in a warfare. We're right on the edge of it. I believe that the world is in a head-on collision course with the Word of God. But it's like the story of Elisha and the servant. The servant saw the strength of the enemy, and wondered why Elisha the prophet was sitting there with his feet up, not doing anything about it. The servant was fearful. But Elisha could see something the servant couldn't. There was another army out there. So he prayed, "Lord, open his eyes. Let him see what I can see." And hey, there are two armies out there. There's our army and there's their army, and those two armies are in conflict with each other. That's what I'm doing here in Ecuador.

> You see constantly how Satan attacks us. I do get really frustrated with how Satan works. Like last year, Satan really attacked in the financial side of the hospital. There was talk about whether we would have to close the hospital down. Then that seemed to be solved, and all of the sudden, Satan attacks with staff. Recently we have had a lot of dissatisfaction amongst the staff, and I really feel that Satan is behind it.

The Second Audience: the Missionary Community

As we shall see, HCJB members tend to express highly ambivalent feelings toward the community of their missionary peers.[17] On the one hand (and most significantly), the group provides necessary affirmation and support for the individual, and helps to sustain the evangelical worldview within which the performance of a mission is made meaningful. The group also provides models for personal missionary performances, along with boilerplate strategies of rationalization that bridge the gap between expectations and reality. But on the other hand, the group gets in the way of individual performances, insofar as these are based on highly personalized myths of moral heroism and strangerhood, in which the individual sets out alone as a messenger to the unsaved.

The HCJB Mission compound in Quito demarcates the physical setting in which the missionaries' within-group conversations and performances take place. A visitor to the compound has the feeling of entering a self-contained, almost cloistered community whose character stands out as alien to the larger social life of Quito, even though there are many Ecuadorian employees who work inside the compound. An HCJB promotional brochure distributed in 1982 captures this feeling in a commendation of the Mission's supporting services department:

> Upon entering the HCJB grounds one immediately feels the effects of Supporting Services . . . the nicely painted buildings, the well-kept gardens and lawns, the friendly Ecuadorian employee who opens the gate. He is willing to help with di-

rections or with calling personnel. The phone system is operated by a national employee who knows most of the staff well and where to find them.

Visitors at HCJB notice the clean grounds and buildings. The missionaries appreciate having clean offices and studios in which to work . . . they are happy about being able to pick up mail at the on-site post office . . . and they are thankful for the commissary where they can pick up food items. If a desk or shelves are needed in an office, the carpentry shop does a beautiful job. . . . [A missionary] serves as a most valuable mechanic with HCJB, keeping the mission's automobiles on the road.

The HCJB compound environs also include a number of missionary homes and apartments, mostly owned by the Mission. As is customary in Quito, all of these houses are secured behind barbed-wire fences or walls with shards of broken glass cemented along the top to discourage intruders. A coordinated system of locks allows missionaries access, with master keys, to the Mission grounds and surrounding residential premises. But for Ecuadorians and nonmissionaries without keys, access to the compound is controlled through a manned guardhouse. Access to residential gates on the Mission lock system is also strictly controlled. For example, official policy on locks and keys states that "house gate keys (with access limited to the gates of the individual house) are available for use by maids or gardeners. No other key should be given to them."

Yet, without a hint of irony, missionaries who are members of this closed community often portray it as if it were a small rural town where everyone is known and trusted. A tenant of HCJB's apartment building adjacent to the compound speaks of his missionary neighbors:

When Jim comes over, he just walks in through the front door. He never knocks. And I love it, because I like people to feel that way about me—that there aren't really any doors. Like Herb, he just sticks his head in the door and hollers, "Anybody home?" We have a big friendly dog, and he's like I am, too. I like people, and I like them to just walk right in.

But, of course, this missionary's open door is situated behind barbed wire and locked gates to which only fellow HCJB members (and perhaps a trusted gardener) have a key. His large dog provides added security.

Likewise, the social and moral boundaries surrounding the missionary community are quite rigidly controlled. For example, a single missionary must obtain permission from the Board in order to be married, or else resign from HCJB. If the single missionary's prospective spouse is not a member of the Mission, he or she is required to join the Mission too, or the marriage will not be approved. Missionaries who are divorced are required to resign from the Mission in almost every case. Candidates who have been divorced and remarried in the past may be considered for membership only if the scenario is reconstructed in one of two ways: (1) the divorce happened "prior to conversion" and the present marriage has lasted three years, showing "every evidence of stability"; (2) the divorced applicant for membership was the "innocent party" in a marriage that ended due to adultery or desertion by an "unbelieving spouse." The Mission bases its divorce policy on the words of Christ as recorded in Matthew's gospel, reprinted in the HCJB workers' manual in the King

James Version: "And I say unto you, whosoever shall put away his wife, except for fornication, and shall marry another, committeth adultery and whoso marrieth her which is put away doth commit adultery" (Matthew 19:9).

Smoking, drinking, profanity, gambling, and practices that American fundamentalists have traditionally seen as immoral amusements are generally forbidden. The Mission's official justification for a strict code of personal moral conduct again invokes the Bible with its metaphors of spartan self-denial in preparation for the rigors of military and athletic conflict:

> With others of like precious faith we accept the fact that when we walk in the Holy Spirit, we will not fulfill the lusts of the flesh but will have the fruit of the Spirit (Galatians 5:16–25). . . . As a mission we feel it important voluntarily to abstain from certain amusements and practices which have compromising factors connected with them and/or which by their nature can result in stumbling blocks for our Christian brother. We are soldiers engaged in crucial warfare. We must happily strip ourselves of unnecessary weights to fight a good fight.

The HCJB worker's manual goes on to cite three Biblical principles, based upon New Testament guidelines that address the dealings of the early church with Gentile converts to Christianity: "avoid contamination; show consideration for the scruples of others, even in things that you don't consider wrong; avoid compromise." Some of the distinctive ways in which the American fundamentalist ethos has applied such principles may be seen in the Mission's statement of "broadcast norms" for HCJB radio and TV productions:

> On all World Radio staff religious programs, participants such as preachers and singers must be Christians. . . . Non-Christian talent may be used as actors in dramatic productions or as instrumentalists.[18]
>
> World Radio looks favorably on wholesome sports. However, we do not approve of news items concerning the following: bull fighting, horse racing, cock fighting and professional boxing and wrestling. . . . World Radio does not broadcast sports on Sunday. . . . Undue emphasis should not be given to the promotion of professional sports, particularly those which take place on Sunday.
>
> . . . We usually omit references to the Roman Catholic clergy unless such items have definite news value.
>
> . . . Anything eulogizing Hollywood movie stars is cut. Items concerning divorces and demoralizing situations are usually cut.
>
> . . . Music with immoral or suggestive words will not be used. . . . Objectionable rhythm or instrumentation will be avoided. Rhythm or instrumentation that absorbs the listener's attention away from or is otherwise inconsistent with the text, harmonic treatment, or melodic pattern, shall not be used, except in cases such as martial music.
>
> . . . We shall not approve the use of any cultural program whose influence would tend to nullify the Gospel message that we proclaim. . . . All music that is generally associated with dances should not be used. In addition, all music whose text has an immoral influence must be eliminated.
>
> . . . NEGATIVE: Music generally associated with modern dancing and dance bands: jazz, rock, etc. . . . Zarzuelas and Latin American pieces should be auditioned to assure their moral content. Dance music from France and Italy, as well as that

from the Caribbean, should be avoided along with popular music in general from Brazil and Argentina.

For such views to be maintained as morally defensible and meaningful, the insular structure of a subcultural enclave is in some sense necessary. Still, that structure represents a significant paradox at the interface between the personal and social axes of missionary identity. The missionary community insulates people whose moral careers and core identities are bound up psychologically with the notion of living precariously, heroically, in touch with a lost world. People who view themselves in this manner tend to feel uneasy in an closed community of like-minded believers. And yet, the enclave provides security, comfort, and certain social resources which, as it turns out, many HCJB missionaries are unwilling to forego.

This community is outstanding. It's wonderful that if you have needs, there are so many people you can go to. I've just written my prayer letter on the subject of friends—to have so many friends, so many people who care. I think it's an exceptional situation. Our gatherings together really promote that—the weekly staff meeting, the Annual Meeting. I find people are very caring. But personally, I wouldn't want it to be any more than it is, because we are missionaries in Ecuador and we should associate with the Ecuadorians.

Here in Quito, I was attracted to the life and the way the missionaries interacted. But the mission compound thing, the subculture—it bothered me. I had a fear that we would get locked in here, and there wouldn't be the opportunity for service that we had hoped for— that we would get caught up in the subculture. Do you know what I mean? Missionary life but not *missionary life*.

The hard times for me came in relating to other Christians in this community. I was criticized. In fact, someone said to me a couple of years ago—an older missionary—"When you first came, I didn't even believe you were a Christian." Well, to maintain your own integrity and your own relationship to the Lord, and still belong to a highly restrictive community— that was very, very difficult. The only way it's worked in my life is that I've withdrawn from the missionary ghetto. For me to survive as a missionary, it was a matter of withdrawing and making my own world, and not depending on the mission world for sustenance.

We've started a dinner club where we eat meals in each other's houses and after a few months trade around and have new people. But it makes you feel guilty, because you're spending all your time with missionaries, and not with Latins.

We do have some friends among Ecuadorians, but not many—and I don't know why. Maybe it's because we're too much of a community among ourselves, too close together, and we have our associations in English church and school that are so isolated from the Ecuadorian community. I think that's why it is—it's just easier to remain in our own little realm. That's human nature, and I think it's very unfortunate. I would never say that's a good thing. I don't think it is. I'm sorry that our missionaries live so close together.

I naturally feel more at ease with people of my own culture, because there's just a built-in understanding of certain things. But as missionaries, we have not wanted to live right in with other Americans and always associate with people of our own kind—as nice as that may be. I want to have different kinds of people in our home—people from different cultures, and different religions. Still, my strongest sense of community is with people of my own culture.

When Jack had his accident, we were all gathered around him in the hospital, and he wasn't as badly hurt as the driver of the other car. We should have spent more time with the Ecuadorian people who were in the other car, who were being treated at the same time. It wasn't that anybody had anger toward the other driver, it was just that we were concerned about *our* man.

We try to work together as people who are open and tender toward the spirit of God, and burdened for one another's ministries. We are a team. We encourage and support one another. We see one another as brothers and sisters in Christ. The whole picture here is for the glory of God. I think being a secretary is just as important—in the eyes of God and to this ministry—as being an engineer or a broadcaster or a doctor.

From the moment I arrived, it was wonderful. I just felt extremely supported and cared for right from the beginning. I remember my first interview, being asked what my interests were and what kind of work I would like to be involved in. They asked me where I wanted to live, instead of telling me I had to live with somebody. There was caring for me as a person. The team spirit I found outstanding.

We are the body of Christ. When one part of the body hurts, the rest of the body is there to rescue and support it. Where this really comes through, like I have never seen anywhere else in my life, is in a time of crisis. You let something serious happen to one of our staff members—auto accident, serious illness—and boy I'll tell you, the body of Christ and the body of HCJB surrounds them, regardless of where they work. When I had a crisis myself, did I ever feel like I had a body of brothers and sisters!

I have one big concern. It's that we have so many missionaries, and we are all together here, so many of us. Too many are just involved for themselves, and their own families and their own community. We do too much on the inside, and not enough on the outside. We get involved in so many things that are not priorities at all. It's nice here.

Like their home nation, the missionary community functions as an ambiguous social symbol. In a cultural sense, it embodies the missionaries' vision of traditional Christian-American values—from Puritan morality to small-town familiarity, order, hard work, and cleanliness. On a spiritual plane, the missionary enclave evokes in its members the New Testament ideal of an organic community of faith in which burdens and blessings, talents and tasks are shared alike; in which every part of the body works together harmoniously in submission to Christ as the head; and in which every person's gift or calling is needed and none is disparaged.

The missionary community gives HCJB members a social context and a sympathetic audience for living out their message. It is their version of the Puritans' shining city on a hill, glorifying God and showing grace to the world. And yet, from the inner vantage point of their strangerhood and divine calling to perform a personal mission, the missionary community also becomes a negative symbol. It becomes a sign of the secure and comfortable world *out of which* missionaries are called individually, and *from* which they are to be set apart sacrificially, in order to bring the gospel to a lost world.

The Third Audience: Evangelicals at Home

The third audience is constituted by supporters in the sending country, typically North American evangelicals and fundamentalists. By accepting monetary pledges and gifts from these people (and churches) back home, the missionary tacitly incurs an obligation to perform on their behalf, and to use the money in a way that fulfills donors' intentions. In addition, a sort of unwritten contract requires the missionary to send intermittent reports from the field, known as *prayer letters*, as well as to make personal appearances on furlough. Thus, a kind of relationship develops between missionaries and their sending communities that is maintained instrumentally by the exchange of field reports and financial donations. This relationship exists in a very specific rhetorical context, which renders the exchange as an exercise of altruistic giving on both sides. That is to say, the missionary's life and the donor's money are each seen as sacrificial gifts to the Lord, intended for the benefit of *neither* the missionary nor the donor, but for the salvation of souls abroad. The typical missionary donor is often portrayed as follows:

> We have some faithful people back home, in our home church, who are struggling to be sure that we are here in the field. We have one dear lady who supports us with five dollars a month. And you know, to her that is a big chunk. She's a widow, and she doesn't have a whole lot of money. But that five dollars—you know, it makes me watch where my money goes. I cannot justify a free expenditure of other people's money. Because they can't be here, they are sending themselves in the form of money. But I think the concept of giving *to the Lord* needs to be taught. Many times, people give to *us* as missionary personalities, and then those personalities are expected to respond with prayer letters.

Prayer letters fulfill the manifest purpose of informing the sending community of the missionary's progress and ongoing needs, and thus maintain a financial pipeline in working order. Yet their ideological significance extends far beyond that. Prayer letters construct a special reality, one that is abstracted from everyday experience in such a way as to maintain (and further elaborate) the missionary myth—not only for the sending community, but perhaps even more importantly for the missionary herself. As such, the prayer letter becomes a primary medium of rationalization—indeed, a primary textual form of the missionary's moral career. The prayer letter demands a selective way of seeing, and provides a genre for the writing and rewriting of life experience, specifically as *missionary* life experience.

> Dear Friends:
>
> Ten years ago I was accepted for service with World Radio Missionary Fellowship (HCJB). . . . For this special anniversary letter I would like to draw excerpts from previous prayer letters as 'memorial stones' down the path that God has led us these ten years. . . . Please pray with me that I may realize in my life the intent of the Scripture . . . "to bring good news to the afflicted . . . to bind up the brokenhearted, to proclaim liberty to captives, and freedom to prisoners, to proclaim the favorable year of the Lord . . . to comfort all who mourn . . ." (Isaiah 61:1,2). . . . I think I carried a lot of preconceived ideas to Ecuador of what my first term would be like and when things didn't work out that way it was difficult for me. . . . Lately the Lord has been showing me that He didn't call me to Ecuador simply to train village health workers. He called . . . me to be a fragrance of Christ to Ecuadorians, and He ordained the experience . . . to conform to His image. . . . And so, our dear friends, God's great adventure goes on. Several of you have been with us in prayer

and financial support since those early days. God has caused our path to cross with others of you at different points along this pilgrimage. For all of you we give our Father deepest thanks.[19]

A missionary writes to her supporters about a young man named Santiago who is nearly killed when an airplane crashes on takeoff. On the ground near the crash, Santiago escapes with his life by running through the fiery wreckage, but burns his hand severely. The missionary then transforms the story into a poetic image of eternal destiny. The poem addresses Santiago directly in the second person, as if intended literally to scare the hell out of him. But of course, the piece is written in English with deep resonances for American fundamentalists—an audience that will respond, in its fiber, to the imagery of the lake of fire.

> *Santiago, please give Jesus your stripped, raw hand*
> *Eternity with Him will be absent of pain*
> *Eternity without Him will be like running*
> *Through the fire you ran through two days ago—*
> *Only it will never end.*[20]

In recent years, HCJB has begun to produce a series of institutional prayer letters in the form of regular fund-raising publications, which individual members can also use to inform and inspire their own supporters. These include three quarterly magazines in English: *Around the World*, a publication for the Mission's general constituency; *Amigos*, for "friends of the HCJB Health Care Division"; and *HCJB Today*, for "alumni and friends." Stories and photographs of *the work* in Ecuador fill these periodicals. While many of the articles are produced by professional missionary writers assigned to the Mission's Department of Publicity and Public Relations, vignettes are included on a regular basis from staff members working in different areas of the Mission.

A 1989 issue of the *Around the World* gives an especially graphic display of the Mission's rhetorical work. Organized entirely around the theme of spiritual combat, the issue includes articles entitled "Deploying the Troops," "Radio Penetrates Communist Bloc," and "Welcome to Basic Training." In an almost literal sense, radio is portrayed here as God's air force. Mission President Ron Cline's column in the magazine is illustrated with the quintessential World War II recruiting poster for the United States armed forces. The stars and stripes have been discretely removed from the figure of Uncle Sam; yet there is no mistaking the stern, goateed, top-hatted icon of American patriotism, thrusting his index finger directly at the reader. In the text of his appeal for funds, Cline portrays a scene from air combat:

> In the ready room. Go over the plan. Last minute equipment check. Planes fueled and ready. "Go." Target sighted. Be aware of the enemy. Drop the bombs. Return to base. Mission completed.
>
> That's how it's done in a war.
>
> And that's the way we are doing it today. Only our bombs carry life instead of death, and we use radio instead of airplanes. But in reality, in the spiritual warfare going on today, we are God's air force and our Commander-in-Chief, the one who directs all of our missions, is the Holy Spirit himself. He travels the same way our life-giving message travels—invisibly, rapidly, through the air.

In my 30 minutes on the air today, I will talk to more people than I will speak with face-to-face in my whole lifetime. . . . As I speak the words, "Good morning, this is HCJB, and we are Heralding Christ Jesus' Blessings," the bomb drops, right on time, right on target. And people learn about life eternal.

Oh, yes . . . there is an enemy. He's called the prince of the power of the air, and we are fighting him everyday right in his back yard. And we are winning. People are turning from darkness to light. They are becoming free—reborn children of God. . . . I don't know why, but during these days we are running low on operational funds to keep up the battle. . . . With your help right now, through a special gift or prayer, HCJB may be able to press the war in some areas so that Satan would lose substantial ground (Cline, 1989:8).

On one level, this passage might be seen as a rhetorical throwback to the World War II imagery of 1950s missions—an appeal to old-line supporters. Alternatively, the proper context of the piece appears to be more contemporary; its extended metaphor reflects a remilitarized U.S. foreign policy of the late 1980s. But what is perhaps most significant to note here is not the *context* of Ron Cline's message, but the *text* itself. In a sense, Cline is not using military conflict as a metaphor for the spiritual work of evangelical missions; for him this is a literal reality—more real and of greater consequence than war between nations. The Holy Spirit actually travels through the air. Satan is a personal being, a real enemy; the territory he holds on earth is real ground. In his 1990 year-end report, Cline draws the battle lines explicitly in geographical terms:

Our primary concern . . . [is a] belt [that] runs from West Africa across the Middle East and through Asia. . . . I believe if Christ gave His great commission—"Arise and go!"—today, He would point to this belt as a first priority. . . . [With] 55 of the least evangelized countries in the world . . . , this belt represents a majority of mankind dominated and controlled by the forces of Satan. They are hungry for food, freedom and the truth. In many cases they have no access to that truth except as we get it to them via radio.

Radio can talk to so many people at once—unhampered by governmental red tape. . . . All we need is you. You will provide the prayer support and the financial support to finish the task. You hold the resources necessary to blitz the belt! (Cline, 1990:3).

While the religious right in America has lost the threat of international communism as an organizing principle, we see in Cline's portrayal an alternative basis for the moral bifurcation of the globe—one that hearkens back to the nineteenth-century colonialist missions' view of Christendom vs. the pagan world, yet employs the idiom of modern media. From an evangelical perspective, this is a more concrete demarcation than that of anticommunism, because it eliminates the intermediate ideological linkage of moral standing to political systems and coalitions. The only thing that matters is whether people have had an opportunity to hear and respond to the Word, the Christian message. And yet, this maneuver is based upon grandiose abstraction. Masses of human beings are conceptually cordoned off together in a huge swath of unevangelized territory far away. Radio, a remote medium that strips the Word to its bare essence, penetrates enemy territory by a strategy of stealth and efficiency. The missionary becomes a disembodied voice from the other side of the world, carried through the air by radio waves.

The medical side of the Mission offers another kind of example of how special rhetoric may be used in the production of images for audiences of missionary supporters in the United States. The following is an excerpt from a typical story published on the front page of the *Amigos* newsletter, entitled "A Gift of Love," by Karen Mace:

> The powers of darkness moved silently and with strength over 13-year-old Angel. The evil was palpable. The pain in the Shuar boy's leg was almost unbearable, but his father the witch doctor insisted on using his power to cure his son. . . . Incantations and calling on dark powers for the healing of his leg had been going on forever it seemed. Finally from among the watching group, someone hesitantly suggested going to Hospital Vozandes-Shell. Arrangements were made with MAF (Mission Aviation Fellowship) to fly the boy to the hospital. Even so, all night before the flight, the witch doctor worked calling on his powers. . . .
>
> [The boy undergoes lengthy treatment at the hands of Dr. Al Dixon in the Mission's hospital in Shell.]
>
> When Angel left the hospital he left behind many friends. But he took with him the Word of God planted in his heart by Joyce Stuck and other faithful servants of the Lord. He also left knowing that his bill was taken care of by the hospital charity fund—a gift of love. . . .
>
> *Postscript*: At press time Angel was back in the hospital. . . . The sad thing is that he thinks he has been bewitched by a witch doctor and that this is the reason for his illness. There are a number of powerful witch doctors in Angel's family, and he finds it hard to remain firm in Christ while he is back with his tribe. Pray that his faith will help him overcome, and that he will be Christ's ambassador to his people (Mace, 1991:1).

The choice of this particular story for publication, its dramatic construction of character and conflict, its narrative form and its rhetorical style, tell us perhaps more about the demands of its target audience in North America than it reveals about the actual events it describes or the lives of its protagonists in Ecuador. The story embodies a kind of mythic ideal of the Mission. Bearing little connection to the daily activities and encounters of most HCJB members, this text employs an idiom that has been honed for specific resonance with evangelical donors' traditional images and expectations of missionary work.

In fact, Mission writers are capable of portraying the same sort of phenomena in an entirely different light, in response to the exigencies of a very different audience of supporters—for example, the secular audience represented by a U.S. government granting agency. To be specific, in the late 1970s, the United States Agency for International Development (USAID) provided grant funding to the HCJB Health Care Division to support a community development project among the Shuar Indians— the same tribe of which the unfortunate boy depicted above was a member. The Mission's final report to USAID is entitled *Primary Health Care Workers in Ecuador: A PVO's* [private voluntary organization's] *Experience*. Leaning heavily on anthropologist Michael Harner's published ethnographies of the Shuar, the Mission report characterizes indigenous healing in a way that contrasts markedly (to say the least) with Karen Mace's portrayal in the *Amigos* article. The witch doctor becomes a shaman. The "palpable evil" vanishes, and in its place we find a "cohesive system of beliefs about illness":

> The Shuars have quite an extensive and cohesive system of beliefs about illness, its causes and prevention, and death. . . . In order for a shaman to cure a patient, he must first ascertain whether or not the illness is due to witchcraft. . . . The Shuar also grow many herbs and medicinal plants and almost everyone knows how to use them. Sometimes a person will get a reputation for being good at treating certain kinds of illnesses and they are called 'the knowing ones' (Risser, 1983:2–3, 6–7).

Missionaries themselves often are quite self-conscious about the process of producing texts that portray their work, with sensitivities quite attuned to rhetorical nuances. Their concern has to do with what is at stake. Quite simply, prayer letters, furlough speeches, and publicity materials produced for U.S. audiences constitute the economic lifeblood of the Mission. For individual missionaries, effective impression management may mean the difference between winning and losing the financial backing that is necessary to stay in the field.

> I lost a lot of churches' financial support because I was seen as a secondary missionary. Because my vocation, as it turned out, didn't fit in to what most churches thought of as being a real missionary.

> At the church missionary meeting on furlough, they gave me ten minutes to speak. And I thought, what will I say in ten minutes? I tried, as best I could, in the allotted time. But I felt that it was a disappointment to people. It went flat, because I didn't tell any missionary stories about the natives. I was made aware of their especially distorted view of missionaries, and what people think of as the mission field.

> One of my close friends is a secretary in the administration office. She finds that difficult because she doesn't feel like a real missionary, and she has to look for information to use for prayer letters that will sound spiritual.

> I don't write anything about what I'm doing here except "real missionary" work. I just don't feel that they need to know the rest of it. I've written them a lot about when I've gone on caravans, and stuff like that. As far as my missionary letters—prayer letters—it is pretty much what they'd like to hear, to fulfill their expectations. . . . They're expecting you to be down here witnessing, winning souls, and that kind of stuff—at least doing something that sounds like missionary-type work. So you just write that, you know. . . . I really got a lot of response from a story about a kid who was supposed to die, and didn't die, and how the family came to the Lord through it. A lot of people appreciated that letter. They have expectations that they want fulfilled.

At some point, probably every HCJB missionary faces the dilemma of how to communicate with supporters in a manner that fulfills their expectations, while still maintaining personal integrity. Indeed, the Mission administration has worried enough about this issue to address it directly in the Worker's Manual, warning members to "Be Careful" in writing prayer letters:

> Very often people at home are eager to read of the "dramatic" incidents or the unfavorable aspects of life on the mission field. . . . A balanced picture should always be given. For example, the impression should not be [given] . . . that all the people who live in Ecuador are "ignorant, poverty-stricken Indians, living in straw-thatched huts out in the jungles, reachable only by mule back." . . . The use of the word "native" in reference to the people of Latin America is to be avoided. The terms "national" or "Ecuadorian" . . . are better.

It is tempting to dismiss this statement as well-intentioned bigotry, of the sort that demonstrates an unseemly prejudice while attempting to preach against it. And yet, there may be more to this official admonition than meets the eye. From the Mission's point of view, there is a certain finesse to it. In the first place, it explicitly acknowledges the issue of audience expectations, thereby lending significance to the matter beyond the unspoken concerns of individual missionaries. Then, it advocates a "balanced picture" by citing a negative example that is extreme to the point of being obviously humorous. The images of ignorant Indians, straw huts, and mule travel amount to a caricature, of course—but one that is recognizable precisely because of its resemblance to many real prayer letters that are written with audience expectations in mind. In effect, the straw-man example fails to address—and thus tacitly condones—the less blatant stylizing of the truth that is much more common and accepted. Indeed, HCJB missionaries do not talk about "the natives" any more; but they do mention "the nationals" with much the same patronizing connotation.

> Impatience or exasperation can turn us prematurely aside from some national believer who is slow to catch on, but who, if properly trained will finally produce far more benefits to the work than the smartest national who is unconverted and rejects the Gospel (Jones, 1966 [1962]: 118).

The Fourth Audience: Targets of Mission

The fourth audience is made up of the targets or *objects* of mission: the unsaved, the sick, the needy, the nationals. These are the missionary's clientele. They constitute various groups, some remote and others present to the missionary. They are encountered in various ways, in different roles: radio listener, hospital patient, Mission employee. As an *audience*, they fulfill two significant functions for the missionary's moral career. First, they provide the objectified *other* to whom a personal mission may be directed. Second, they enable missionaries to maintain the ideology of otherworldly strangerhood as the foundation of their personal identity. Themes of set-apartness get worked into the composition of missionaries' lives in complex patterns, creating painful ironies. Missionary conversation about the people outside their world becomes a sort of fugue of cultural alienation:

> If God wanted me to speak Spanish better, he would have given me the ability. Some people can master the language, and some people can't, and I'm one of those people who can't. But with the Indians, it's very interesting. You take a Spanish person in there, and they won't listen to him—but they will listen to a gringo. Sometimes we'll go out with a Latin. And the Latin will preach, and nothing happens. And the Quichua will preach, and nothing happens. And the gringo will preach, and there will be a number of people accept the Lord! Now the message is basically the same. But I can command more attention than the Quichua or the Latin. The only thing I can think of is that they're awed, and they have to listen hard to hear what this strange person is trying to say. These people know that you're more educated than they are, and they want to learn. They know also that you have something more than they have. How did you get it? If they can listen hard enough to learn how you got it, they might be able to get it too.

> All I have to do is prepare myself to say it well—to speak the message. I don't have to do anything else. I go into the studio, I speak, and people tens of thousands of miles away are

able to listen. What a tremendous capacity! I compare the radio work—our work—with the work that the Lord did when he was here. He is the creator of the whole universe, but when he was here he had to walk—up the hills and down, along the roads from village to village, to bring the gospel to those people. We, on the other hand, have the capacity to preach the message from this one location, and thousands of people in thousands of villages can hear it at the same moment.

In Ecuador I've really grown in self esteem. Being a foreign-trained professional, one is given a higher place. Last year I was asked to conduct a seminar at the university. At home, I would be the one attending seminars to learn new things. At first I was really afraid to do it because of my Spanish. I was afraid they were going to ask questions and I wouldn't know what they were talking about. But I found that I really could present new ideas to them. They wouldn't have been new ideas at home, but they are new here. Also, in the church, I've come to see myself in a different role here. I never thought of myself as a spiritual leader before. I just never was a leader in the church at home. I think part of it is lack of understanding on the part of the Latins, or a lack of maturity perhaps.

As a supervisor, I really try to get to know the employees on an individual basis. I know most of their families. I've met their wives, their kids. I've been in some of their homes. I've visited them, shared with them, studied the Word with them. We've prayed together. When one of them gets sick, or a kid is in the hospital, I try to go and visit them and pray with them. Any of the employees on the compound, I'll always speak to them coming and going. I call them by name, and they call me Don Pancho.

For a missionary nurse it's difficult, because when you do try to say something spiritual to the patients, they'll often tell you they are evangelical Christians just because they think they'll get better care in the hospital. I'm not sure I'm really *talking* to anybody. That's one of my biggest frustrations. You know, you feel you're supposed to be down here serving the Lord and reaching all these people. You're supposed to be out there, making friends with the Latins and bringing them into your home and witnessing and talking to them. And then you can't even talk to anybody because you don't have the time, and when you do have the time you can't really do it anyway and you feel really guilty. I'm thinking, you know, if I were to go home on furlough tomorrow—what would I tell the people? What would I say, in terms of praying with patients, in terms of speaking with them about spiritual things? I would like to see much more evidence of people personally touched—not just physically, but spiritually.

I have heard some deep criticisms of the missionary conglomerate. To Latins on the outside looking in, we seem to be all-encompassing. If it's radio, it's us. If it's medicine, it's us. If it's engineering, it's us. If it's hydroelectric, it's us. If it's community development, it's us. Wow, we do everything. Now, it's a human trait to be critical of something large and successful. And I have had Latins say to me, "Missionaries should not be allowed in this country. They ought to be sent out of the country." Well, I try to get them to put a face on it, because I am "it." In order to bring that home, I respond by saying, "When do you think I should leave?" And they will say, "Oh, we don't mean you. We know you, and you're different." By not defending ourselves, we make ourselves even more vulnerable than they had intended to make us. You kind of have to disarm them.

The Latins don't take responsibility. That's a real hard thing to accept. If something goes wrong at the hospital, you know, a patient falls or doesn't get a certain treatment, [they say] "It's not my fault, it's somebody else's, I haven't done anything!" They don't seem to care. It's hard to work with Latin people, because they don't take responsibility as we do. They don't care as much. If they can do it easier, so much the better. They don't care if a patient is going to get completely contaminated because they dropped a dressing on the floor. There's not that sense of caring that we're so used to. And they don't treat people with respect. Nobody gets treated with respect unless they have money—then they get lots of good care. That's one of the hardest things. They're very difficult to work with. You've got to be checking up on them all the time to make sure they've gotten done what they were supposed to. They say they'll do something, but then they won't do it.

We went on vacation with an Ecuadorian couple, who are among our closest friends. We took them to Los Cerros [a missionary camp on the coast]. They were the only nonmissionaries there. Well, for several months after that they resented us, and the wife wouldn't even take communion at our church. It turned out that they thought we were accusing them of stealing our camera, when we innocently asked if they had seen it.

We've always lived out among the Ecuadorians away from the compound, but that doesn't really make us a part of that community. We're still the *extranjeros* in that neighborhood. People are nice to us, but we are not assimilated.

With Ecuadorians, friendship only goes to a certain point, in my experience. I have Ecuadorian friends. They'll confide in you to a certain point, and then it stops. You're invited into their homes. You'll talk about things—but suddenly you'll come to a place where it really has to become internal and intimate friendship, and there's a wall. *They* will not break through it. As a foreigner, you never have a friendship such that you get past a certain point. But maybe as foreigners, as Christ has asked us to be, maybe that's as far as we're supposed to go.

Each of these passages includes talk about the people to whom missionary effort is directed. In the most literal sense, such people represent the *primary* audience for missionaries, their most immediate *other*. Yet the connection of these *others* to missionary identity is ambiguous. Insofar as identity is reflected in community, then this fourth audience is the most peripheral of all, the farthest removed from the missionary group's shared context of meaning and dialogue. And yet, insofar as missionary identity depends on the imagination of *strangerhood*—a glance from nowhere—then people who exist as the external objects of mission are essential to the sustaining of a missionary self. Taken together, their own statements make it poignantly clear how deeply these missionaries remain set apart from the Ecuadorian world.

In the pages to follow, we shall examine ways in which various audiences of interest to HCJB members are juxtaposed in their conversation about one of the most significant ideals of missionary life—the ideal of material sacrifice. We shall see, once again, how HCJB members develop strategies of rationalization and mystification in order to maintain a missionary self in the presence of dissonant facts of experience. At different moments in this process, particular audiences take on significance not only as they provide warrant for alternative performances of mission, but as they provide the components of membership and language for reconstruction of the missionary's identity.

The Sacrifice of Sacrifice

In my generation, we looked for sacrifice on the mission field. We looked for ways to demonstrate that we were hurting or deprived, because that was the traditional concept.

The missionary was thrown in with people of extreme poverty, and so he became a person of poverty himself. But this was the situation of first entry, the pagan situation first being invaded by the pioneering missionary. Today, missionary work is being carried on in many places where the gospel has become quite well known, if not well received. Also, there is much more affluence and development in the countries where missionaries are working, and it no longer necessitates the material deprivations.

Prospective HCJB members often do not realize that their economic means as Quito missionaries will exact little material sacrifice, and in fact will afford them a standard of living far beyond the dreams of most people in Ecuador. Their tidy replicas of American middle-class suburban life, with family cars and modern homes perched in the upscale hillside neighborhoods of north Quito, stand out in gilded relief against images of sacrificial poverty in the missionary myth—and indeed, against the actual setting of a Latin American city with desperate urban slums, beggars in the streets, and ragged children working to feed smaller siblings. Whatever their intentions, missionaries join the ranks of the wealthy, not necessarily because they acquire more resources than they previously had (though they may do so), but because the masses around them have much less (see Bonk, 1991).

As these individuals confront the discrepancy between the missionary myth and their position of relative wealth, feelings of disappointment and guilt vie with pleasant surprise and relief. A second-generation missionary illustrates the ambivalence that emerges in the gap between the sacrificial ideal of his parents' era and the present reality for HCJB members in Quito. Others relate similar experiences.

> I was embarrassed when I came and saw the house people had gotten for us to rent—you know, with a telephone and running water. I expected us to be living in something at the level of my parents. When my parents came to visit, I remember I was really self-conscious about the house. It had nice parquet floors. It had furnishings. And I felt guilty, because I knew where they came from. I knew the very inhuman conditions they put up with for forty years. And I felt really guilty. It took me a long time to conquer, because— it wasn't a point of pride, but it was a feeling that I wasn't a "real missionary" if I didn't suffer the way they did. I feel like I have given up nothing to come here from the States. That's my biggest problem. I feel like I should be giving up something.

> I wasn't called to live in the lap of luxury. So it doesn't help living in such a nice place and having life so easy. I came down almost expecting to live in a mud hut, and was horrified at all the china and sterling silver that the missionaries had.

> When we got to Ecuador I was very surprised. We were invited out the first week to meals in people's homes. The people who invited us, of course, were quite settled—but it was certainly more elegant than I had ever expected. We were with D. S. and Erma Clark, and they had a beautiful home. They rang a bell and a maid came. I was amazed. I had never eaten in homes that were as well put-together and as orderly. I was surprised.

> I remember when we first came, it all seemed too good for me, for what I had thought would be my lot in life. I remember we looked for apartments, and I had been totally ready to live in *whatever.* Then we got a nice place with a bathtub and a fireplace and parquet floors. While we enjoy it, I do feel that as missionaries we have too much, live too well, spoil ourselves with VCRs and microwave ovens. I feel that much of the time we are not

very good stewards of what we have. We are inclined to take advantage of the fact that we are foreigners with more assets.

I expected it would be a sacrifice. And that's not the way it is. We've sort of got a utopia here in Quito. We've got the most beautiful climate—year around—in all the world that I know of. We've got the most beautiful produce and the best meat that you could buy in any market. I can go to the finest restaurants in Ecuador, a lot cheaper than I can go to restaurants in the States.

On the surface, this problem looks like a simple variation on the theme of disenchantment; life in the mission field turns out to be different than missionaries expected. But there is a twist to it. While in one sense life turns out to be *better* than they thought (a pleasant surprise), the missionary ideal reverses the definition of the terms of a good life: better can be worse. Moreover, the conflict is not merely internal; there is the practical matter of communicating with financial supporters who share these expectations about missionary sacrifice. One missionary put it succinctly: "In my supporting churches they put missionaries on a pedestal as being completely self-sacrificing, and living just on the edge of poverty all the time." These images die hard, not only because supporters are removed from the concrete realities of missionary life, but because the images are deeply embedded in the very idiom of communication between missionaries and supporters, i.e., prayer letters to raise funds. Some HCJB missionaries do try to "dispel the myth" as it applies to their own situation. But they find that this is not as easy as they think; nor is it always practical.

I think supporters thrive on a certain missionary image. I really believe they don't *want to* know what I do. They don't want to know how nice my home is. They don't want to know that I drive a regular American car, and that I have a nice office, and that I eat food just like they do, and that my kids go to a good school, and that I live very much in the same lifestyle that they do. I really believe that they don't want to know that today's missionary, for the most part, is living in a big city and living pretty well. I have had people come here and visit me, actually be here, and still ask me these stupid "missionary questions." It's almost like their minds would not allow them to say, "Boy, he's not hurting at all! He's really comfortable. He's got a good life." Maybe they would feel guilty saying that about a missionary, because a missionary is supposed to sacrifice.

It's always a problem communicating to people back home. You can't, unless they come and see it for themselves. And it's something I always remind Bill about, because he's got an almanac of stories that he can tell about primitive situations. I mean, he can go on all day and all night. And then I have to remind people—we drive a nice car, and we live in a nice home, and we can buy anything we need, and our kids have shoes on their feet, and we live in a big city. I try to give a balanced picture because Bill tends to be a little more dramatic than he ought to be sometimes. That's the human element, you know. Missionary—the word itself just seems to say you live in a primitive situation.

Once again, the HCJB Worker's Manual allows us to place these individual views in the context of a common problem for the Mission membership, and to see how the dilemma is constructed officially. The manual is particularly useful for understanding the dynamics of this issue from the inside out, because it is written for inside consumption. Hence, the document does not simply express the ideal of missionary sacrifice, but renders it as a sort of ideological challenge in the context of the missionary's symbolic performances for different audiences. Strategies for resolving both the internal and external conflict surrounding missionary economics again require the use of special rhetoric and mystification. The handbook demonstrates these maneuvers implicitly in the way it frames the problem.

THE MISSIONARY AND HIS OUTFIT

a. General Policies

In his thinking and planning, every missionary should emphasize the importance of spiritual preparation and a life of consecration to Christ. . . . He should seek a balance between austerity and the wise obtaining of the necessary equipment that will make the missionary efficient and will adequately care for his physical and material needs.

He should also keep in mind the effect an excessively large or elaborate outfit has on the following:

1) *The Nationals to Whom He Will Minister*

Their economic situation is generally less favorable than his. They will accept without offense some differences in living standards. However, when that difference becomes glaring, it may prove a stumbling block to them.

2) *His Home Constituency*

When a missionary talks about the sacrifice needed to fulfill the Great Commission and then departs for the field with an outfit that shows little or no sacrifice on his part, it is likely to create an adverse reaction among those who by their own sacrifice maintain the missionary on the field.

3) *His Fellow Missionary*

The right of individual preference is recognized among missionaries of World Radio and no attempt is made to legislate exactly how each person should live. At the same time, an attempt is made to maintain a more or less equal standard of living among the missionary staff.

4) *Himself*

. . . A large outfit [requires] expense and effort that may prove an encumbrance and a hindrance in the fulfillment of his basic purposes as a missionary. . . .

b. Guide to Total Value of Personal Outfit

. . . It is up to the individual to determine his own budget, but the aim should be to stay below the limits which have been established. Some missionaries are willing to make considerable sacrifices in order to get to the field.

A new missionary should not feel that he is entitled to bring as a first-time outfit all that a missionary who has resided on the field for 10 or 20 years may have accumulated.

Several features of this passage deserve comment. First, the most significant solution to the problem of material possessions is embedded in the definition of the topic: the missionary and his *outfit*. Possessions are not for consumption or comfort; they are cast as "equipment" for carrying out the Great Commission. All material properties of the self thus become vocational tools, as the self becomes isomorphic with mission. Secondly, the pragmatic advice to missionaries on relating to different audiences carries two messages; one message upholds the mythic ideal, while the other subverts it with rationalizations and shifts the issue away from the missionary. Thus, on the one hand new missionaries are cautioned not to bring a "large outfit" lest it become an "encumbrance and a hindrance" to their basic purpose. On the other hand, they are admonished not to insist too quickly on having all the material goods that senior missionaries have accumulated. Such pronouncements are made, of course, in the vein of elder missionaries imparting accrued wisdom to new recruits; by example and implication, this is a lesson in how to do *well* by doing *good*.

In particular, while "austerity" is of moral value, it is not supposed to stand in the way of missionaries' "material needs," nor prevent them from getting things to improve their "efficiency"—which can mean anything from a new suit to a new car, personal computer, or video camera. We learn that while nationals are in a "less favorable" economic position than missionaries, they will accept this "without offense." (Indeed they will have to, if they desire employment with HCJB.) Still, missionaries should avoid flaunting an ostentatious living standard in front of the nationals. Why? Because it may become a "stumbling block *to them*" (i.e., to the nationals). Missionaries should not *talk* about sacrifice to their financial backers and then fail to *show* sacrifice as they depart to the field. Why? Because this "might create an adverse reaction." Hence, missionaries should avoid the appearance of using supporters' donations to acquire things for themselves that the supporters' are doing without, in order send people to the mission field.

Missionaries themselves are often acutely aware that the sacrificial ideal can be used to mask an underlying motivation for personal gain. As one member put it:

> I have often seriously questioned the motives of missionaries. I think a lot of them come from situations where they have not been happy, where they have not done well, and they think that they will come here and find a utopia. They often do find that they have much greater economic chances and opportunities here than if they were living in the States. But then they also find themselves, as Americans in Ecuador, looked-up-to and hated at the same time.

While a number of HCJB members concur with this narrator's opinion, it is probably quite rare that someone actually joins the Mission for the conscious purpose of attaining a comfortable lifestyle. It is hardly rare, though, for missionaries to become a good deal more affluent than they were—or even would have been—in their home country. But while HCJB missionaries enjoy and take pride in their homes and possessions, they also typically feel some conflict about their material wealth in a poor country, which requires rationalizations of one sort or another.

> We have a comfortable apartment. And I told my wife I don't care how nice it gets, as long as it doesn't get so nice that I don't want to go out to the Indians. But it's important for me to have a nice place to come home to after I have been out there. As far as identifying with the poor—you will never have a place where someone doesn't feel uncomfortable coming to your place. You could live in a rat hole—then your middle class and your upper class are going to feel uncomfortable coming to your place. If you have a nice place—if you even have a modest, decent place—the Indians will not feel comfortable coming. We have invited any number of Indians to come to eat in our house, and we've yet to have the first one come. They've said they're going to come. We've prepared for them. But they've

never come. So it's much easier for us to go down—to sit around the Indians' humble little fire and eat their soup—than it is for them to come here and wonder what the devil all these forks are for, and what all this stuff is.

I'm faced with a tremendous unanswered question: What do I do about the poverty? How do I relate, as a person, as a servant of God, when I'm confronted with such poverty? How does one deal with that? I've had to look at myself in a different light.

We get in a habit of walking by beggars, and ignoring people at our gate who are hungry. And it happens to me. And then I think, how can I do that? I mean, here I am, a big rich American—what is ten sucres to me? I could throw that on the sidewalk and never turn around and look at it. I could give that to anybody who comes around to my door. What is ten sucres? Nothing.

I'm the one who yells and screams that we should bring our own salaries down, and raise the level of our national workers' salaries. I'm very ill at ease about the discrepancy there that is so very, very obvious. I don't want to be receiving a lot more than others.

A few missionaries attempt to resolve this issue by placing moral responsibility for poverty squarely on the backs of the poor themselves. Thus, the missionary's social obligation reduces to setting a good example by living uprightly and well, thereby teaching the values that will enable the lower classes to pull themselves up by their own bootstraps.

If you try to reach the low class by going down and living like they live, they would look at you and say, "What a fool! We know he's got more than that, but the way he lives is no better than we live." Now, if you're into community development—are you developing them by living at the same low standards that they do? Or is development going to come because you live different? I'm here to teach them spiritual values, but also things like cleanliness, neatness, organization. As they see me, it gives them a goal to try to reach.

When I first got here, one missionary told me, "You know, all these people that beg in the street—you shouldn't give to them." Somebody else said, "No, I've never been hurt by giving to them." You do have these type of people who come to your door, and probably would just keep coming forever if you gave them money. I think it never hurts to give them a little. But you've got to put some limitation on it. When they come back and start asking for clothes and stuff, you've got to put a stop to it, because they will never do anything but beg for the rest of their life if they can get away with it.

More commonly, HCJB members resolve this conflict through a more sophisticated ideological transformation of economic status into a matter of cultural identity and lifestyle choice. By a subtle mystification, poverty and wealth can be viewed not primarily as *concrete conditions* with moral relevance to human relationships, but as *subjective assessments* in the neutral zone of culture and personal preference. This maneuver effectively masks inequities in the distribution of resources, power, and privilege, by redefining them as equally valid expressions of different people and different *ethoi*. It then enables missionaries to invoke arguments for cultural respect, personal authenticity, and "pure evangelism" to justify their superior position over the human objects of their mission. Consider a parable from the life of a senior HCJB missionary.

Let me tell you the experience that we had in Illacu, a mountain Quichua Indian town. After we had been going in there with medical caravans for three or four years, the Indians all got together and they said, "We'd like to have a little place for you to stay, so that you can stay here with us." So they built it. When they got it done, they invited us to come and they showed it to us, hoping that we would move there and stay, I suppose. In the first room, they had bought a table with chairs—brand new. In the kitchen, a gas stove. They had bought dish ware—spoons, knives, forks, plates, cups, saucers, bowls—everything, you know, just like you were in one of the restaurants in town. And for cooking, they had bought cookware that was modern. Then we went into the next room, and it was a sort of study. They had bought us a writing desk, a table, a lamp. And in the bedroom, there were bunk beds with mattresses, sheets, blankets, pillows, pillow cases—everything. And I walked in, and I said "What is happening here?" —because I know these people, and none of them has a table. They do not have a gas stove. They do not have a bed. They sleep on the floor on straw mats. But they only said, "Mil disculpas"—"A thousand pardons"—excusing themselves for the very small effort that they had made to make us comfortable. After awhile, I began to talk with them, and I said, "Why did you do this?" I said, "I know that none of you has a table like this. Why did you buy it for us?" And do you know what they said? They said, "We are Indians. We will always be Indians. And to have these things is not part of us. But this is part of you. We know you. And in comparison to where we know you came from, this is just a very meager effort. We would not want you to come down and degrade yourselves to live like we do. Never." That, to me, was a real insight. It said to me, you can live with the Indians, but they don't expect you to live like them. They expect you to live like who you are. What they are also saying is, "Don't expect us to live like you. Let us live the way we are."

Set in larger context, this intriguing story turns on a series of ironic reversals. First, the role of the rich man is played by someone who, as it happens, grew up poor—in a rural, fundamentalist home in North America. But he has entered a vocation in which he is viewed *as if* he were a person of wealth choosing to become poor for the benefit of strangers. When he arrives in Ecuador, his position is reversed again, and he finds that he actually is one of the rich. The role of the poor in the story is played by people who go out and acquire a houseful of material wealth, and then divest themselves of it by giving it to the rich missionary. In the end, the lesson of the story justifies the position of the wealthy, but it is spoken in the voice of the poor.

The affluent missionary thus keeps his possessions as accouterments of an authentic cultural self, but is relieved of any burden of guilt. Absolution is declared by the very people who are presumed to be oppressed by the unequal distribution of wealth. The living conditions of the dispossessed are romanticized; by their own admission, they enjoy living without all the gadgets that encumber the rich. The Indians could have all these things if they wanted them—after all, they somehow got together and acquired them for the missionary. They welcome the missionary's help as long as it allows them to continue living in the simple, happy manner to which they are accustomed. Thus, if we take at face value what the Indians in this story say, missionaries are relieved not only of guilt, but of social responsibility. They don't have to protest the structures that keep Indians in poverty; they don't have to identify with the Indians by living simply themselves; they don't even have to give alms to the poor. From a Marxian perspective, this might appear to be a classic example of how ideology serves class interest through systematic distortion of the views of the oppressed, so that they are unable to see the reality of their own condition and thus remain dependent and powerless. First the ideology of power creates its own version of reality; then this new reality consolidates power by hiding its ideological scaffolding where it can least be suspected as such—in the minds and voices of the weak and poor. And yet, such a rendering may give the Indians less credit than they deserve. By seeing the story only as missionary mystification, we fail to see the sense in which the Indians have taken an ideology thrust upon them and used it creatively for purposes of their own. On the surface, their gesture embraces the missionary and brings him into their midst. (He portrays it as a fetching attempt on the part of these simple folk to win his presence among them.) But its much deeper effect is to objectify the missionary-as-stranger through an iconography of his alien accouterments. Most importantly, moral power is thus transferred from the missionary to the Indians, as the tables are turned and he becomes the recipient of *their* grace and altruism. In the subtext of this missionary's story, then, the Indians emerge as a free and autonomous community—not needing what he has to provide—while he ends up beholden and estranged from them.

It has not been unheard of for an HCJB missionary actually to try living at the economic level of an average Ecuadorian. Stories still circulate about past missionaries who adopted this strategy, at least for a time; but almost invariably it is defined negatively in terms of imitating Ecuadorian culture and rejecting one's own. According to common wisdom, the problem is that Ecuadorians will not take at face value such an affectation by someone from outside their culture. Rather, they will see it for what it is—a disingenuous performance. No charade will make someone an Ecuadorian. Thus, from an ideological point of view, the imitation strategy is useful to missionaries not as an actual mode of evangelism, but because its patent falseness justifies going to the other extreme. It becomes part of the repertoire of mystifications that HCJB missionaries have developed to rationalize the pursuit of the American middle-class dream in a mission enclave in Ecuador. Economic comfort is coopted as being true to one's own cultural identity.

> I think the standard of living is a difficult issue, and it's a very personal thing. But I've seen the other extreme. I knew some missionaries who decided they were going to live like the Indians. Well, it was a shambles. They weren't respected, they got sick, and they were next to useless because of the stand they took to look like the Indians. They went home very discouraged, and not willing to return. That was a very bad example. Here, most of the people in the Mission live in very nice situations. I do not think it makes any difference to your communication with the nationals. I think it's your attitude, and God working in you.

> In my own society of America, I would not classify myself by a long shot as being rich. But when you compare me to the poor Ecuadorian, I am rich. It could bother me, but I don't let it. The fact is that I am here, and in order to do my job here there are certain requirements for me to live. Now, I could say, the average Ecuadorian lives on one hundred dollars a month; if he can do it, I can too. But if I went down and started living on his level, he would not accept me for any more than I really am. That does not make me an Ecuadorian. I could get a sun tan, I could talk eloquent Spanish, but that does not make me an Ecuadorian. I have no difficulty with the standard I live on in Ecuador. I think that if I would try to bring myself down and live like he lives, I think he would look at me and say, "You idiot, what in the world are you trying to do and who are you trying to convince?" They see through that as a false way of trying to communicate with people.

We are born and raised with certain tastes, certain ways. You cannot eradicate those by living in a foreign country, and I would be foolish to try, because they are me. I am very grateful that my Latin brothers accept me with my baggage. They don't have any trouble with my being a gringo, so why should I fight it? If I were to try somehow to become a Latin, I would not be a true person. They would not respect me, because there would be something false there.

I don't feel any great desire to be more integrated into Ecuadorian society. I am an American, and I really cannot become an Ecuadorian. However, I want to be careful not to look down on them as being inferior. I try to look at them as just being different—although some things I feel *are* inferior.

There are some missionaries who try to get totally involved in Latin culture, and before long they've lost their identity, of who they are, and what their real purpose is here. And I don't think the Latins want you to do that. I think they want you to be a good gringo. I think that sometimes it's the culture and the people themselves that keep you separated. There never is a full acceptance, no matter what you do. You're always the gringo. You can wear their clothes, you can eat their food, but you always will be the gringo.

Perhaps the most intriguing rationalization that missionaries have developed in this context is one that shifts the mission field directly into the province of the upper class—a sort of evangelistic equivalent of trickle-down economics. After all, the conservative well-to-do in Ecuador are the people with whom HCJB missionaries are often identified by default, whether they want to be or not. If the missionaries can see themselves as *called to evangelize* these privileged few, then they can feel justified in living as upper-class people themselves. In fact, this becomes a conscious strategy of identification, a scheme to attract converts—and not just any converts, but influential elites.

Now you could even argue that in order to contextualize the gospel message, and really become culturally acclimated, the missionary may need to assume a certain level of affluence. I mean, he could argue that way because of the affluence of the people with whom he is dealing. It's the reverse situation from missionaries who are working with people of poverty.

I think in urban evangelism these days we need to figure out which groups aren't being reached, and perhaps the poor people are being reached better than any other. Perhaps we need more people witnessing very openly to upper-class people. Rather than saying everybody should live poorly, we should plan our standard of living . . . according to which groups most need to be reached. Those groups could very well be the middle and upper classes.

At the racquetball club, two of the guys there are very close to accepting the Lord. They're very open. Basically, inside they're searching. And from there it goes. Several people who have come to our home Bible study group were contacts I made playing racquetball.

Whatever people's social situation, I see anybody without Christ as basically without purpose in this life and without hope for a life hereafter. We have neighbors, here in the condominium where we're living right now, who need the Lord just as much as the poor. So I don't feel guilty. I'm in a place where I can minister to them, because I'm in a living situation that's not far from their own. We have a four-bedroom condominium with off-white shag carpeting. I mean, when we go on furlough it's a step down from here.

Some large contradictions emerge here. These are missionaries who are viewed back home as sacrificing worldly gain to work in a poor country. Whether they consciously promote it or not, their image of altruistic poverty helps motivate donations, which (as it turns out) enable them to sustain an affluent lifestyle abroad. The missionaries then justify their affluence (to themselves) by saying it allows them to identify with affluent Ecuadorians—that is, to evangelize them on their own turf. But this is the same strategy they reject, in favor of authenticity, when it comes to evangelizing the poor. On an abstract level, they view the incarnation of Christ as the archetype for missionary identification. Concretely, they must renegotiate what it means to imitate a Christ who "had no place to lay his head," and who made it more difficult for a rich man to enter heaven than for a camel to pass through the eye of a needle.

HCJB missionaries do sometimes admit that the gospel is supposed to redeem the wealthy from the particular sins that go along with being rich. But this means that they must distinguish themselves—in some morally significant way—from their well-to-do neighbors:

> Now, I do want to relate to them in a redemptive way. I get all steamed up when I hear them talking about themselves as *buena gente,* and being so disparaging of the lower classes. I want to relate to them in openness and love, but fight that kind of social classism. Hopefully, we've gotten things together enough in our own relationship to God and to our calling, that they're seeing differences in our lives, as compared to their own.

And yet they tend to reject, on moral grounds, any protest against the existing structure of economic and social relations that keeps people in poverty. When labor strikes occur in Quito, HCJB missionaries often side privately with the business owners against the laborers—in spite of the Mission's official policy of neutrality, and even though they affect a pose of benevolent concern for the poor in their arguments for the *status quo*:

> I get so upset over these strikes and protests and what they're about. It's really just *outside people* taking advantage of the poor. When they do these strikes and protests it just hurts the poor. It's a futile activity that's supposed to do one thing, and in reality does the opposite. I think, as an outsider myself, I can see it a little more objectively.

Oddly, it is when they go home on furlough that many of these missionaries finally acquire the sense of loss and sacrifice that they originally thought would mark their life on the field. It is not the same kind of sacrifice they expected. Nevertheless, it serves to confirm their original sense of calling to live in dependence upon God, their earlier commitment to set aside the trappings of worldly success in favor of a spiritual vocation. Furlough provides an alternative map that reorients their experience to the axes of sacrifice, altruism, and calling. It offers a reference group in which missionaries may feel impoverished, and a setting in which they can imagine a life of wealth and social standing as their road-not-taken:

> I don't regret being a missionary. It hits Janet, though, when we go back on furlough, to see the people we were in school with. And now they have their nice homes, and they're well established, and they have their friends and their social circles. And you know, we're

sort of floaters, and we come back and we have to ask for a car. But back home, they think we're a very special breed. Our old acquaintances, they just shake their heads and say, "We couldn't do what you've done." I guess what they're saying is they couldn't live with the insecurity. For them, having their home, having their job is security. I guess by their definition, we are a reckless type of people. Insecurity doesn't seem to bother us. If you spiritualize it, I guess you'd say that the Lord has given us the gift of faith so that we can depend on the Lord, more so than others. . . . In a sense, we *are* a special breed of people, in comparison to folks at home.

Once again, the larger context of this narrative gives it an ironic twist. The missionary portrayed here *has indeed* left community, friends, security, and material comforts. In fact, he has left these things behind in Ecuador to go on furlough. He has to "ask for a car" as if he had none—yet he is renting out his own automobile to colleagues in Quito while he is away. Here we see the essential ambivalence as well as the transforming ideological symbolism in missionaries' set-apartness from their home community. The vision is negative at first, but then shifts and becomes a positive confirmation of the missionary vocation. Marginality from a former group becomes membership in a special breed. Coming home and encountering others with more possessions becomes a symbol of being set apart by God on the mission field. The missionary myth doubles back on itself.

5

Missionary Strangerhood and American Evangelical Identity

The preceding chapters have illustrated how various layers of strangerhood combine to form a complex ideological theme in the self-understanding and social experience of missionaries. We have seen how a group of American evangelicals in a foreign setting may appropriate the rhetoric of calling in order to interpret diverse conditions of cultural and existential estrangement in their lives. We have examined ways in which missionary identities are shaped through generalized ambivalence arising from repeated experiences of withdrawal and engagement, conflict and embrace, dependence and autonomy. We have seen, in particular, how missionaries may elaborate moral careers as they reflect on their experiences over time, in the light of culturally stylized ideas about *life-as-conversion-testimony*. Finally, we have noted that such missionaries are able to resolve developmental predicaments, domesticate foreignness, and transcend disenchantment through a reformulation of the traditional imagery of *mission-as-sacrificial-hero-quest*.

My goal in this final chapter is twofold. First, I will try to encapsulate and reinforce the book's overall argument about strangerhood and calling in missionaries' moral careers, using selected quantitative findings from the attitudinal survey that I administered to 129 HCJB members, illustrated by a few selected quotations from interviews. Second, I will discuss in a broader context the relationship between these missionaries' reflections on their lives and the shifting cultural identity of contemporary American evangelicals and fundamentalists in general. The questions to be addressed, in the end, are these: What does this study's argument amount to? And what larger social realities do missionaries' lives represent or illuminate?

Meaning, Belonging, and Identity: A Survey

The story of how a calling based on strangerhood develops in moral careers is to be told largely in the subjective accounts of individual missionaries. But we gain important perspective on these personal views by examining group parameters in a statistical form as well. Once we see composite patterns and trends in the missionaries' general attitudes toward themselves and their social surroundings, we acquire a firmer context in which to interpret individual accounts. In turn, the narratives provide ideas about what the group patterns may mean. To these ends, I developed a standardized questionnaire toward the end of my year of field work, with the goal of uniformly assessing

151

HCJB members' sense of attachment to various sources of meaning, belonging, and identity. Most of the fixed-choice items that I constructed were developed directly from my record of things missionaries at various career stages had said spontaneously, i.e., in the narrative-style interviews that I conducted first.

A caution about method must temper any conclusion that the statistical differences between cohorts represent the actual unfolding of careers over time; clearly, these are not longitudinal data. While it may be tempting to assume that newcomers and veteran missionaries are the same people at separate stages, in fact they are not. As compared herein, they are different people who entered the vocation at different historical moments and were subjected to different influences. Selection processes were at work as well; many original members of now-senior cohorts did not stay beyond one term, for reasons related to the very phenomena being considered here. If they had been around to be studied, the data would look different. Nevertheless, significant trends associated with years of experience may be viewed as suggestive of career patterns as well as reasons for persistence in the missionary vocation, especially when they are consistent with ideas that emerge from the life story interviews. With that caveat, let us now examine some relevant general findings from the survey.

Of the 129 missionaries who returned the questionnaire, 70 percent reported that they had been able to *fulfill their original sense of missionary calling* almost completely, if not completely, in the course of their career with HCJB. The most important determinant of this variable was whether one's Mission job provided frequent chances to *share the gospel verbally*. The two-thirds of the group who said they did have such opportunities included radio preachers, evangelists, nurses who witnessed to patients, but also some support-staff members who felt they had a "ministry to the national employees." Specifically, whatever their role in the organization, those whose activities included the frequent *speaking* of the gospel were significantly more likely to report that they were fulfilling a personal missionary call (80 percent compared to 53 percent; p<.01).[1] Second, these frequent witnesses were more likely to identify themselves personally with the Mission organization, as indicated by a significantly higher rate of strong agreement with the following statement: "When I am asked to talk about myself, I usually talk a lot about the Mission (HCJB)" (47 percent compared to 28 percent agreed; p<.05).

Two veteran mission members illustrate well the notion of fulfilling a personal missionary call through personal witnessing as well as through membership and participation in a corporate effort to evangelize the world:

> The greatest thing that keeps me going is getting out into the mountains and seeing these Indian people accept the Lord. The second is seeing my department in the black, growing and doing an acceptable job for the Mission—and just being a part of this great organization that is getting the gospel out to the whole world through radio.

> How do I describe what I do for a living? What I do for a living is I work for the Lord Jesus Christ. HCJB is an agency for the man I really work for, who is the Lord Jesus Christ. All our radio programs contain some portion of the Lord Jesus Christ. We always get in there the fact that one needs to be born again in order to get into the Kingdom of Heaven. We're out there proclaiming the good news, that there is a way of eternal life after death. We are a group of 250 people, and we basically cover the world with our radio signal, broadcasting the gospel around the clock, six programs at a time.

In contrast, the following statements were made by first-term missionaries, a radio engineer and a hospital nurse, neither of whom could say they had fulfilled a personal missionary call through their work with HCJB:

> The problem I have—and some other engineers have the same feeling—is that you don't feel you're a real missionary. When I was in the States preparing to come here, I got to speak in churches, I talked to people, and I did a lot of things directly with people. But here, if you're an engineer you're not doing direct work with people. And I don't really see myself, personally, as having directly influenced people very much.

> As a missionary, I feel guilty that I just work a set shift in a hospital, eight hours a day, five days a week. You feel you might as well be back home doing the same thing. And in reality, if I were working in a hospital back home I would feel almost more like a missionary than I do here, because I could communicate a lot more. Here I still have a lot of trouble with the language.

The survey data suggest a linkage between three elements that tend to develop in parallel in the missionary's moral career: (1) the identification of self with the Mission organization; (2) a sense of supportive social-spatial connection to the missionary community; and (3) the reconstructed experience of a missionary calling. For example, of those who said their talk about self usually included a lot of talk about the Mission entity, 94 percent also identified with their co-workers as "neighbors and closest friends," compared to 69.3 percent (significantly less, $p<.001$) of those who did not identify as strongly with the Mission organization. A description by a Mission manager illustrates the dense social webbing of the core HCJB group:

> I would say that most of our relationships in social type situations are also related in the work situation. Andy [a co-worker], for example, lives next door. Andy and Sue and Mary and I are close friends. We're involved in Bible studies together. We'll go out to dinner. Andy and I'll go fishing together. Sue and Mary will go shopping together, and they'll get involved in women's groups together. It's the same with Don and Janet—we have taken vacations with them, and Don is my boss. And Frank, who works here in the office, was on vacation with us. And we get involved with our singles. We've got a lot of single people on the staff—more women than men—and we try to bring them into our lives. For example, we were invited to two of our single girls' home last night for dinner.

HCJB missionaries also expressed somewhat ambivalent feelings about their insular community, as we have already seen. On the questionnaire, about three-quarters of the respondents admitted they felt uncomfortable that "so many missionaries remain aloof from the culture and society of Ecuador." They seemed to sense that the very existence of the enclave in some ways contradicted the premise of their calling. And yet, those who (like the narrator above) tended to view their HCJB colleagues as "neighbors and closest friends" were significantly more likely to report a personal missionary call experience, compared to those who apparently lacked this sense of neighborly belonging to the HCJB community (77.0 percent vs. 57.7 percent, $p<.05$).

These findings appear to be consistent with two complementary interpretations of the development of missionary calls over time, both of which highlight the socialization of individuals within the missionary community. First, those who had a specific, epiphanal sort of calling before joining the Mission were more likely to fit in from the beginning, to identify with elder role models in the group, and to persist in the field. Second, those who arrived without a specific missionary call, but who nevertheless were drawn into the heart of the missionary community, were more likely over time to acquire (or construct) a call, i.e., as a mediated experience in line with the subcultural texts that sustain the collective identity of the Mission group. For such people, the personal missionary call becomes narrative truth.[2]

Perhaps not surprisingly, the prevalence of divine calling among the missionaries was found to vary with another (somewhat more solid) criterion as well, which is housing arrangement. The Mission owns a number of houses and apartments in and around the compound of Quito, as well as around the Shell hospital and the Pifo transmitter site; about one third of the missionaries said they had lived in these Mission-owned homes during most of their careers. Of this group of Mission tenants, 88.1 percent said that they had a missionary call, while only 65.5 percent of those who lived in non-Mission homes (away from the compound) reported the call experience (p<.05).

Once again, this finding probably has to do with cohort and period as well as selection effects: Both the call and a history of living in Mission housing were found to be more prevalent among senior than among junior missionaries. In the early days of the Mission, virtually all of the "HCJB family" in Quito lived within a three-block radius of the compound, including a street named for the Voice of the Andes (*Avenida Vozandes*). This situation has changed partly because the increase in missionary personnel has far outpaced the supply of Mission-owned residences, and partly because missionaries in recent years have often preferred to live away from the compound. Hence, while 60 percent of those with 20 or more years of experience have been Mission tenants during most of their time in Ecuador, only 14 percent of first-year newcomers were living in homes or apartments owned by HCJB.

Due to the proximity of the Mission's houses to the compound and the familiarity that it breeds, and also as a consequence of the Mission tenants' relative longevity, the HCJB tenant group stood out in some ways from their colleagues who had chosen other housing arrangements. In a sense, they represented the core of the internal social network of the Mission. This is vividly illustrated in the previous passage in which a Mission manager described his friendships with HCJB colleagues. It is probably not a coincidence that all of the people he mentioned lived near each other in homes or apartments owned by the Mission. Ninety-one percent of Mission renters said they appreciated their HCJB co-workers as "neighbors and closest friends," while a significantly lesser proportion of those in other housing (73.8 percent, p<.05) viewed the HCJB group in this way. The Mission tenants were also more likely to endorse the aforementioned statement equating talk about the self with talk about HCJB (53.7 percent vs. 33.3 percent, p<.05).

Figure 5.1 portrays four of these variables as a function of categories of years experience. The 129 respondents are classified into five groups: those with 0–2 years, 3–4 years, 5–9 years, 10–19 years, and 20 or more years of missionary experience in Ecuador. Responses were plotted for each group on four variables, as measured in the following terms:

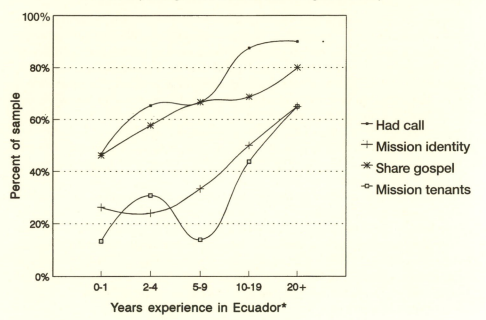

* Mantel-Haenszel chi square test showed significant linear association
between years of experience and each variable displayed; p<0.05 to p<0.001.

Figure 5.1. Calling and mission identity among HCJB members in Ecuador by years in
the field.

1. *Call*: reported experience of a definite call to be a missionary.
2. *Mission tenants*: reported living in Mission-owned housing at least the majority of time in Ecuador.
3. *Mission identity*: reported that they agreed or identified with the statement, "When I am asked to talk about myself, I usually talk a lot about the Mission (HCJB)."
4. *Share gospel*: reported that during the past year they very often have had opportunities to share the gospel verbally in the course of doing their Mission job.

The graph shows a fairly linear and parallel increase in the prevalence of these four conditions among missionaries with greater experience in the field. The four rates range from 14 percent to 47 percent among first-year missionaries, and from 65 percent to 88 percent among those with twenty or more years of experience. The Mantel-Haenszel chi-square test showed a significant linear association of each of the four variables to years of experience (i.e., experience coded into five categories of increasing interval width). To be clear, Figure 5.1 does not demonstrate direct *causal* association among the four variables; it only shows that all of them independently were found to be more prevalent among missionaries with greater experience.

Concerning other-worldly evangelical beliefs as a general dimension of meaning and belonging for these missionaries, a number of attitudinal measures confirmed for the whole group what many expressed individually: a pervasive sense of set-apartness from the world, linked to ideas about membership in a transcultural Kingdom of God. Of the 129 respondents, 92 percent agreed that they would "feel more comfortable with an evangelical Christian from a foreign culture than with a non-Christian from [their] own culture, because with the Christian [they] would share the same basic worldview." A similarly high proportion (86 percent) reported that they felt "uncomfortable with the way most people in [their] home culture view the world." A substantial majority (80 percent) endorsed a statement that "the only really important citizenship is that of the Kingdom of Heaven." Virtually everyone (95 percent) agreed that "all the problems of human society are caused by sin in the lives of individual men and women who need Jesus Christ." There were no significant differences in these variables by years of experience.

It should be noted that since these statements were composed to express a somewhat commonplace ideology of spiritual strangerhood among conservative evangelicals, the act of affirming them on a questionnaire could amount merely to "giving the right answer" almost without thinking. In that sense, the more interesting respondents might be the handful who disagreed with the rhetoric. Still, the fact that such a large percentage of HCJB missionaries did recognize and identify themselves personally with these other-worldly expressions serves to highlight them as, indeed, significant contours of their common experience and belief.

Some prominent differences within the missionary group emerged along the lines of attachment to their home country and to Ecuador. One important facet of cultural attachment might be framed as the *psychological location* from which missionaries tend to view the past—encompassing their own store of memories as well as a larger sense of history. When missionaries imagine history leading up to the present moment, where do they imagine themselves to be standing? Upon reflection and given a choice of national perspectives on past events, would they identify a place in the mind closer to their home country or to Ecuador? How might this vary by experience in the field? Two general questions were asked, one about each country, to allow for the possibility of viewing history from two primary national or cultural perspectives at once. The meaning of these perspectives was left to the individual. In addition, the missionaries were asked whether their viewpoint on history was essentially a spiritual one, i.e., that the past revealed nothing so much as "the hand of God in the course of events over the ages."

The result was that 63 percent of the missionaries said they tended to view history primarily from their home nation's point of view, while 28 percent claimed to view it from the perspective of the host nation, Ecuador. Fifteen percent endorsed both points of view as primary to their sense of past events, while 23 percent endorsed neither. Perhaps not surprisingly, virtually everyone (97 percent) claimed a spiritual interpretation of history, that it revealed the hand of God through the ages. (Similarly, 95 percent endorsed a parallel statement that revealed their template for considering the future: "I imagine it largely in relation to the events foretold in the Book of Revelation, culminating in the final coming of Christ and His Kingdom.")

Figure 5.2 juxtaposes the percentage of responses corresponding to the two national viewpoints on history, configured along the axis of years in the field. The pattern is striking and statistically significant. Almost all of the first-year newcomers affirmed that the United States provided their primary point of view on history, and almost none

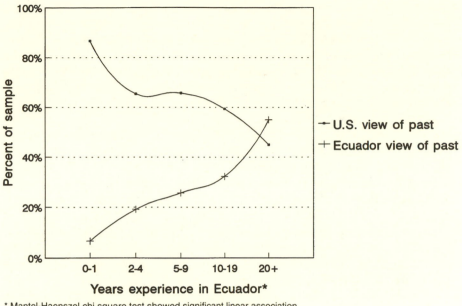

* Mantel-Haenszel chi square test showed significant linear association
between years of experience and each variable displayed; p<0.01.

Figure 5.2. HCJB missionaries' views of past and history from perspective of Ecuador vs.
United States, by years of experience in Ecuador.

affirmed Ecuador. Among twenty-year veterans, these proportions converge: 45 percent endorsed the home country while 55 percent endorsed the host country. (I will have more to say later about what the pattern in Figure 5.2 could mean.)

Another facet of attachment may be set in the context of civil authority and extended to international relations: Do conservative evangelical missionaries view themselves as obligated to U.S. national interests over those of their host country of Ecuador? This topic takes on salience in light of the sort of argument made recently by David Stoll: that the U.S. government throughout the 1980s attempted to use the evangelical movement in Latin America to expand or consolidate its military-political hegemony; that it garnered support at home by capitalizing on "a theocratic vision [of the religious right] reviving confusion between Christian mission and North American empire" (Stoll, 1990:xvii). Stoll contends that while some evangelicals have challenged the way their own missions operate in the Third World, and while Latin Americans at the popular level are using imported religion for purposes of their own, nevertheless evangelism continues to be employed as an instrument of a militarized U.S. foreign policy supported by the religious right.

The questionnaire did not address in detail the nuances of missionaries' nationalistic loyalties. Nevertheless, some general questions revealed a complex phenomenon in keeping with missionaries' general ambivalence toward government authority, stemming from their position as other-worldly strangers in Ecuador. Which nation has primary claim to govern missionaries' actions—the home country of their citizenship, or the host country in which they live? Just over half (54 percent) of the 129 respondents identified their home nation's government as the primary civil authority to which they were subject, even though they were living within another country's borders. In answer to a separate, parallel question, almost the same proportion (55 percent) regarded Ecuador's government in that role. Once again, these responses were not constrained to be mutually exclusive but could overlap; and in fact, 20 percent of the missionaries ascribed primary civil authority to *both* countries, while 11 percent endorsed *neither* as such. Perhaps most significantly, 91 percent of the respondents affirmed that they were "under God's authority first, and only secondly subject to human civil authority."

There were no cohort differences in the missionaries' inclination to affirm God's authority over all human government, as this idea was held almost universally by HCJB members regardless of how long they had been in the field. However, the locus of their sense of civil obligation *per se* (home vs. host country) did appear to shift with years of experience, though not in a strictly linear pattern. Among the newcomers (0–1 years), percentages were 71 percent endorsing the home country vs. 41 percent endorsing the host country as primary civil authority. Among those with 5 to 9 years of experience, the proportions were reversed to 41 percent for the home country vs. 64 percent for Ecuador. But in the most senior group, the two converged at 60 percent and 65 percent respectively.

These data appear consistent with the missionaries' narrative portrayals of their own ambivalence regarding national loyalties and, in general, toward the cultural components of their identity.

> My wife and I talk about Ecuador as being "home." And we talk about wanting to stay here even if missions are eventually thrown out. I believe with all my heart that I want to do that. And when we get home on furlough—but did you notice what I just said? I said *home* on furlough, without even thinking. When we get home on furlough we are always talking about going home, meaning come back to Ecuador. . . . But there is still something about the American soil, the American culture, the American financial backing—I am still an American. I naturally swing my eyes up to the North, because that's the country that provides for my economic needs.

In large part, such ambivalence stems from a paradox inherent in missionaries' sense of agency: They are emissaries of a gospel that is supposed to stand above all nations and cultures, but they are also citizens of a foreign nation that they see as superior—culturally, economically, and politically—*due to its evangelical heritage*. America thus becomes a symbol of the other-worldly Kingdom. From that point of view, missionaries make moral judgments about Ecuadorian culture, in such a way as to blur the line between *American* and *Christian*:

> I am the product of a thinking society, a very ordered society. So there are points at which I come dashing up against the culture here, because Ecuadorians are feeling people much more than thinking people. You get into the area of male-female relationships in this society, as opposed to the Judaeo-Christian viewpoint of America—I'm sorry, but sometimes you see people here living almost like animals in their physical relationships. And it's just so difficult to bridge from our Christian point of view to their understanding. Then there's the whole area of truth vs. untruth in their perception of things. You get an Ecuadorian's point of view and you get an American's point of view, and they are not the same. What is truth? There is something in me, in my fiber, in my understanding of God's word, that cuts through this. But it poses a real wrestling match, a boxing match, at some points.

Americans are clean, and they wash their hands before they eat. Ecuadorians somehow don't make the connection between hygiene and sickness. . . . I can't compute the Latin culture. I try, but trying isn't enough. I think you'd have to be born and raised here to understand their ways of thinking. For example, automotive maintenance—it's just not something that comes naturally to their mind set. I have yet to find a mechanic in Ecuador who has a real concern for the driver of the car that he's fixed—that the tire won't blow out or the fan belt won't break, out in the middle of nowhere. . . . And they mistrust each other. Outwardly, they express affection, but there's no real *esprit de corps* like we have.

There are cultural things about Ecuador that will always bother me. The system of justice. The way Ecuadorian men treat women. Class structure. The poverty. There are a lot of things. The graffiti on the walls that says *Yankee Go Home*—that hurts.

The "America" constructed by these missionaries stands implicitly for rationality, order, truth, purity, and a whole list of social mores construed by evangelicals as Biblical absolutes. Missionaries' sojourn away from this mythical Puritan land to the North provides an imagery for their pilgrimage below. Ecuadorian culture, on the other hand, stands for *the world* out of which people must be saved. In the first passage above, the missionary's portrayal of Ecuadorians as living "almost like animals in their physical relationships" evokes traditional images of paganism—the dark, inhuman backdrop of *life in the flesh*, against which to highlight the missionary's own ideals of *life in the spirit* as human culture redeemed by the gospel. By constructing such images of the foreign culture from which they are set apart, the missionaries thus assert their own salvation and spiritual status.

And yet, America stands as an ambiguous moral symbol. Missionaries also paint a picture of contemporary secularized America using stark contrasts and dark hues, in the style of the religious right. In this portrayal, America has become a spiritual wasteland; even the churches are passive, complacent, insulated from the spiritual warfare going on around them. A number of HCJB members even cite their reaction against the tepid religious environment in America as a key influence in their missionary calling. Living away from it often intensifies feelings of moral estrangement, even as the myth of a traditional Godly America remains strong.

I believe that in America, the lifestyle and the cultural changes are moving directly away from the Word of God. And the pastors are going to have to go one way or the other. They cannot continue to support the lifestyle and the cultural changes in America, and still preach the Word of God. . . . Where is the church in America? Abortion—millions of babies killed. Where is the church? Where was the church when prayer was thrown out of the public schools? Why do we just build the walls higher and higher around the church, to keep the sin out, to keep the faith in, and disassociate ourselves from the world around us?

I have a desperate feeling that the churches in America do not understand that Satan is out there as roaring lion, trying to devour the church. Many of them are going innocently on their way, and letting him do it.

The idea of cultural change bears profound significance for missionaries, though their lives imbue it with contradictions. They decry the "cultural changes" that signal the decline of Puritan America, seeing themselves as representatives of those traditional values that once favored America in the eyes of God. But then they defend themselves against charges of imperialist complicity by insisting they are not out to impose their culture on others, only to share the gospel which is translatable into any and all cultures. Finally, they attribute to spiritual conversion a wide range of cultural, social-structural, and economic changes that tend to occur in communities under their influence—changes that may be used to rhetorical and actual advantage not only by themselves, but by their home government's foreign policy. The question phrased by Stoll (1982) becomes acutely relevant here: Are missionaries "fishers of men or founders of empire?" Often they are both, in spite themselves.

> You've seen the Quichuas, how dirty they are as nonbelievers. They get drunk and it looks like someone dragged them through a mud pile and they haven't washed. Well, as believers, we taught them that they have a responsibility to take care of themselves. And boy, they really caught on. As Christians they don't drink. They wash their hair, they come in new clothes. You see them now and they're just beautiful people. . . . Now with close to a thousand believers they want to build a church. And so we were involved in designing it and helping them get the loans. The other thing is we were involved in helping start [farm] cooperatives. We have two Christian cooperatives in this area, and it has just revolutionized the economic base of these communities. They have vehicles, tractors, everything. There's also a non-Christian cooperative, and last year the Christian cooperative earned 30 percent more than the non-Christian. Of course, we have tried to help them in their seeding and their technology. The next thing is we wanted to incorporate the health dispensary as a ministry of the church to the community. There are 10,000 Quichuas in that valley, and so the need for curative care is very great. Also, with proper health education, many deaths could be prevented. So we thought, if we can formulate a good health program that really takes care of the people, it would be a fantastic ministry of the evangelical church to the community. And now it's all being done by nationals. We are just advisors. It's moving into a stage where it's going completely indigenous, completely self-supporting. If the Lord takes us home, I know it's going to walk on its own.

The speaker in this passage would not think of himself explicitly as a propagator of American economic, cultural, and political influence abroad. (One might observe that farm cooperatives are not an especially American idea.) Indeed, his intended point was that the Quichua community has achieved positive development on its own initiative by the transformative power of Christian belief, with the missionaries' help and advice only in the beginning. Nevertheless, he has acted as an agent of broad-based change, the implications of which go far beyond the interests of the Quichuas in adopting evangelical beliefs. Indeed, given the size and inchoate political significance of the Indian population in South America, it could easily be argued that these changes extend to the realm of national and international interests. And yet, significantly, the missionary has done this not as a would-be member of the local community with a personal stake in its future, but rather as a foreigner who comes today and leaves tomorrow. In spite of his activist role among the Quichuas, his stance has placed him permanently outside their community looking in (or rather, above it looking down). He has come with the hope that one day his imported religion will permeate every aspect of Quichua life and culture, that it will redeem, dominate, and transform their life-world from the inside out, even as he himself becomes (somewhat paradoxically) more and more removed from their community.

In both the interview and related questionnaire data, the majority of HCJB members endorsed the notion that they would "never really fit into Ecuadorian society or culture." While this seemed to cause them some discomfort, most accepted it as an intrinsic feature of their role as foreign missionaries. Even if they were to spend most of their adult lives in Ecuador, HCJB members expected to return to their home country eventually. Still, the thought of returning home to stay also produced discomfort for many of them. Responses to two questionnaire items in particular revealed their ambiguous social position in relation to both their home society and Ecuador. The first question was whether the missionaries had the feeling that they "would not fit in" if they went back to stay in their home country. Second, they were presented with a hypothetical situation: What if the Mission organization moved out of Ecuador? In that event, could the missionary stay behind as an individual with a sense of purpose and belonging in the host country?

The answers to the first question were most clearly related to years of experience, as shown in Figure 5.3. While only 19 percent of newcomers felt they would not fit in back home, over 55 percent of those with ten or more years of experience felt this way. The relation of this variable to years in the field was statistically linear, though it peaked in the group of ten-year veterans. Of course, the language of categories used here (these would fit in, these would not) is in some sense an artificial imposition for the purpose of analysis. Actually, such feelings probably occur with varying intensity at moments in every missionary's career and are part of the ambivalence in-

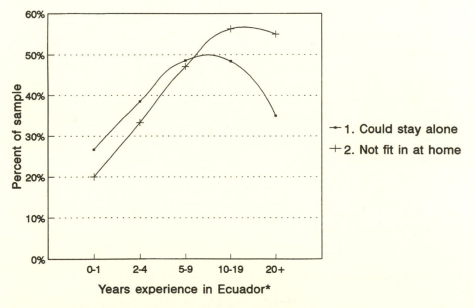

* Mantel-Haenszel chi square test showed significant linear association between years of experience and variable 2 (p<0.001) but not variable 1.

Figure 5.3. HCJB missionaries' attitudes about staying in Ecuador on their own, "not fitting in" upon return to home country, by years of experience in Ecuador.

herent in the vocation itself. Nevertheless, such feelings are significantly more prevalent among missionaries with longer tenure in the field.

One interpretation of this finding, and of the previous ones about perspectives on history and civil authority, would be to render the missionary career as a road leading away from home. The journey changes the traveler and his sense of self, while the home country also changes in his absence, placing more and more distance between the two. Hence, the longer one travels, the more probable it becomes that the thought of going back will seem strange and difficult. And of course, those who do not feel this sense of strangeness tend to turn back early, making it even more likely that feelings of not fitting in back home will characterize those who continue in the field. This is perhaps a standard portrayal of the immigrant saga, and it does fit these missionary data to a limited degree, as illustrated by a prayer letter from an HCJB member on furlough:

> There have been times when we have felt very alone since July. The familiar and comfortable world for us seems back in Quito. Although it is wonderful to see family, to renew old acquaintances . . . we feel out of place occasionally. Many things have changed in the past decade which we did not notice. . . . We have changed as well. . . . [These experiences] have increased our sense of not belonging. Some days have been difficult. Please pray that we will know the faithfulness of God. . . . [3]
>
> "The road goes ever on," sings Bilbo Baggins at the conclusion of J.R.R. Tolkien's *The Hobbit* (or *There and Back Again* as the author preferred). Our journeys have continued during our time of home ministry assignment. . . . Bilbo is right. The road goes ever on and ever shall until we reach our final home.[4]

But the other side of the coin is this: even among veteran missionaries with twenty or more years in the field, only a bit more than half reported feeling that they would not fit in if they went back to their home country to live. The other 45 percent of the senior missionaries apparently felt most of the time that they could go home again; that home was a welcoming place awaiting their return. In the Mission newsletter he edits, HCJB member Harold Goerzen wrote about making the transition on his recent furlough:

> This wasn't our first furlough, so reverse culture shock came unexpectedly. We were dazzled by wide, runway-like highways, sprawling supermarkets, Nintendo video games and 24-hour weather channels. We had to adapt to a fast-paced, clock-controlled lifestyle where efficiency is all important.
>
> At first we felt abandoned and lost, but soon we started to fit in. Old friendships were rejuvenated; relatives showered us with love and kindness; we caught on to the latest gadgets; and our home church began to feel like home again. . . . As the leaves turned yellow and cold north winds returned, we remembered how it felt to change seasons. Ecuador seemed far off and distant. We were at home . . .

In this light, consider the answers to the second question displayed in Figure 5.3, about staying in Ecuador if the Mission were to leave. Again, responses were tabulated by categories of seniority in the field. If we look only at the three groups with less than ten years of experience, a linear pattern once again seems to emerge: While little more than a quarter of the newcomers answered in the affirmative, almost half of those with five to nine years in Ecuador said they could stay on their own without the Mission organization. To a point, then, the curve might suggest an increasing individual acculturation in Ecuador as part of the unfolding of the missionary's career. But then a downturn occurs, so that twenty-year veterans are virtually less likely than two-year veterans to say they could stay in Ecuador on their own without the Mission.

According to a linear acculturation model, the missionaries who have been in Ecuador the longest should be the most likely to feel connected as individuals to the larger social surround of the host country, to feel inclined and empowered to stay even without the Mission structure. But on the contrary, only 35 percent of HCJB missionaries with more than twenty years of experience could imagine themselves faring well in such a situation. One veteran missionary put it straightforwardly:

> Missionaries do not somehow fit in as other immigrants in this country. I think most of them would be ready to climb on the plane tomorrow if political unrest were to put the Mission in jeopardy, rather than wanting to stay here and be a part of this country.

This statement evokes one of the most significant themes in HCJB members' narratives about their continuing strangerhood in Ecuador—their sense of impermanence in a country where, in many missionaries' perception, latent political hostilities lurk beneath the surface of friendly attitudes toward Americans and Protestant religious workers. During the 1960s, Mission founder Clarence Jones amplified on this theme with explicit Cold War rhetoric:

> Having enjoyed unusual liberty and acceptance by the government of Ecuador during the years of its existence, HCJB and the WRMF need to keep a constant vigil over this happy relationship. Many of our personnel may not always appreciate to the full the extremely fortunate position we occupy . . . With the rise of hypernationalisim this situation could always change. "Yankee-go-home" is a ready and potent rallying cry to the rabble rousers.
>
> With Castroism and Communism spreading like a cancer over Latin America, Ecuador itself has already felt the tangible effects of guerrilla warfare within its borders, red-inspired riots in its streets, and commy elements in its national and city governments.
>
> Some of these political phenomena point to the wisdom of not having "All our eggs in one basket," and the WRMF needs to have its top administration free to watch developments along this line constantly and carefully (Jones, 1966 [1962]:113–114).

When I interviewed Mission members two decades after Jones exhorted them with these words, such stridently political language was seldom heard, but similar sentiments were common nonetheless. Despite their long tenure and comfortable life in Ecuador, many HCJB members still had a way of speaking as if they did not expect to stay very long. They alluded to a day—almost with a strange sense of anticipation—when missionaries might be evicted from the country.

> There are leftist groups here who hate the very sight of our light-colored hair. I am very aware of the possibility that missionaries may not be welcome in this country within the next decade.

I suspect someday we'll all have to go, and the Lord will continue his work through Ecuadorian believers. As we withdraw, or as we're forced to leave, I believe God's work will go on. The Station won't continue, and the hospital may not operate in the same way. But I don't believe God's work will cease.

When I pick up a newspaper and read about what people are experiencing in other parts of Latin America, I get very concerned. Part of what happens when you live in another country is you realize that people and nations don't live in isolation. I view what's happening in Central America with just about as much concern as I would a riot downtown, because I think they are very closely related. They influence each other.

We don't have a sense of permanence. We're here now, and there's work to be done. But if the government changes, we could be out of here.

The handwriting is on the wall. It's just a matter of time, and I don't feel we are preparing. It makes me shudder to see the little progress we have made toward equipping nationals to take over should we get a phone call saying, "Be out in twenty-four hours." That's a serious concern. But it's what I see as the logical future for missions in Latin America. I think if we follow what the Bible teaches, the Apostle Paul is the greatest example of a missionary. And he didn't put his roots down too deep. His effectiveness was based on the fact that he could go in and equip people to handle the job themselves, and then leave, and keep in contact through letters, providing strong guidance that way. I would like to see more of that model.

It is possible that HCJB could cease to exist in Ecuador because of a government order—next week. What would I do? Well, I would wait for the Lord to give me direction. Of course, I try to look at my future from the point of view of the Lord's return. When the Lord returns, then my future is with him.

Clearly, these statements should be interpreted in the early-1980s context in which they were made—against the backdrop of a remilitarized United States foreign policy under the Reagan administration, and the spectre of American involvement in the war in Nicaragua and El Salvador. Moreover, some HCJB members were reacting to the expulsion of the Wycliffe Bible Translators—their collegues and friends—from Ecuador and Peru. In any event, the question of whether HCJB missionaries' situation in Ecuador was, in any way, politically precarious is not a matter I can take up here. What is significant is that many of them *imagined* it to be precarious, and that this mode of thinking has symbolic significance in their moral careers.

For many evangelicals, the urgency that characterizes the missionary ethos rests upon the millenialist doctrine of the Last Days, the expectation that Christ may return to judge the earth and snatch up the faithful literally at any time. For HCJB missionaries in Ecuador, the possibility of a government takeover forcing them to leave has become an eschatological metaphor—a concrete way for them to apprehend the Biblical injunction *to work while it is yet day, for the night is coming fast.*

And yet, as these missionaries begin to reflect on the idea of reentry to their home country, it seems to evoke in them a sense of set-apartness that resonates even more profoundly with their construct of spiritual identity:

I think I would have to make some real cultural adjustments if I were to go back home. I would accept it from the Lord and try to fit in, but not without some rough adjustments. We're turned off by the shallowness that we see in people in the United States, and we find it harder to like people there. But if we went back, our lifestyle, and the "missionary" part of it would basically stay the same. We would still be trying to reach people with the saving message of what Christ can do, and trying to live that honestly before them. Just showing people what Christ can do in giving them a purpose and a reason to live and a hope for eternity. A missionary isn't so much what I do as *who I am* and how I am related to the people around me.

To take on the identity of a missionary was hard, because of all the things that people assume that you are and do, and you know that it's not all true. I had a hard time with that. But I know that if I ever went back to live in the States, I would take back with me a sense of mission—to the United States. That would be the great lesson of my missionary experience, that the sense of mission belongs with any Christian, no matter where you live.

And so they remain—strangers abroad, strangers at home. In the end, these missionaries' experiences of set-apartness, of withdrawal and alternative engagement, are not to be seen merely as mile markers passed by on the way to some final destination where vocation and life story converge in a coherent whole. Strangerhood is not a condition to be overcome through a missionary pilgrimage. Rather, it emerges as a defining theme that is present from the beginning and continues to the end. If there is any completion of a lifelong mission, it involves returning—actually or symbolically—to the place from which one was sent. But where is that place? For many missionaries, the sense of truly coming home remains elusive.

Missionaries Today: Remnants or Representatives of Evangelical America?

While HCJB missionaries' moral careers may appear to be spun out in a web of meanings peculiar to their occupation and foreign setting, in many ways they deal with the same contemporary dilemmas that face evangelicals in general (as well as other people with strong vocational or religious commitments.) Indeed, much of what missionaries are doing through self-conscious autobiographical reconstruction is attempting to discern some spiritual significance and narrative coherence in the seemingly disconnected fragments of their experience in the modern (and postmodern) world. Thus, the analysis of missionaries' moral careers—and particularly the interpretation of ambivalence and strangerhood in missionary testimonies—may reveal new facets of the tensions described lately by a number of social scientists (e.g., Ammerman, 1987; Bellah et al., 1985; Berger 1979; Greeley, 1989; Hunter, 1982, 1987; Lawrence, 1989; Warner, 1988; Wuthnow, 1988a, 1998b) in their observations of the encounter of American religiosity with modernity.

The question of how exactly missionaries today *represent* some sort of Christian-American culture is a complex one. Certain recurring themes in HCJB testimonies seem to suggest, on the one hand, that the Mission attracts a fringe group of evangelicals—those with separatist leanings who reject the worldly and accommodationist stance of nominal religiosity in their home country. Indeed, in some cases the foreign encounter seems to fuel reactionary views; we see evangelicals becoming fundamentalist ideologues—Christian soldiers on a spiritual battlefield. And yet, other narrative themes suggest that many HCJB missionaries are pushing out against the sectarian envelope—purveying an inclusive gospel and accommodating their lives significantly to a pluralism of cultural ideas, values, and ways of being in their foreign surround. For these individuals, the missionary experience seems to have an effect just the opposite of intensified separatism; here we see evangelicals becoming more open and tolerant of cultural others, less controlling and condescending.

The HCJB missionary community thus appears to combine different types of fundamentalists and evangelicals with different stances vis-a-vis cultural outsiders: One type faces inward with the goal of *separating from the world*; another type faces outward with the goal of *redeeming the world*; and still another tries to face in both directions with the goal of somehow *accommodating* an evangelical ethos to the surrounding world and to modernity. Actually, however, these stances do not so much characterize distinct groups of people in the Mission, but rather tap into disparate attitudes coexisting (often uneasily) in the same people—producing a persistent tension and a cultural ambivalence that may be found among contemporary evangelicals generally, but which stands out perhaps more visibly in missionaries.

Alternative ways of casting missionaries' relationship to their communities of origin—as fringe, exemplar, microcosm, aberration, caricature, reflected, or refracted image—may highlight distinctive contours of the evangelical and American character at different moments in history. At the peak of the early-modern foreign missions movement in the late nineteenth century, the missionary personified at once the quintessential Christian and the paradigmatic American: The ideals of both identities were fused into one sort of ambassadorial role, illuminated against the dark backdrop of a "vast pagan mission field." As rendered by novelist John Hersey (1985) in the voice of a memorable missionary character in *The Call*, many talented young Americans who were "ambitious for the Lord" felt strongly that they had been "chosen . . . for the high honor of carrying to the unevangelized nations of this earth the very and only word which can ease the lost of those forgotten and backward nations." The mission task was construed, then, as a heroic rescue operation assigned "by God to the Republic of the United States" and requiring "manfullness and brain power and skills of captaincy and courage, no less than evangelical zeal."

But now, as the twentieth century draws to a close, mainstream Christian scholars in America find themselves pondering an ambiguous legacy of that earlier mission. Many are chastened with feelings of self-doubt. On his return from a spiritual sojourn in Peru in the mid-1980s, Henri Nouwen (1983) observed:

> After many centuries of missionary work during which we, the people of the north, tried to give them, the people of the south, what we felt they needed, we have now come to realize. . . . A treasure lies hidden in the soul of Latin America, a spiritual treasure to be recognized as a gift for us who live in the illusion of power and self-control. It is the treasure of gratitude that can help us to break through the walls of our individual and collective self-righteousness and can prevent us from destroying ourselves and our planet in the futile attempt to hold onto what we consider our own. If I have any vocation in Latin America, it is the vocation to receive from the people the gifts they have to offer us and to bring these gifts back up north for our own conversion and healing (Nouwen, 1985:188).

It is my argument that the American missionary identity today—if it is the remnant of a traditional calling built on heroic ideals—is equally a product of the social conflicts and cultural tensions experienced by contemporary evangelical believers. Some of those tensions are the result of fairly recent developments on the American religious landscape; others go back much further, and indeed define a historical ambivalence in evangelical views of American society.

With a large survey of students attending Christian colleges and seminaries in the 1980s, James Hunter (1987) announces the coming of a new generation of evangelicals—kinder and gentler but more ambivalent and "worldly," as seen in the loss of this very term's traditional nuance. While the ranks of evangelicals have grown, Hunter suggests the new faithful are a new breed. On the theological front, Hunter's subjects—whom he claims represent the movement's leadership in decades to come—manifest an almost reluctant (if not faltering) commitment to orthodoxy. He portrays them as far less hard-bitten than their parents' generation in their views of such doctrines as scriptural inerrancy, the literal existence of hell, and the condemnation of those unreached by the gospel.

In their attitudes toward work and the self, Hunter's coming generation no longer exhibits the sort of "vocational asceticism" that Max Weber noted as a hallmark of Luther's "priesthood of believers." Indeed, Hunter observes a dramatic reversal of the older Protestant attitudes of self-denial and renunciation. Now, his data show, young evangelicals are consciously concerned with self-fulfillment and personal development. In their judgments of morality, a sizable proportion of the ascendant generation endorses liberalized social attitudes and personal practices that their predecessors would have condemned unequivocally. For example, only about half favor a ban on abortion, while about seventy percent favor a ban on prayer in public schools, and less than twenty percent condemn drinking alcohol as morally wrong. In their personal commitment to share the faith with others, Hunter's subjects favor an "ethic of civility" that eschews confrontational witnessing in favor of "lifestyle evangelism." They not only tolerate, but closely resemble their nonevangelical middle-class neighbors and co-workers. In short, Hunter's representative sample presents a detailed picture of young American evangelicals differing sharply from the media-hyped images of reactionary militancy attributed to the religious right.

Since the 1970s, a number of social scientists have observed the concurrent trends of evangelical growth and mainline Protestant decline, and have interpreted these trends jointly as evidence for the success of theological orthodoxy, moral absolutism, and traditional religious idioms in attracting disaffected mainline Protestants to the evangelical camp. But Hunter's study calls into question the simplistic version of this claim. If, indeed, American evangelicals have made some gains in the fallout of mainline Protestant decline, they have done so at the cost of considerable accommodation to modernity, thereby losing certain distinctive qualities of an ethos once strongly identified with fundamentalist faith.

In any event, the important question for us to consider here is how this apparent erosion of the traditional evangelical worldview and ethos might alter typical interpretations of the missionary calling, and might thus reshape the moral career pathways of young evangelicals attracted to mission work abroad. According to Hunter, some young evangelicals now entertain ideas about world mission that would have made their fundamentalist forbears queasy—for example, that social action for justice, peace, and human wellbeing should receive equal emphasis with preaching the Bible's salvation message on the grounds that both are necessary components of an authentic Gospel witness. Meanwhile, significant numbers of young evangelicals are now signing up for short-term missions almost as if for a study-abroad tour—intending to broaden their own horizons while engaging in some meaningful (though brief) service to humanity, but with little thought of a traditional missionary career.

How do we interpret HCJB missionary narratives in light of these changing evangelical attitudes in the coming generation? Do missionaries reflect or resist cultural changes at home? Could they even be instrumental in bringing about such changes in the sending environment? These questions become especially salient here, since many HCJB workers in Ecuador are alumni of the very colleges from which Hunter drew his sample of students, and the data for both studies were collected about the same time.[5] HCJB thus seems as good a place as any to look for ways in which Hunter's "coming generation" may be defining a new ethos of mission abroad.

Interestingly, such an analysis produces two seemingly contrary insights. Indeed, on the one hand, there does appear to be a new breed of missionary corresponding to Hunter's new breed of evangelical. Quite common in the youngest cohorts of HCJB missionaries is an increased concern with professional career development and a sense of professional identity that transcends mission work. This new professionalism often places a higher value on personal success, upward mobility, and even material affluence. Moreover, many of the new missionaries maintain a professional skill-based portability, which tends to produce short-term commitment to any one organization or service locale. Perhaps related to these attitudes, younger cohorts in the Mission are somewhat less likely than their senior colleagues to use the rhetoric of divine calling to explain their underlying motivation.

But on the other hand, in my view, HCJB missionaries generally represent the forces of reaction against the accommodating and relativizing moves of American evangelicals. In their global focus on "unreached people groups" and "the world by 2000," HCJB recreates the early modern (nineteenth century) mission motivation with metaphors evoking conquest, perishing pagan masses, and apocalyptic urgency. Ironically, their resistance to the deconstruction of Anglo-dominated missions is perpetuated as much by their dependence on modern media as it is by their commitment to an antimodern message. While the Mission's continued creedal affirmation of salvation only through belief in Christ is what sets them rhetorically against any sort of universalist accommodation, it is the economic and technological exigencies of a global radio network that structurally prolong foreign hegemony in the Mission's financial base and power elite, and in the cast of its rank-and-file technician-missionaries.

While HCJB missionaries are mostly inclined to deny the values and motives of material acquisition, they nevertheless apply capitalist imagery to the corporate task of world evangelism—with talk of investment and return, market expansion, productivity and competition. At the same time, they are prone to resurrect and reformulate the Protestant-theological valuation of mundane work—of inner-worldly vocational asceticism and commitment—when their highly personalized religious callings dissolve into routinized labor in a Mission bureaucracy. And finally, (as someone has said) quite a few missionaries who set out to do good, end up doing "right well."

In the final analysis, I regard HCJB missionaries as a kind of representative sample of American evangelicals—though not in the statistical sense, but rather in the way they personify core evangelical impulses, cultural themes, and tensions. As should be clear by now, people who leave home to join a religious mission in a foreign country do have some selective life experiences, both preceding and following their vocational commitments, which tend to distinguish them from their peers who stay home. Nevertheless, in their basic religious ideology and approach to the modern world, HCJB members are for the most part a group of conservative, committed Anglo-American evangelicals who happen to be working in Ecuador. A number of them try to make this point explicitly, even if at other times they speak of being "called" and of feeling "set apart." As one put it:

> I am labeled a missionary because I work with HCJB in a foreign country and I depend on the offerings of people in my home churches for support. But that doesn't make me any more spiritual or somehow a better Christian than they are. Really, I don't see myself as different than any other believer who takes the Gospel seriously and who is open to the Lord's leading in their daily life and witness. Every Christian is supposed to be a missionary in whatever location the Lord calls them to serve, in whatever field. It could be in the local church or in a business or in the home or in a foreign country. Any place can be a mission field. . . . This is my assigned place of service for now, but it could change if the Lord decides he wants me someplace else.

On one level, this kind of statement indicates a superficial pose that evangelical missionaries often strike; and perhaps more than genuine continuity with the vocations of their nonmissionary brethren, it expresses the requisite self-effacing style of "service in the Lord's infantry". But even as such, the notion that "every Christian is a missionary" expresses something extremely important—especially coming from professional missionaries. It suggests that missionary discourse not only *includes* all evangelicals in its audience of insiders, but that it *typifies* a core aspect of their identity—of what it means to be an evangelical anywhere.

A good example is seen in a March 1992 prayer letter from Gordon and June Gustafson[6] to the supporters of their Florida-based ministry among U.S. military service personnel:

> "I just wish I knew what the Lord wants me to do!" Have you ever pondered that question? The basic answer "trust and obey" Bill has been learning to do since that all important decision to receive Jesus Christ as His Lord and Savior.
>
> But now it's decision time again, and the question is, "Should I give up my commission in the Navy as a maintenance officer . . . and train for missionary service . . . or stay in the Navy where my financial support is sure and *consider it my mission field*."
>
> Pray for Bill as he wrestles with this question in his eager desire to please God. . . .
>
> Thanks again for your part in helping us fulfill the Great Commission.

When missionaries use phrases such as "fulfilling the Great Commission," "leading people to a saving knowledge of Jesus Christ," "accepted Christ as my personal savior," "the Lord's will for my life," "in the world but not of it," "reaching the world in our own generation," "spiritual warfare," "the rapture," and even "secular humanistic influences," they speak for themselves—but also for millions of American evangelicals and fundamentalists. They let us hear with extraordinary clarity the common voice of an interpretive community within which these phrases are imbued with special meaning (Boone, 1989). In this sense, HCJB members in Ecuador are interesting not only in the ways they differ from their coreligionists in North America, but also in the ways they accurately represent defining views.

While this sort of linkage is instructive, it begs several questions: Don't missionaries produce distorted images of "ordinary" American evangelicals? Aren't their stories colored by the need to fulfill the expectations of special constituencies of missions-minded churches and individuals upon whom they remain financially dependent? And of course (to reiterate), hasn't the evangelical ethos in America shifted in ways that missionaries in foreign countries may not accurately reflect? My response to these questions is that a group like HCJB indeed reveals something more than a mirror image of American evangelical culture at a given moment in history. Missionaries' lives highlight a number of cultural themes that are of defining significance to the evangelical experience, but that remain somewhat opaque in the lives of rank-and-file evangelicals who often blend into the scenery of their communities in North America. At the same time, missionaries' private accounts of their lives show how various traditional as well as novel ideas about mission may be played out in ways that serve individual needs, but that differ substantially from the publicly stated ideals, goals, and motives of contemporary missions theorists and other evangelical elites (e.g., Van Engen, Gilliland, and Pierson, 1993; Hesselgrave, 1988; Bonk, 1991; Bosch, 1991; Carpenter and Shenk, 1990; Neill, 1986; Taber, 1991).

Missionaries and the Cultural Tensions of American Evangelicalism

When examined through the lens of the missionary vocation as it confronts other religious worldviews and cultural communities, the experience of *strangerhood* stands out in bold relief as a theme that is intrinsic to (but often submerged in) the larger evangelical-fundamentalist culture of North America. Likewise, the continuously crafted testimony of the missionary—the quintessence of the altered and the altering self—highlights evangelical nuances of the Christian life conceived as a pilgrimage that both proceeds *from*, and leads *to*, the experience of personal transformation.

Missionaries' strategic attempts to bring about the other-worldly transformation of the other—in a cultural surround to which they themselves are malapropos—manifest layers of meaning that are latent in the metaphor of spiritual warfare and in the ambiguous ideal of being "in the world but not of it." Thus, the ambivalence arising in the gap between missionaries' militant rhetoric of set-apartness and their attempts to recreate an affluent, peaceful, small-town Christian-American lifestyle in Quito echoes these larger themes and tensions in evangelicals' views of American culture and history. In sum, the rhetoric of HCJB members, quoted throughout this book, offers a distilled essence of the cultural contradictions in the evangelical-fundamentalist ethos and worldview—of a people trying to be comfortable in a world that is not their home.

One of the most important conflicts involves the tension between missionaries' anti-modern spiritual worldview and their inner-worldly, corporate-technical ethos. In fact, they might be characterized as a group of modern-media technocrats organized around a message that rejects the premises of modernist thought. This highlights a basic cultural paradox that has to be integrated by fundamentalist ideology. As Lawrence (1989) has noted:

> [Fundamentalists] accept implicitly the benefits of modernity, often thriving through their use of technology, while explicitly rejecting modernism as a holistic ideological framework. They are moderns but not modernists. . . . [F]undamentalism [is] a religious ideology differentiated but not separated from that which it opposes, namely the modernist worldview. While fundamentalists challenge the hegemonic presuppositions of scientific positivism, they are willing adepts of contemporary technology, especially as it applies to mass communications and the media. Distancing themselves from moral relativism, they accept technical efficiency as an instrumental good. They are tenaciously ambivalent (Lawrence, 1989:17,20).

George Marsden (1984) makes a similar point regarding evangelicals in general, insisting on the importance of distinguishing premodern from early modern (Enlightenment period) and late modern (twentieth-century) views when interpreting the evangelical "confrontation with modernity":

> Evangelicals are in many respects very modern people. They are among the masters, for instance, of the use of technique—for promotion, advertising, and so forth—in modern culture. But the structures of their thought, aside from biblical influences, are distinctly early modern as opposed to later modern (that is, twentieth-century modern). . . . Evangelicalism as a distinct phenomenon was early modern in its origins and hence early modern in its assumptions. . . . Evangelicals have been, on the whole, champions of common sense, empiricism, and scientific thinking (Marsden, 1984:98).

The Mission of HCJB epitomizes this sort of tension. Self-descriptions of the Mission, whether official or not, almost invariably include two elements: (1) its innovative use of "the latest technology," (e.g., massive shortwave transmitters, television production facilities, hydroelectric power generators, computer systems, and medical advances); (2) its "faithfulness" in proclaiming the traditional Biblical message of salvation through personal trust in Jesus Christ. When mission members are asked to describe what is distinctive about their group, they almost invariably rise to the occasion by ticking off their colleagues' technical specialties: "We have engineers, doctors, nurses, radio and TV production people, computer specialists, managers." But this is a set-up—quickly followed by an affirmation of core evangelical identity and common purpose: "The thing that unites us all is our desire to get the Gospel out to a lost world."

The narrated careers of HCJB missionaries thus offer exemplars of what Lawrence (1989) calls fundamentalist "countertexts" of the modernist vision; they self-consciously employ the material elements of modernity in a vocation that implicitly counteracts the secular underpinnings of a late-modern worldview. In the case of missionaries, though, these countertexts double back to reveal the deeper nature of evangelicals' ambivalent views toward historical progress.

More specifically, HCJB members objectify the audiences for their Gospel message in terms of targeted "people groups" around the world whose cultures represent
to them the entire sweep of historical development—from stone age tribal groups listening to their newly acquired radios in isolated Amazonian villages to jaded
university students in European capitals. The missionaries continue to insist it is the
same timeless message—salvation through faith in Jesus Christ alone—that is desperately needed by all of these groups. Moreover, they maintain that the Bible's
simple plan of salvation, by whatever communications medium it is received, demands a personal commitment on the hearer's part which enables a divine
transformation not only of a human self, but of the sinful elements of any culture.
Significantly, the textual format of such transformations—the shape and style of their
telling and retelling—is provided by a missionary reading of the Bible itself.

Two passages from HCJB's recent fund-raising publications illustrate these important nuances in the evangelical doctrine of individual and social conversion. In
the excerpts to follow, what is most important to note is that the stories were chosen
and presented by missionaries to appeal specifically to an audience of their likely
supporters; as such, the stories reveal perhaps more about the ideology of North
American evangelicals who finance missions than they do about the actual human
events they purport to describe. In my view, the critical question to ask here is not
"What really happened?" but "Why (and to whom) are these stories being told here?"
and "Why do they work?"

The first piece appears in the Spring 1992 issue of *Amigos*, a front page story entitled "From Communist to Pastor" written by missionary Marlene Goerzen. The tale
unfolds of a former leftist guerrilla in Peru—a onetime enemy of the Gospel now employed with the Mission in Quito—whose zealous "search for truth" and a "just
cause in an unjust society" leads him from Marxist philosophy and illicit drugs to the
study of the Bible and a personal encounter with Jesus Christ. As an idealistic university student in a third world country, Rigoberto Chamoro takes on the mantle of
a Marxist revolution, but later becomes disillusioned with the hypocrisy of "Communist leaders [who] would fervently preach one thing and practice another." He
then proceeds to investigate "many religions" but is left confused and dissatisfied.
Finally, he discovers the Word of God:

> Once he began reading, he couldn't put the fascinating book down. "Studying the
> book of Revelation is what finally got me," Rigo says. "It made me realize that with-
> out Christ there was no hope. So one day after reading until early morning, I got out
> of bed, knelt down and accepted Christ as my Savior."
>
> Then Rigo realized he wanted to meet other believers. He sought out a local
> evangelistic church and told the leaders what had happened to him. The congre-
> gation there nurtured and discipled him.
>
> Rigo's intense desire to communicate Christ to the rest of the world led him to
> study in an Assemblies of God seminary in Peru. He later started a church and de-
> veloped a radio program for youth. . . .
>
> "I've been a Christian for 16 years now," Rigo concludes. "The thing that keeps
> me going is seeing the change that Christ can make in people" (Goerzen, 1992:1).

There is a certain euphony in this riff—unmistakable to fundamentalists, perhaps lost on the ear unattuned by a certain reading of the Acts of the Apostles. But

the intended audience for Marlene Goerzen's rendition will feel in their bones the story's resonance with the Biblical texts wherein Saul of Tarsus, Pharisee of Pharisees and zealous persecutor of Christians, encounters Jesus on the road to Damascus and is in due course transformed into Paul, Apostle to the Gentiles. For them, this is quite literally, a *textbook conversion*—precisely the kind of story that serves to powerfully reaffirm the evangelical worldview and clarify its social and psychological boundaries.

In addition to its implicit citation of a Biblical archetype, several features mark this testimony as an especially significant one for its audience. First, the mention of Communism and illicit drugs as elements of Chamoro's preconversion state implicates a two-pronged enslavement of mind and flesh, bearing a distinctly American signature of the Devil. In political terms, while Communism as a global enemy has lost its Cold War ability to evoke the cosmic arena of the Eschaton and thus to galvanize the millenialist sensibilities of the religious right, a morally equivalent battle may still be joined in the Andean hinterlands where Marxist insurgency, drug trafficking, and Satanic ritual have regrouped in a new conspiracy of evil—one that penetrates from the south and ultimately seems to threaten the borders of the American family.

Second, Chamoro's conversion occurs simply as the result of *reading the Bible*, unassisted by any other human witness. While it appears to celebrate the mind of a young man whose rational inquiry leads him to the truth of the Gospel, there is also a strongly anti-academic and anti-humanist message encoded here. Chamoro's secular university education offers him Marxism, whose pantheon and latter-day followers turn out to be whited sepulchers. His investigation of alternative religions only brings confusion, as he tries to hear the "real truth" in the cacophony of competing claims. But his God-given rational acuity finally exposes the falseness and sophistry of all secular philosophies and religions of human origin, and leads him squarely to The Book. Chamoro finds Christ *in spite* of his secular education, not because of it.

Moreover, his decision is made completely alone, kneeling by his bed in the wee hours of the morning. It is only afterward that he "[seeks] out a local evangelistic church and [tells] the leaders what [has] happened to him." Here, again, we see the American evangelical notion of conversion as a quintessentially individual experience, unmediated by community or cleric. Even in the sweep of revivals when the Spirit slays mortal hearts in mass, the sawdust trail is finally a lonesome valley—and "you've got to walk it by yourself."

Then, as I have noted, there is the peculiar rhetorical vessel for this story; it appears in a mission newsletter as a report from "out there" in the foreign field. The medium suits the message; this is no home-grown testimony of the sort one is likely to hear within the fundamentalist fold. This is a conversion of the radically *other*; Chamoro is a true defector from enemy territory. Precisely for this reason, the fact that his testimony conforms so closely to the domestic ideal type—in its narrative shape and delineation of cognitive categories—gives it much more power, both to validate evangelical reality and to motivate continued support of foreign missions.

The second passage comes from Donelle Barnes's "Drama in Tonampare," featured in the Autumn 1990 issue of *Amigos*. It details the story of a young woman of the Waorani tribe, whose pregnancy nearly ends in tragedy. In the throes of complex labor, the woman is airlifted out of her jungle home by missionary airplane and taken to HCJB's *Hospital Vozandes*:

> The woman later delivered a baby girl; the rescue had been timely and successful. But the drama didn't end there. The baby was born without a left forearm. In North American culture this would not be considered a severe handicap; in traditional Waorani culture babies born with physical defects are drowned or left to starve to death. In jungle communities where only the strong survive, the disadvantaged are not greatly valued. However, these customs are now changing among the Waorani with the arrival of the gospel.
>
> Whether this little girl would have survived after being born in the jungle is uncertain. But she was born at Hospital Vozandes-Shell and mother and daughter began bonding closely to each other. By the time the two were able to return to their village, they were a family (Barnes, 1990:1).

In this text, the theme of salvation cuts down through several layers of meaning. On the surface, it is the technology and skill of modern Western medicine that saves the lives of mother and child. But salvation is also wrought by the imported values of "North American culture," set up as the moral antithesis of "traditional Waorani culture" in which "babies born with physical defects are drowned or left to starve." More specifically, "North American culture" is linked (not too subtly) with the Gospel—objectified as a vessel that "arrives" with the substance of new life, allowing a deformed infant to survive. In this light, one might see this story's obstetrical rescue as a metaphor for the missionaries' larger agenda of spiritual midwifery, delivering new members into the family of God. The bonding of mother and child thus becomes a transparent sign of divine reconciliation, the infant's deformity a mark of human failing that is covered by God's grace.

Less apparent, however, may be the story's function as an evocative parable of conflicts much closer to the lives of its intended readers to the north. The negative power in the phrase "where only the strong survive" arises from its historical allusion to fundamentalist anathema—its encoding of a battle call against the barbarism of modernist thought. In the ellipses, a cry for salvation is heard from the distant shores of home. And the image of the slaughter of innocents doubles back in a crusade for the Right to Life, galvanizing Christian sensibilities. The pregnant woman and unborn child are the inchoate Family, threatened with annihilation in the moral equivalent of a jungle. In its photographic negative, "North American culture" becomes the savage; the dog is in the manger.

Evangelical historian Bruce Shelley[7] expresses this idea less subtly, sounding the call to remissionize an America profaned by pluralism. In his book, *The Gospel and the American Dream* (1980), Shelley ruminates:

> [M]assive immigrations to metropolitan areas have made pluralism a fact of life. Consensus under the Puritan vision of a moral America is a distant memory. The values of the secular tradition, especially the exclusion of churches from seats of power, have been welcomed by too many for too long. . . . Does this mean the Christian mission to America has been rescinded? Must Christians settle for winning individual souls here and there? Not at all. Christians are a vital part of America's future. Evangelism remains a mandate. The preservation of the traditional family, the multiplication of spiritually vibrant congregations, the Christian education of the

young and newly converted, and Christian ministries of compassion in the public realm remain priorities for Christians in America. Only now, *in the presence of these secular barbarians*, these ministries must be conducted as strategies of a minority, not the party of power (Shelley, 1980:175, emphasis added).

In my view, this passage illustrates how the American missionary impulse continually recenters itself on the margins of a social order that it confronts and attempts to convert. From the alternative center, it recalibrates the progress of history by the metric of a spiritual journey. And the pilgrimage moves in two directions—pressing onward by hearkening back, penetrating inward to the heart even as it radiates outward to the world. Indeed, while the modern secular humanists are being *called back* to the Bible, the primitive tribes are being *brought forward* to it. Cultural conversion is demonstrated by the reinstallation of "family values" in the first world, matched by "community development" in the third.

Even as it thrives on the margins of contemporary secular culture, the evangelical imagination posits a sort of temporal *axis mundi* of Christian civilization to which all redeemed cultures will gravitate, a prefiguring of the Kingdom of Heaven. While impossible to define, it is a kind of mythic time, place, and way of life that evokes for them the ideal of first-century Christian community (albeit shaped by a few qualities one might associate as well with seventeenth-century Massachusetts Bay, nineteenth-century Victorian England, and twentieth-century Wheaton, Illinois).

The opposing reflexes bound up in ideas of redemptive mission and historical progress relate, of course, to a more basic dilemma faced by evangelicals—how to negotiate a Biblical identity that both confronts and transcends the conditions of modernity. On the one hand, they must try to maintain a view of the Bible and of the Christian story as standing apart from the actual unfolding of history, thus remaining unscathed by the acids of scientific discovery, critical scholarship, cultural transformation, and the ambiguities of a what some would call a post-Christian and postmodern age. Evangelicals who adopt this stance are able to integrate novel cultural experience only by reformulating it to sustain "historically transcendent truths" (i.e., traditional categories of thought). But on the other hand, for evangelicals the enduring authority and power of Scripture dependes on its literal historical truth and accuracy, i.e., as a record of God's dealings in a concrete human time that is continuous with their present experience. Indeed, it is the belief that such divine dealings persist in their own moment that allows evangelicals to appropriate a Biblical past as their own—to literally read themselves into the sacred text. Consider HCJB President Ron Cline's 1990 year-end report:

> HCJB's staff takes seriously the commission Jesus gave the early church in Acts 1:8. If we were to personalize this verse for HCJB, it would read, "You will receive power . . . and you will be my witnesses in Quito, and in all Ecuador and Latin America, and to the ends of the earth."
>
> It was in Quito that the first missionary radio station went on the air. The other ministries sprang up to reach out to people in our host country—local radio and TV, hospitals and clinics, evangelism and discipleship, education, community development, literature and, of course, the personal involvement of each of our missionaries.
>
> From this base, our commitment spreads to all of Latin America. . . . Our World by 2000 commitment is to the "ends of the earth"—that each man, woman and child

will be able to turn on his or her radio and hear the gospel in a language he or she can understand, no matter how remote the location (Cline, 1990:1).

Cline's message here reveals the inherent dilemma for evangelical action in the world. It is (to add a twist to the Biblical aphorism) how to be *inside* history but not *determined* by it; how to bring a desired future into being—a "World by 2000"—yet still believe that human events are sliding relentlessly toward a cataclysmic end to ordinary affairs on earth.

George Marsden (1984) renders this tension with a description of the architecture of two buildings facing each other on the campus of Wheaton College, the evangelical center west of Chicago. Blanchard Hall, a "Victorian conception of a medieval fort," brimming with towers and parapets, seems to speak metaphorically of evangelicals' militant opposition toward modernism. In contrast, the "colossal colonial" style of the Billy Graham Center suggests harmony with culture. The one holds high the standard of dispensational theology, as if to barricade the company of the saved while urgently beckoning sinners outside to turn and flee the present secular age before its imminent cataclysmic end. The other evokes the traditional myth of a Christian America, an image of the heavenly city right here on earth. In this light, the gap between HCJB missionaries' rhetoric of spiritual warfare and their actual attempts to recreate a peaceful, affluent, small-town Christian-American lifestyle in Quito echoes these larger themes in evangelicals' views of American culture and history.

The notion of progress underlying this sort of missionary thinking implies the necessity of conversion that is both a momentary transformation and a continued movement toward a unified and purified self, family, and surrounding cultural whole. Through the prism of missionaries' moral careers and their rhetoric of the self, we discover that the evangelical ideology of progress—especially in its American signature—is structured in ways that maintain evangelical ideology in taut suspension from its own cultural matrices. We see a significant linkage—an aesthetic synergism—between the ongoing narrative reconstruction of individual selves in the format of Christian testimonies, and the ambiguous recasting of an American past in a way that simultaneously posits an unbroken thread of advancing "Christian civilization" through various crises, yet necessitates world denial and cultural conversion. In their style and thematic connections, the testimonies of missionaries reveal polarities underlying a larger evangelical mythology that has construed American history itself *as* a missionary testimony. Interposed in their accounts of self are the contrary facets of being set apart in a grander scheme—the Redeemer Nation's self-righteous sense of destiny and divine calling, combined with a fallen sinner's abject unworthiness.

In the book, *How Does America Hear the Gospel?*, evangelical theologian and missionary William Dyrness (1989) illustrates such themes. In the first place, Dyrness observes an American tendency in the viewing of history that bears no accidental resemblance to the process of life storytelling among fundamentalist Christians: "The way Americans deal with the past," he writes, "is a function of our approach to life. Fundamentally, we have two ways of dealing with it: we idealize it or, when this is impossible, we forget it. In our remembering of history we tend to make it an image of what we would like our present to be." By the logic of a national testimony, moral shades of gray in past conflicts become black and white on either side of redemptive moments.

A second theme emerges, however, as Dyrness critiques televangelist Robert Schuller's "theology of self-esteem." Contrary to Schuller, Dyrness (1989:30) implies that the purpose of all this amazing grace God shed on the face of America is, after all, to save wretches like us:

> Discussion of Christian life in America will characteristically include references to emotional failure and personal feelings of inadequacy. But these discussions must be reformed in the light of Scripture. Emotional pain will be the expression of a basic rebellion and inability to listen to God's word; inadequacy will only be properly recognized when we see ourselves as the prodigal son who has consciously fled from the father's house.

The complex interplay between these contrasting mission themes in the fundamentalist worldview is especially apparent in Robert Flood's book, *America: God Shed His Grace on Thee*. An illustrated rendering of the nation's history for young readers, this volume was published in 1975 by Moody Press on the upswing of what its author calls "the evangelical renaissance." As Flood would have it, the destiny of America has been wrought by God through the words and deeds of protofundamentalist Christians beginning with Christopher Columbus: "Secular historians have underplayed the greatest single driving force behind the voyage of Columbus: the impact of the Bible upon his life."

Significantly, Abraham Lincoln and Dwight L. Moody each rate one of the book's twelve chapters[8]; each illustrates a different facet of fundamentalists' view of their mission identity in relation to American history and culture. On the one hand, Lincoln represents the idea that America's exemplary role in the world arises out of the Biblical principles that have conceived and preserved the symbolic architecture of a Christian civilization—specifically by means of divine guidance appropriated by its leaders at key moments.

With some reluctance, Flood admits that Lincoln was a human vessel of grace; during his days in New Salem he "struggled with his faith" and "held a view of universal salvation—from his misinterpretation of such verses as 1 Corinthians 15:22." But basically he portrays Lincoln as a man so engaged with God and so steeped in the Scriptures that he almost becomes a Biblical figure himself, lifting America into the Good Book with him. Lincoln's lifelong refusal to join a church is turned into a sort of fundamentalist snub of humanistic religion: "Nor did he care for creeds. He preferred to draw his convictions directly from the Scriptures rather than from what he regarded as man-made abstracts. . . . He firmly saw [slavery] as a moral evil, an injustice that would surely bring the wrath of God upon the nation. Common sense, coupled with the Bible he so frequently read, drove him to these conclusions."

On the other hand, D. L. Moody, the famed shoe-salesman-turned-evangelist who called thousands to personal faith and missionary commitment during the late nineteenth century, represents the theme of individual conversion and set-apartness from a sinful world as key to the fundamentalist stance toward culture: "Daily Moody pressed almost everyone he met in Chicago with the question, 'Are you a Christian?' One by one, men were converted" (Flood 1975:133). Leave it to Lincoln to stay the nation's moral course; it was Moody's job to convince people "one by one" to renounce their individual sin and be born again, and then to share their new birth with others as he himself had done. Flood (1975:142) quotes Moody:

> Some day you will read in the papers that Moody is dead. Don't you believe a word of it. At that moment I shall be more alive than I am now. . . . I was born of the flesh in 1837, I was born of the Spirit in 1855. That which is born of the flesh may die. That which is born of the Spirit shall live forever.

The juxtaposition of two themes in Flood's book epitomizes the tension under-lying American fundamentalists' identification with their own nation, and their sense of its destiny and mission in the world. On the one hand, in his portrayal of America's symbolic spiritual foundations and special historical role, Flood invokes the aura of the redeemer nation with its roots in Puritan theocracy:

> Anyone who grasps the flow of history and the purposes of God will sense America's role in this divine world plan: the remarkably late discovery [by Europeans] of the continent itself, the unique Christian foundations, the revivals which sent forth from this land the seeds for spiritual revolution among other peoples of the earth (Flood, 1975:183).

> The men who wrote the Constitution . . . in no way suggested that God could be ig-nored in the governmental affairs of men. In fact, they assumed the very opposite—that God is above any human government—and this assumption was so unanimous that it was not even debated!

> The conviction that government is responsible to God, even in a democracy, per-meates many of the documents of our nation. . . .

> Not all our early leaders were necessarily fundamental in theology. But they sensed *God's sovereign hand in human affairs*, and they believed that "except the Lord build the house, they labour in vain that build it" (Psalm 127:1) (Flood, 1975:164, emphasis added).

On the other hand, Flood laments that "our society today is a pluralistic one as never before, [and] the tide of secularism has swept away many of our spiritual values." The "real danger" facing America, says Flood in a chapter called "Who is Under-mining Our Republic?", lies in "the movement afoot today which is chipping away at the spiritual timbers built into the framework of our nation" (Flood, 1975: 164–165). And at the end of his chapter on D. L. Moody, Flood seems to character-ize the general trend of American history as one of inevitable moral decline, barely held in check by a tiny remnant of godly people in each generation:

> Had not God singled out a handful of individuals in each century who could help re-verse the *inevitable degeneracy in the hearts of men*, America even by now may have died (p.146, emphasis added).

Both of these kinds of statements presume determinism, but one takes an opti-mistic stance while the other is pessimistic: "God's sovereign hand in human affairs" somehow coexists with the "inevitable degeneracy in the hearts of men." In the end, Flood resolves this paradox with a poetic flourish, quoting the third stanza of *"America the Beautiful"*:

> America! America! God mend thine every flaw,
> Confirm thy soul in self control, Thy liberty in law!

Thus, a patriotic anthem becomes a fundamentalist paean; the individual conversion story, a testimony of national identity.

In this light, then, we may see the missionary's moral career as a kind of symbolic repository of America's evangelical past. It is, after all, the missionary's story which speaks of the mending of a flawed self, the confirmation of a soul in self control. As such, it evokes a once youthful nation's sense of itself emerging from strangerhood, forging its own character through redemptive suffering, and responding to a sacrificial calling to teach and to heal the world. Finally, though, the culmination of the heroic stranger's journey is an ambiguous return home, which beckons America to return as well—back from its lonely and bewildering adventures to a destination of communal repose in its collective imagination—to a place that never really was.

Conclusion

Sociologists have long recognized the paradoxical value of the person on the boundary—for the maintenance of social order on the one hand, for the impetus to change on the other, and for the task of jointly interpreting both of these phenomena. One whose very presence calls into question a group's taken-for-granted reality can bring into sharp relief the group's most important norms, values, and ideas about the world. The very ways in which some persons are defined and treated as deviant or marginal can highlight the key features of a group's shared identity. Moreover, the outsider perceives important nuances of detail which the insider does not notice. And perhaps we can learn most about the universal human need for community by listening to persons whose membership in a community is ambiguous, tentative, or threatened.

This study values the missionary's position on the boundary not only for these reasons, but also for a subtly different one: Being set apart prevents people from taking their own experience for granted and thus constrains them to interpret a greater portion of their experience *morally*. The key sociological question about missionaries, then, is not only: What can people on the social boundary tell us about meaning at the center of social life? It is also: How does life on the boundary come to be experienced *morally* first and foremost? In answering this second question, perhaps the most obvious lesson to be learned from missionaries in our time is that the subjective conditions of estrangement are formed by conflict at the interface between personal and social definitions of the self—which is precisely where moral interpretation is most called for. But there is another lesson that is less apparent: that the experience of strangerhood can be transformed, by the imagery of an other-worldly vocation, into a coherent (even practical) understanding of human development, finally producing positive change and transcendent meaning on the margins of social life.

At the end of his journey the wise man of Ecclesiastes wondered, "What does man gain by all the toil at which he toils under the sun? A generation goes, and a generation comes, but the earth remains forever." Yet even as he pondered the meaningless sameness of existence, the wise man rendered vivid images of movement and dynamic reversals in the nature of things—the sun rising and setting, the wind blowing north and south, and streams flowing to the sea. Like the writer of Ecclesiastes, we may choose to view human life as a cycle forever repeated, devoid of progress or

objective purpose. Still, in our personal experience of the world, real change confronts us as the central fact and the central fear of consciousness. Each of us *is* the
world unto herself or himself, yet the world exists as *not us*; the trajectory of our lives
pulls us relentlessly away—starting the day we are born—farther out and away from
the unity of things until the moment we die and only the briefest ripple on the surface
of history would let anyone know we had once been a living, breathing part of a
world. In a way, it is this highly personalized modern recognition of what the *fact of
change* ultimately must mean to us that defines the universal experience of strangerhood—as an incurable set-apartness at the core of the human self—the knowledge
that the world and our own kind will very soon go on without us.

Missionaries, as we have seen, exemplify these modern predicaments of the species through a pedagogy of paradox; their condition is universalized and humanized
insofar as they are set apart from sources of community. They highlight the power of
death by urgently proclaiming its overcoming in salvation. They let us see the importance of reflective self-discovery, even as they set out to discover and manipulate
the possibilities of conversion in others. They, perhaps more acutely than most
people, experience life in confrontation with change—both as subjects and as agents.
But even as their views of life provide an imagery of transformation rendering human
identity itself as a kind of strangerhood, missionaries' stories challenge us to construct change as human development toward unity, toward a sense of belonging and
meaning grounded in transcendent generativity which—as John Kotre put it—may
"outlive the self." The story of missionaries teaches us, finally, to choose to act on
the hope (even if it turns out to be false) that one can make a positive difference in
the world, not only for oneself but for others, both here and now, and in whatever
world may come.

Notes

Chapter 1

1. Perhaps better known by the call letters of its radio station, HCJB (Heralding Christ Jesus' Blessings), the group that I studied will be identified throughout the book by several names used interchangeably in quotations from missionaries and in my own discussion: World Radio, HCJB, the Voice of the Andes (*Vozandes* in Spanish), or simply the Mission.

2. Latourette devoted to the nineteenth century three of the seven volumes in his monumental *History of the Expansion of Christianity*, (1937–1945). See volumes 4–6, *The Great Century, 1800–1914*.

3. See Bosch (1991) for a discussion of mission theology in the context of postmodernity. See also Grant Wacker's essay, "Uneasy in Zion: Evangelicals in Postmodern Society" (in Marsden, 1984).

4. See Roberts and Siewart (1989) for a comprehensive survey of U.S.–based Protestant missions throughout the world.

5. Nevertheless, I did end up with some quantifiable information which the reader will find on display mainly in the final chapter of this book. I collected two sets of primary data: tape-recorded interviews with 107 missionaries, and written questionnaires returned by 129 missionaries. The first group is largely a subset of the second. Of all those interviewed, eight did not return the questionnaire. Of all those who returned the questionnaire, 30 had not been interviewed. In sum, ninety-nine missionaries (about half the total staff of 200 in Ecuador) are included in both data sets, and 137 missionaries (68 percent of the total staff) are included in at least one of the data sets. In any event, I conducted the interviews as a first step. These were open-ended, wide-ranging discussions eliciting personal life stories, accounts of the missionary call and other religious experiences, reflections on the meaning of missionary work—the motives, rewards, and tensions inherent in missionary careers—and so forth. I designed and administered the written questionnaire subsequently, with the intent to provide a descriptive overview of the group based on the frequency of, and correlation between, certain attitudes, experiences, and conditions identified in the interviews.

6. A fellow graduate student, Nancy Ammerman, steered me in Erikson's direction as he was guiding her own work on a study that eventually became *Bible Believers: Fundamentalists in the Modern World* (Ammerman, 1987).

7. He had written two award-winning books: *Wayward Puritans* (1966), which examined how deviance was defined and responded to in the Massachusetts Bay Colony, and *Everything in its Path* (1976), which was about the loss of community in the aftermath of a disastrous flood in Buffalo Creek, West Virginia.

8. Quoted in Marsden (1980).

9. Along these lines, see Barbara Myerhoff's *Number Our Days* (1978), an illuminating account in which an anthropologist-author weaves her own life story and personal quest for meaning into an ethnographic study of her elders in a Jewish retirement home.

10. See Carpenter and Shenk's *Earthen Vessels* (1990) for an excellent collection of historical essays that chronicle various aspects of American evangelical missions from 1880 to 1980. For a recent collection of essays on evangelical mission theology, see Van Engen, Gilliland, and Pierson (1993).

11. See Tod Swanson's Chicago dissertation, "A crown of *Yage*" (1988), concerning the encounter of native South American cosmologies with Christian missions, and the social and religious consequences for indigenous people from colonial times through the present. See also Bowden (1982), Dussel (1981), and Pike (1993).

12. See Thomas Cole's *The Journey of Life* (1992) for a comprehensive history of American ideas about the moral self and progress through the life course.

13. See Leslie Harman's *The Modern Stranger: On Language and Membership* (1988) for a theoretical overview and synthesis of previous sociological analyses of the concept, including such related images as "the marginal man," "the lonely crowd," "other- and inner-direction," "the homeless mind," "reflexive crisis," and "the trained observer as stranger."

14. A composite of passages from David Brainerd's diary, edited by Jonathan Edwards (Brainerd, 1949 [ca. 1745]).

15. A composite of passages from Jim Elliot's diary, quoted in Elisabeth Elliot (1958).

16. See Najarian (1982) for a symbolic-interactionist account that applies the *stranger* concept to interpret the experience of nineteenth-century Protestant missionaries in China. See also Cohen (1990), Mittelberg (1988), and Gittens (1989).

17. See Snow and Anderson (1987) for a discussion of the concept of identity work as a socially reflective process that motivates the construction and revision of autobiographical narratives, applied specifically to the marginalized experience of homeless persons.

18. Schutz (1944), described a cultural pattern as encompassing "all the peculiar valuations, institutions, and systems of orientation and guidance . . . the network of plans, means-ends relations, motives and chances, hopes and fears, which the actor within a particular social world uses for interpreting his experiences of it." Schutz viewed this pattern metaphorically as a map which, in order to be useful, includes not only symbols of the group's external boundaries and internal structure, but also a representation of a given person's own position with respect to the group.

19. Among missionaries to the Indians in colonial America, the best known is David Brainerd. Although he worked among the Indians for only three years, Brainerd became Jonathan Edwards's greatest spiritual hero during the final years of his short life. In 1749 Edwards edited and published Brainerd's soul-searching journals, later to have a remarkable impact on an English cobbler named William Carey, as well as on many others who followed him in the modern missionary movement (Ahlstrom, 1961).

20. Carey's personal accomplishments were remarkable. He started several churches and a college, planted botanical gardens, worked to bring about various reforms, translated the Bible into numerous languages, and produced notable works of scholarship in Bengali and Sanskrit (DuBose, 1979).

21. It took Adoniram Judson almost half a year to reach India, which was long enough for him to change his views on infant baptism.

22. This story is told in two books: Frank Cook's *Seeds in the Wind* (1961) and Lois Neely's *Come Up to This Mountain: The Miracle of Clarence W. Jones and HCJB* (1980).

23. See George Marsden's *Fundamentalism and American Culture* (1980) for an illuminating discussion of the religious and cultural climate in evangelical America around the time when World Radio and other "faith missions" were founded. See also Dana Robert's essay (in Carpenter and Shenk, 1990) on the origins of independent evangelical missions during the period 1880 to 1920.

24. From a World Radio Missionary Fellowship brochure, 1983. See Alan Riding's 1984 *New York Times* article, "From High in Andes, Bible's Message Carries Far," for a mainstream media report on the impact of HCJB in the short-wave listening world.

25. Joel Carpenter (1990) mentions the founding of WRMF in his historical discussion of fundamentalist faith missions, many of which eventually became more moderate and mainstream evangelical organizations.

Chapter 2

1. A total of 99 missionaries (about half the staff of 200 in Ecuador in 1982) were included in both data sets; 137 missionaries (68 percent of the staff) were included in at least one of the two data sets.

2. See Kotre's *Outliving the Self* (1984) and Rosenwald and Ochberg's *Storied Lives* (1992) for excellent examples of life-story production and thematic analysis in the social and behavioral sciences.

3. All names applied to missionaries in this study are pseudonyms. Material that appears in quotation was transcribed from tape-recorded interviews. I have minimally edited some passages from these transcripts, to eliminate redundancy and improve clarity, but have preserved the speaker's actual language and context. In a couple of cases, I arranged life story events in chronological order, e.g., when a speaker later recalled and mentioned an incident that clearly preceded in time something he or she had already talked about. Also, certain incidental details that would have revealed a subject's identity have been omitted or changed. However, the features of significant events are rendered as narrated by the subject. To the extent that some of the interview material includes life-historical details that these subjects also shared in public testimonies—things well known about them by their friends in the community—it is possible that certain speakers may be recognizable to insiders. However, I consider all of these narratives to be anonymous.

4. See Kroll-Smith (1980), Harding (1987), and Boone (1989) for discussions of testimonies—especially testimonies of conversions—as rhetorical devices fulfilling significant functions for evangelical and fundamentalist Christians' social and personal identity.

5. My application of the terms sacred and profane is informed by Mircea Eliade's 1959 treatise, *The Sacred and the Profane*, although I put these concepts to a somewhat different use. Eliade's primary dimension of comparison was historical. He referred to people in archaic societies who oriented their lives according to circular notions of time and sacred space at the center of being. Such people lived entirely in a sacred world, according to Eliade; their sense of order was derived from human-divine homologies (as body-house-cosmos, and female-earth/male-heaven) expressed in myths and rituals. Eliade radically distinguished the sacred world of the ancients from the disenchanted world of modern people, for whom the vital experiences of sex, eating, work, and play have been desacralized. But he noted that even for nonreligious people, space was not entirely homogeneous, and time is not entirely linear. Secular rituals still mime the actions of the gods, recorded in ancient myths. Diverging from these sorts of comparisons, my use of sacred and profane refers primarily to a tension in the lives of modern people who are religious, but who see themselves as living in a sort of exile within a nonreligious world. The rhetoric and the rituals of conversion and religious strangerhood express that separation.

6. Snow and Machalek propose, for example, that converts tend not to use analogical metaphors showing how their religious beliefs are *like* other beliefs, but iconic metaphors (such as "God is love," or "I've been born again") that emphasize the uniqueness of their system of meaning.

7. As theologian Harvey Cox (1984) has noted, the testimonies of born-again Christians in general tend to resemble each other, but this does not make them "untrue." In part, this is because key events in their lives are expected to follow a recognized sequence and are in-

terpreted similarly by a pervasive religious tradition in certain communities. He cites the Rev. Jerry Falwell's depiction of himself as a "ne'er-do-well headed for perdition until the Lord turned him around on his personal road to Damascus" as an example of the "power of religious traditions to shape life cycles in similar ways, especially in a region where such a tradition pervades the atmosphere."

8. See Meissner (1984) and Jones (1991) for a discussion of psychoanalysis and religion, including recent developments. Beginning with Freud, psychoanalysts have mostly held a demystified and pathologized view of religion, i.e., one sharply at odds with religion's general esteem in popular culture. As summarized recently by Jones (1991), Freud developed at least two accounts of the origins and psychological foundations of religious devotion (neither of them flattering to believers.) In *Totem and Taboo* (1913) he proposed that religion arose out of primal guilt over the unconscious Oedipal wishes of sons to kill their fathers—a myth with historical origins in primitive times, Freud argued. Guilt was then assuaged through idealization of the dead patriarch and by obsessional repetition of rituals of devotion. This amounted to a diagnosis of religion as collective neurosis. In *The Future of an Illusion* (1927), Freud offered a somewhat more sociological explanation: Religion existed because it fulfilled certain infantile needs for a developing humanity—needs for consolation and security, and for the taming of asocial instincts. As Jones (1991:2) rendered it, Freud was suggesting that "through fantasy, religion reduces the terror of an uncaring nature by personalizing the natural order, removes the fear of death by providing an illusion of immortality, and reconciles us to the social necessity of self-denial by promising to reward us for it in the hereafter." Contemporary psychoanalysts have recognized the limitations of these reductionistic Freudian formulations. As summarized by Meissner (1984:137), "The two primary criticisms that have been leveled against Freud's view of religion are that he based it on the notion of the internalization and re-externalization exclusively of a paternal imago—derived from the vicissitudes of the father-son Oedipal relationship, with its inherent conflict and ambivalence—and that he provided an account of religious experience that looks in a rather limited and prejudicial fashion at the more infantile dimensions and derivatives of religious experience." Post-Freudian analysts such as Meissner and Jones tend to be more accepting of religion as a potentially healthy, mature feature of the experience of human beings in their "relatedness" to one another and to the world around them.

9. See Ullman (1989) for a discussion of the psychodynamic significance of parental death—particularly the death of the father—in interpreting adolescent conversion experiences.

Chapter 3

1. As the missions historian Charles Forman (1984:2) expressed this view, a personal call "needs to find confirmation from the body of Christians before that person can fully accept it as God's calling. So Paul sensed his call to preach the gospel to the Gentiles, but this was confirmed by the church in Antioch before he started out and was reaffirmed by the council in Jerusalem as he continued."

2. See I Corinthians 7:24, and surrounding verses. Weber observed that Luther rendered with call (in German, *Beruf*) a Greek word that had two quite different meanings; in one context it meant the call to salvation through Christ, while in the other it conveyed something similar to the Latin *status* (or German *Stand*), as in "status of a servant" or "status of marriage." See Max Weber's *The Protestant Ethic and the Spirit of Capitalism* (1904:207–209).

3. Writing four years after *The Protestant Ethic* was first published, Lutheran theologian Einar Billing (1909:8–12) offered support for what he saw as Weber's case against the Calvinists while he tried to recapture the true meaning of vocation as Luther had taught it. Billing

pitied the person who "actually lives in the thought" of double predestination. "It acts as an open sore to keep the soul ever in anxiety over his eternal welfare," he wrote. "The Roman Catholic takes refuge in the church. The Lutheran takes refuge in the presence of Christ. But the Calvinist? If in his achievements he can discover such great progress that he must admit a power greater than his own, then he knows that God is working in him and that he is of the elect." In order for the Calvinist to discover this, it is necessary for him to "fill every second of time with hard work," and to "center life on a unifying task, a *call*." But Luther's concept of vocation was different, according to Billing: "The call is the forgiveness of sins. . . . My call is the form my life takes according as God himself organizes it for me through his forgiving grace. Life organized around the forgiveness of sins: that is Luther's idea of the call." He went on to note that for Luther, work in a calling had a threefold value: (1) it provided a discipline for the body, a crucifixion of the old sinful self; (2) it provided a means for serving one's neighbor; and (3) it contributed to community life, order, peace, and security.

4. An early example of the application of rational scientific methods to the missionary task was given by Rev. John Clifford (1901:91). Reporting to the Student Volunteer Convention in London, he said: "We need students—men who will work upon the facts of religion as Richard Owen amongst fossils and Sir Joseph Hooker on plants; scientific students, exact, severe, painstaking, hating inaccuracy as they hate a lie in their reasoning, never passing a single datum however repulsive, nor accepting an illusion however full of charm; eliminating the possibility of error by the repetition of experiments and the accumulation of observations, and so furnishing the churches and their workers with that knowledge of the realities of life without which energy is wasted, mistakes are made, and work is marred."

5. The Macedonian cry is a reference to a vision reported by the Apostle Paul on his second missionary journey—a man from Macedonia calling for Paul to "come over and help us."

6. For some of these people, the missionary call was merely a special case of a regular occurrence of "hearing God's voice." For example, when I asked one man more specifically about the voice he heard when he received a missionary call, he answered that he hears God speak to him fairly often: "I have the experience where I hear an audible, quiet little voice. The Lord doesn't hit me with bricks or lightning—just that quiet little voice talking to me. It is something beyond my conscience, speaking to me. I know it. Well some people laugh at me and say, 'Oh, so you have little voices that speak to you.' But you know what I'm talking about, don't you?"

7. See Chapter 2, pages 38–39 and 64–65.

Chapter 4

1. This is the subtitle in Harman's (1988) theoretical reformulation of the stranger as a social type.

2. Alfred Schutz used the map metaphor in his discussion of cultural patterns, which he defined as "systems of orientation and guidance . . . the network of plans, means-ends relations, motives and chances, hopes and fears, which the actor within a particular social world uses for interpreting his experiences of it" (Schutz, 1944:499–500).

3. I would generally include here symbolic-interactionist and social-constructionist theories informed by phenomenology.

4. Hammond (1988) notes that identity consists of both immutable and constructed elements, and that religion can be either one—or both—depending on the social context and historical moment in which the individual encounters religion.

5. In an essay on the missionary enterprise and theories of imperialism, Arthur Schlesinger (1978) has noted that the expansion of Western culture throughout the world has been, from the point of view of the actors involved, "overdetermined" (in the Freudian sense).

6. Clifford's (1982) biography of Leenhardt, aptly titled *Person and Myth*, is enriched by the missionary-scholar's own reflective writing throughout his career.

7. This also served the purpose of clarifying and maintaining the boundaries of the group. In one sense, unconverted employees provided an opportunity for evangelism—as Jones put it, "a mission field within a mission field." But in another sense, unsaved workers were infiltrators from *the world* who posed a threat to the character of the Mission. Hence, Jones warned his colleagues to "guard against having a predominant proportion of unsaved to Christian in any department" (Jones, 1966 [1962]:117).

8. Maurice Leenhardt's biography superbly illustrates what I mean here by *utopia*, namely the *elsewhere* that the missionary imagines as a virgin spiritual ground upon which to sow his faith (Clifford, 1982:20).

9. Shaffir notes further that "every act of witnessing anchors the belief system deeply in the emotions of the believer" (Shaffir, 1978).

10. This is the Mission's official estimate of average weekly attendance in 1982.

11. An allusion to I Corinthians 3:4.

12. In addition to English Fellowship Church, another factor that contributes to the persistent cultural isolation of the missionary enclave in Quito is the presence of an English-language Christian school accredited in the United States. The Alliance Academy was founded in 1929 by the Christian and Missionary Alliance (CMA) as a school for missionaries' children. Various mission organizations provide teachers in exchange for tuition credit for their members' children. The Academy has helped bring together a large number of missionaries in Quito and has tended to focus their family life away from the Ecuadorian culture and community.

13. See my discussion of Weber's notion of calling in Chapter 3.

14. This claim sometimes produces an odd superficial alliance between missionaries and cultural survivalists, whose real means and ends could hardly be further apart (Stoll, 1982).

15. Ricoeur (1986) elucidates this important link between the social and the individual contours of ideology, by connecting Erik Erikson's and Clifford Geertz's notions of its function. While ideology operates as a guardian of culture, it also accomplishes the integration of identity. To think of ideology only in suspicious, negative terms as distortion or legitimation is to miss its positive significance acquired through conversation. "In conversation we have an interpretive attitude," says Ricoeur, through which we may "recognize a group's values on the basis of its self-understanding" (Ricoeur, 1986:255).

16. The transcript has been edited to eliminate redundancy and improve clarity, while preserving the actual language and rhetorical interplay among speakers.

17. In my role as an interviewer asking questions for a research project, I myself provided the primary, most immediate audience for the statements that appear throughout this book. However, I was also perceived as a member of the second audience, the community of other missionaries. Having grown up in Ecuador as the son of HCJB missionaries, I was treated as an insider. In that sense, the conversations that I recorded occurred in the vein of "backstage" talk between missionaries, and should be interpreted as such.

18. This is an intriguing distinction; one can only speculate on the underlying rationale for it. On the surface, it appears to be a pragmatic compromise necessitated by the scarcity of Christian talent for broadcast productions. Assuming that to be the case, one might understand why the Mission would draw a line between preachers and instrumental musicians. While a preacher actually speaks *the word* through which the power of the gospel must pass, a flute player merely accompanies the word, uplifts the spirit, evokes a lyric. An unsaved preacher is a fraud; an unsaved flute player is a minor embarrassment, or an opportunity for evangelism. But why split the hair between singers and actors? Probably the reason is that gospel singers are assumed to believe what they sing, whereas actors are understood to be putting on a false *persona*.

19. Newsletter from Glenn and Bonnie Brawand-Lafitte, 1991.
20. Newsletter from Glenn and Bonnie Brawand-Lafitte, 1984.

Chapter 5.

1. Strictly speaking it is not appropriate to discuss these data in terms of statistical significance. The questionnaire respondents do not constitute a representative sample, but a small population. Hence, the data are purely descriptive. *Statistical* inferences to a larger population really ought not to be made, though in conceptual terms these data may yield general insights about missionaries as a category of social actors. Nevertheless, I include probability values for chi-square tests to give some idea of the magnitude of differences observed in various percentages of interest. A probability value less than 0.05 should be given the following interpretation here: If these subgroups had been random samples drawn from a population in which no real differences existed on the parameter in question, we would expect to find sample differences as large as these less than 5 times in 100 by chance.

2. See Donald Spence's (1982) discussion of narrative truth vs. historical truth from a psychoanalytic point of view.

3. Newsletter from Rob and Barb Quiring, 1990.

4. Newsletter from Rob and Barb Quiring, 1991.

5. The Mission actively recruits on these campuses through chapel addresses and representation at student mission conferences. More broadly, evangelical foreign missions and Christian colleges share a constituency; families who send their children to schools like Wheaton, Westmont, Bethel, Gordon, Taylor, and Asbury also tend to support evangelical missionaries through their churches. Reciprocally, missionaries often send their children to such schools. Further, the Mission has linked itself to Christian colleges through formal programmatic ties, e.g., it has served as an extension site for degree programs in communications offered by Wheaton College and Azusa Pacific University. A number of Mission staff and board members (President Ron Cline among them) have served as faculty and administrators at various colleges in the Christian College Consortium. In sum, HCJB and the Christian colleges that provided Hunter with a representative sample of young evangelicals are part of the same subculture and social network.

6. The Gustafsons are not members of HCJB. They are among a number of other American evangelical workers whose prayer letters I received.

7. Shelley is a seasoned academic with a PhD from the University of Iowa, who claims in his preface to *The Gospel and the American Dream* (1980) that his thinking has been shaped by the writings of Robert Bellah, among others. Despite his academic credentials, Shelley appears also to be the kind of committed believer that Jerry Falwell would gladly claim as a fellow fundamentalist. Thus, he not only understands academically the kinds of cultural tensions that I am grasping at here, but he articulates them as an insider in a way that resonates with the actual experience of conservative Christians.

8. Flood devotes other chapters to explaining "How Evangelicals Launched the Ivy League," "Who is Undermining our Republic?" and "America's great missionary role" ("Through All the Earth Abroad").

References

Adeney, D. (1955). *The Unchanging Commission*. Inter-Varsity Press, Chicago.

Ahlstrom, S.E. (1972). *A Religious History of the American People, Vol.II*. Yale University Press, New Haven.

———. (1961). "The American Frontier and the Protestant Missionary Response." In *History Lessons for Tomorrow's Mission*. World Christian Student Federation, Geneva.

Ammerman, N.T. (1987). *Bible Believers: Fundamentalists in the Modern World*. Rutgers University Press, New Brunswick.

Austin, J. (1962). *How to Do Things with Words*. Harvard University Press, Cambridge.

Baldwin, M.S. (1901). "Essential Spiritual Qualifications of the Volunteer." Report to the Student Volunteer Convention, 1898. In *The Call, Qualifications and Preparation of Candidates for Foreign Missionary Service: Papers by Missionaries and Other Authorities*. Student Volunteer Movement for Foreign Missions, New York.

Barnes, D. (1990). "Drama in Tonampare." *Amigos* Autumn:3.

Bell, D. (1980). "The End of American Exceptionalism." In *The Winding Passage*. Random House, New York.

———. (1976). *The Cultural Contradictions of Capitalism*. Basic Books, New York.

Bellah, R.N., Madsen, R., Sullivan, R., Swidler, A., and Tipton, S. (1985). *Habits of the Heart: Individualism and Commitment in American Life*. University of California Press, Berkeley.

Berger, P.L. (1979). *The Heretical Imperative*. Doubleday, Garden City, New York.

Berger, P. and Luckmann, T. (1966). *The Social Construction of Reality*. Doubleday, New York.

Billing, E. (1964). *Our Calling* [1909]. Conrad Bergendoff, tr. Fortress Press, Philadelphia.

Bonk, J. (1991). *Missions and Money: Affluence as a Western Missionary Problem*. Orbis Books, Maryknoll, New York.

Boone, K.C. (1989). *The Bible Tells Them So: The Discourse of Protestant Fundamentalism*. State University of New York, Albany.

Bosch, D.J. (1991). *Transforming Mission: Paradigm Shifts in Theology of Mission*. Orbis Books, Maryknoll, New Jersey.

Bowden, H.W. (1982). *American Indians and Christian Missions Studies in Cultural Conflict*. University of Chicago Press, Chicago.

Bower, S. (1966). "Conquest by Air." Evaluation Study Report of World Radio Missionary Fellowship, Inc. Christian Service Fellowship, Inc., Fort Morgan, Colorado.

Brainerd, D. (1949). [diary, ca. 1745]. In Jonathan Edwards, ed., *Life and Diary of David Brainerd*. Moody Press, Chicago.

Campbell, J. (1949). *Hero With a Thousand Faces*. Princeton University Press, Princeton.

Carey, W. (1979). "An Enquiry into the Obligations of Christians to Use Means for the Conversion of the Heathens" [1792]. In Francis DuBose, ed., *Classics of Christian Missions*. Broadman, Nashville.

Carpenter, J.A. (1990). "Propagating the Faith Once Delivered: The Fundamentalist Missionary Enterprise, 1920–1945." In J.A. Carpenter and W.R. Shenk, eds., *Earthen Vessels: American Evangelicals and Foreign Missions, 1880–1980*. Eerdmans, Grand Rapids.

Carpenter, J.A. and Shenk, W.R. (1990). *Earthen vessels: American evangelicals and foreign missions, 1880-1980*. Eerdmans, Grand Rapids.

Cassel, E.T. (1911). "The King's Business" [1902]. In H. Rodeheaver and B.D. Ackley, eds., *Great Revival Hymns*. New York.

Chamberlain, J. (1901). "The Call to Foreign Missionary Work" (*The Intercollegian*, November, 1900). In *The Call, Qualifications and Preparation of Candidates for Foreign Missionary Service: Papers by Missionaries and Other Authorities*. Student Volunteer Movement for Foreign Missions, New York.

Clifford, J. (1982). *Person and Myth: Maurice Leenhardt in the Melanesian World*. University of California Press, Berkeley.

———. (1901). "The Need of Thinkers for the Mission Field." Report to the Student Volunteer Convention, 1900. In *The Call, Qualifications and Preparation of Candidates for Foreign Missionary Service: Papers by Missionaries and Other Authorities*. Student Volunteer Movement for Foreign Missions, New York.

Cline, R.A. (1990). "HCJB World Radio Year-End Report." The World Radio Missionary Fellowship, Quito, Ecuador.

———. (1989). "Come Fly with Us!" *Around the World* Spring:8.

Cohen, E. (1990). "The Missionary as Stranger: A Phenomenological Analysis of Christian Missionaries' Encounter with the Folk Religions of Thailand." *Review of Religious Research* 31(4):337–350.

Cohler, B.J. (1988). "The Human Studies and the Life History." *Social Science Review* 62:552–575.

Cole, T.R. (1992). *The Journey of Life*. Cambridge University Press, Cambridge.

Cook, F.S. (1961). *Seeds in the Wind*. World Radio Missionary Fellowship, Quito, Ecuador.

Cox, H. (1984). *Religion in the Secular City*. Simon & Schuster, New York.

Dawson, L. (1990). "Self-affirmation, freedom, and rationality: Theoretically elaborating 'active' conversions." *Journal for the Scientific Study of Religion* 29(2):141–163.

Downton, J.V. (1979). *Sacred Journeys: The Conversion of Young Americans to Divine Light Mission*. Columbia University Press, New York.

DuBose, F. (1979). *Classics of Christian Missions*. Broadman, Nashville.

Dussel, E. (1981). *A History of the Church in Latin America: Colonialism to Liberation*. Eerdmans, Grand Rapids.

Dyrness, W. (1989). *How Does America Hear the Gospel?* Eerdmans, Grand Rapids.

Eliade, M. (1959). *The Sacred and the Profane*. Harcourt, Brace and World, New York.

Elliot, E. (1958). *Shadow of the Almighty: The Life and Testament of Jim Elliot*. Harper & Brothers, New York.

———. (1957). *Through Gates of Splendor*. Harper & Brothers, New York.

Erikson, K.T. (1984). "Sociology and Contemporary Events." In Walter W. Powell and Richard Robbins, eds., *Conflict and Consensus: A Festschrift in Honor of Lewis A. Coser*. Free Press, New York.

———. (1976). *Everything in Its Path*. Simon & Schuster, New York.

———. (1966). *Wayward Puritans*. Wiley, New York.

Fahs, C.H. (1933). "Recruiting and Selecting New Missionaries." In Orville A. Petty, ed., *Laymen's Foreign Mission Inquiry, Vol. VII*. Harper & Brothers, New York.

Flood, R. (1975). *America: God Shed His Grace on Thee*. Moody Press, Chicago.

Forman, C. (1984). "Missionary Vocation." Unpublished paper.

Freud, S. (1961). *The Future of an Illusion* [1927]. James Strachey, tr. W.W. Norton, New York.

Geertz, C. (1988). *Work and Lives*. Stanford University Press, Stanford, California.

Gensichen, D.H.W. (1960). "Were the Reformers Indifferent to Missions?" In *History's Lessons for Tomorrow's Mission: Milestones in the History of Missionary Thinking*. World's Student Christian Federation, Geneva.

Gergen, K.J. (1990). "Warranting Voice and the Elaboration of the Self." In John Shotter and Kenneth J. Gergen, eds., *Texts of Identity*. Sage Publications, London.

Gittins, A.J. (1989). *Gifts and Strangers: Meeting the Challenge of Inculturation.* Paulist Press, New York.

Goffman, E. (1961). "The Moral Career of the Mental Patient." In *Asylums.* Doubleday, Garden City, New York.

Goldschmidt, W. (1990). *The Human Career: The Self in the Symbolic World.* Blackwell, Cambridge.

Greeley, A. (1989). *Religious Change in America.* Harvard University Press, Cambridge.

Hammond, P.E. (1988). "Religion and the Persistence of Identity." *Journal for the Scientific Study of Religion* 27:1.

Harding, S.F. (1987). "Convicted by the Holy Spirit: The Rhetoric of Fundamental Baptist Conversion." *The American Ethnologist* 14:167:81.

Harman, L.D. (1988). *The Modern Stranger: On Language and Membership.* Walter de Gruyter & Co., Berlin.

Hendrix, E.R. (1905). "The Call and Qualifications of a Missionary" (lecture delivered at the Missionary Training School).

Hersey, J. (1985). *The Call: An American Missionary in China.* Knopf, New York.

Hesselgrave, D.J. (1988). *Today's Choices for Tomorrow's Mission: An Evangelical Perspective on Trends and Issues in Missions.* Zondervan, Grand Rapids.

Houghton, A.T. (1956). *Preparing to Be a Missionary.* Inter-Varsity Fellowship, London.

Hunter, J.D. (1987). *Evangelicalism: The Coming Generation.* University of Chicago Press, Chicago.

———. (1982). *American Evangelicalism: Conservative Religion and the Quandary of Modernity.* Rutgers University Press, New Brunswick.

Hutchison, W.R. (1987). *Errand to the World: American Protestant Thought and Foreign Missions.* University of Chicago Press, Chicago.

Jessup, H. (1901). "Who Ought Not to Go as Foreign Missionaries" (*The Student Volunteer*, February, 1895). In *The Call, Qualifications and Preparation of Candidates for Foreign Missionary Service: Papers by Missionaries and Other Authorities.* Student Volunteer Movement for Foreign Missions, New York.

Jones, C.W. (1966). "Appraisal" [1962]. In S. Bower, ed., *Conquest by Air. Christian Service Fellowship, Fort Morgan, Colorado.*

Jones, J.W. (1991). *Contemporary Psychoanalysis and Religion.* Yale University Press, New Haven.

Kane, J.H. (1980). *Life and Work on the Mission Field.* Baker, Grand Rapids.

———. (1975). *The Making of the Missionary.* Baker, Grand Rapids.

Kirkpatrick, L.A. and Shaver, P.R. (1990). "Attachment Theory and Religion: Childhood Attachments, Religious Beliefs, and Conversion." *Journal for the Scientific Study of Religion* 29(3):315–334.

Kotre, J. (1984). *Outliving the Self: Generativity and the Interpretation of Lives.* Johns Hopkins University Press, Baltimore.

Kroll-Smith, J.S. (1980). "The Testimony as Performance: The Relationship of an Expressive Event to the Belief System of a Holiness Sect." *Journal for the Scientific Study of Religion* 19:16–25.

Lambert, J.C. (1907). *The Romance of Missionary Heroism: True Stories of Intrepid Bravery and Stirring Adventures with Uncivilized Man, Wild Beasts, and the Forces of Nature in All Parts of the World.* Lippincott, Philadelphia.

Larson, M. (1957). *117 Ways to the Mission Field.* Christian Service Foundation, Moline, Illinois.

Lathern, J. (1884). *The Macedonian Cry: A Voice from the Lands of Brahma and Buddha, Africa and Isles of the Sea and a Plea for Missions.* Briggs, Toronto.

Latourette, K.S. (1949). *Missions and the American Mind*. National Foundation Press, Indianapolis.

———. (1938–1946). *History of the Expansion of Christianity* (seven volumes). Harper & Brothers, New York.

Lawrence, B.B. (1989). *Defenders of God*. Harper & Row, San Francisco.

Lhamon, W.J. (1899). *Heroes of Modern Missions*. Fleming Revell, New York.

Lofland, S. and Stark, R. (1965). "Becoming a World Saver: A Theory of Conversion to a Deviant Perspective." In B. McLaughlin, ed., *Studies in Social Movements*. Free Press, New York.

Lowrie, J.C. (1882). *Missionary Papers*. Robert Carter and Brothers, New York.

Marsden, G. (ed.) (1984). *Evangelicalism and Modern America*. Eerdmans, Grand Rapids.

———. (1980). *Fundamentalism and American Culture*. Oxford University Press, New York.

Marty, M. (1984). *Pilgrims in Their Own Land*. Little, Brown & Co., Boston.

McAdams, D.P (1985). *Power, Intimacy, and the Life Story: Personological Inquiries into Identity*. The Dorsey Press, Homewood, Illinois.

Meissner, W.W. (1984). *Psychoanalysis and Religious Experience*. Yale University Press, New Haven.

Mittleberg, D. (1988). *Strangers in Paradise: The Israeli Kibbutz Experience*. Transaction Books, New Brunswick, New Jersey.

Mol, H. (1978). *Identity and Religion*. Sage, Beverly Hills.

Myerhoff, B. (1978). *Number Our Days*. Simon and Schuster, New York.

Najarian, N. (1982). "A Symbolic Interactionist Approach to the Religious Stranger Concept: Protestant Missionaries in China, 1841–1910." Diss. Drew University.

Neely, L. (1980). *Come Up To This Mountain: The Miracle of Clarence W. Jones and HCJB*. Tyndale, Wheaton, Illinois.

Neill, S. (1986). *A History of Christian Missions*. (Revised for 2nd ed. by Owen Chadwick). Penguin Books, Harmondsworth, Middlesex, England.

———. (1964). *Colonialism and Christian Missions*. Random House, New York.

Neitz, M.J. (1987). *Charisma and Community: A Study of Religious Commitment within the Charismatic Renewal*. Transaction Books, New Brunswick.

Nouwen, H.J.M. (1983). *Gracias*. Harper & Row, San Francisco.

Ostling, R.N. (1982). "The New Missionary." *Time*, Dec. 27.

Phillips, C.J. (1969). *Protestant America and the Pagan World: The First Half Century of the American Board of Commissioners for Foreign Missions, 1810–1860*. East Asian Research Center, Harvard University, Cambridge.

Pike, F.B. (1992). *The United States and Latin America: Myths and Stereotypes of Civilization and Nature*. University of Texas Press, Austin.

Reed, J. (1983). *The Missionary Mind and American East Asia Policy, 1911–1915*. Harvard University Press, Cambridge.

Ricoeur, P. (1986). *Lectures on Ideology and Utopia*. George Taylor, ed., Columbia University Press, New York.

Riding, A. (1984). "From High in Andes, Bible's Message Carries Far." *New York Times*, Wednesday, May 23.

Risser, S. (ed.) (1983). "Primary Health Care Workers in Ecuador: A PVO's Experience." World Radio Missionary Fellowship, Quito.

Robert, D. (1990). "'The Crisis of Missions': Premillennial Mission Theory and the Origins of Independent Evangelical Missions." In J.A. Carpenter and W.R. Shenk, eds., *Earthen Vessels: American Evangelicals and Foreign Missions, 1880–1980*. Eerdmans, Grand Rapids.

Roberts, W. and Siewart, J. (1989). *Mission Handbook: USA/Canada Protestant Ministries Overseas: 14th Edition*. Zondervan, Grand Rapids.

Rosenwald, G.C. and Ochberg, R.L. (1992). *Storied Lives: The Cultural Politics of Self-Understanding.* Yale University Press, New Haven.

Schlesinger, A. (1974). "The Missionary Enterprise and Theories of Imperialism." In Fairbank, John K., ed., *The Missionary Enterprise in China and America.* Harvard University Press, Cambridge, MA.

Schutz, A. (1944). "The Stranger: An Essay in Social Psychology." *American Journal of Sociology* 49(6):499–507.

Shaffir, W. (1978). "Witnessing as Identity Consolidation." In Hans Mol, ed., *Identity and Religion.* Sage, Beverly Hills.

Shelley, B. (1980). *The Gospel and the American Dream.* Multnomah Press, Portland, Oregon.

Shenk, W. (1991). "Introduction." In Charles R. Taber, *The World is Too Much with Us: "Culture" in Modern Missions.* Mercer University Press, Macon, Georgia.

Simmel, G. (1959). *The Sociology of Religion* [1906]. Curt Rosenthal, tr. Philosophical Library, New York.

———. (1950). "The Stranger" [1904]. In Kurt Wolff, tr., *The Sociology of Georg Simmel.* The Free Press, Glencoe, Illinois.

Snow, D.A. and Anderson, L. (1987). "Identity Work Among the Homeless: The Verbal Construction and Avowal of Personal Identities." *American Journal of Sociology* 92(6):1336–1371.

Snow, D.A. and Machalek, R. (1983). "The Convert as a Social Type." In Randall Collins, ed., *Sociological Theory.* Jossey-Bass, San Francisco.

Speer, R. (1901a). "What Constitutes a Missionary Call?" In *The Call, Qualifications and Preparation of Candidates for Foreign Missionary Service: Papers by Missionaries and Other Authorities.* Student Volunteer Movement for Foreign Missions, New York.

———. (1901b). "Qualifications Desired in Missionary Candidates as Indicated by a Tour of the Fields." In *The Call, Qualifications and Preparation of Candidates for Foreign Missionary Service: Papers by Missionaries and Other Authorities.* Student Volunteer Movement for Foreign Missions, New York.

Spence, D.P. (1982). *Narrative Truth and Historical Truth: Meaning and Interpretation in Psychoanalysis.* W.W. Norton, New York.

Stanley, B. (1990). *The Bible and the Flag: Protestant Missions and British Imperialism in the Nineteenth and Twentieth Centuries.* Apollos, England.

Stark, R. and Bainbridge, W.S. (1980). "Towards a Theory of Religious Commitment." *Journal for the Scientific Study of Religion* 19:114–128.

Stoll, D. (1982). "Fishers of men or founders of empire?" *The Wycliffe Bible Translators in Latin America.* Zed Press, London.

———. (1990). *Is Latin America Turning Protestant?* University of California Press, Berkeley.

Swanson, T.D. (1988). "Crown of Yage: Mission Christs and Indigenous Christs in South America." Diss. University of Chicago.

Taber, C.R. (1991). *The World Is Too Much with Us: "Culture" in Modern Missions.* Mercer University Press, Macon, Georgia.

Thomas, G. (1986). *Christianity and Culture in the 19th Century United States: The Dynamics of Evangelical Revivalism, Nationbuilding, and the Market.* University of California Press, Berkeley.

Tillich, P. (1952). *The Courage to Be.* Yale University Press, New Haven.

Ullman, C. (1989). *The Transformed Self: The Psychology of Religious Conversion.* Plenum Press, New York.

Van Engen, C.E., Gilliland, D.S., and Pierson, P. (eds.) (1993). *The Good News of the Kingdom: Mission Theology for the Third Millennium.* Orbis Books, Maryknoll, New York.

Van Engen, C.E. (1990). "A Broadening Vision: Forty Years of Evangelical Theology of Mission, 1946–1986." In J.A. Carpenter and W.R. Shenk, eds., *Earthen Vessels: American Evangelicals and Foreign Missions, 1880–1980* Eerdmans, Grand Rapids.

Warner, R.S. (1988). *New Wine in Old Wineskins: Evangelicals and Liberals in a Small Town Church*. University of California Press, Berkeley.

Warren, M. (1944). *The Calling of God: Four Essays on Missionary Work*. Lutterworth Press, London.

Weber, M. (1963). *The Sociology of Religion* [1922]. Ephraim Fischoff, tr. Beacon Press, Boston.

———. (1958). *The Protestant Ethic and the Spirit of Capitalism* [1904–1905]. Talcott Parsons, tr. Charles Scribner's Sons, New York.

Wenegrat, B. (1990). *The Divine Archetype: The Sociobiology and Psychology of Religion*. Lexington Books, Lexington, MA.

Westphal, M. (1984). *God, Guilt and Death*. Indiana University Press, Bloomington.

Wilson, G. (1901). "Christ's Call to Missionary Service" (*The Student Volunteer*, February, 1897). In *The Call, Qualifications and Preparation of Candidates for Foreign Missionary Service: Papers by Missionaries and Other Authorities*. Student Volunteer Movement for Foreign Missions, New York.

Wingren, G. (1957). *Luther on Vocation* [1942]. Carl C. Rasmussen, tr. Muhlenberg Press, Philadelphia.

Wittgenstein, L. (1953). *Philosophical Investigations*. G. Anscombe, tr. McMillan, New York.

Woodbridge, J.D., Noll M.A., and Hatch, N.O. (1979). *The Gospel in America*. Zondervan, Grand Rapids.

Wuthnow, R.J. (1988a). "Sociology of Religion." In Neil Smelser, ed., *Handbook of Sociology*. Sage, Newbury Park, California.

———. (1988b). *The Restructuring of American Religion*. Princeton University Press, Princeton, New Jersey.

Index